OLD
NEW ZEALAND
HOUSES

1800–1940

OLD
NEW ZEALAND
HOUSES

1800–1940

Jeremy Salmond

To the memory of my parents

Published by Heinemann Reed, a division of Octopus Publishing Group
(NZ) Ltd, 39 Rawene Road, Birkenhead, Auckland. Associated
companies, branches and representatives throughout the world.

ISBN 0 7900 0027 X

© Jeremy Salmond 1986

First published 1986
Reprinted 1987, 1989, 1990

Cover photograph by Robin Morrison
Designed by Silverfish
Printed in Singapore

Contents

Part II: Victorian villas and cottages 1860-1910

Part III: The bungalow and beyond 1910-1940

Acknowledgements

In preparing this book I have been helped in many ways by other people and by various institutions. I want to thank them all warmly, even though they may not recognise their contributions in the text:

The Winstone Centenary Education Trust for a generous grant of $500 towards the costs of the research; The University of Auckland Architecture Library; The Auckland Institute and Museum Library; The New Zealand Room of the Auckland Public Library; The Alexander Turnbull Library; The Hocken Library; The Victoria and Albert Museum Library; The Royal Institute of British Architects Library; The New Zealand Historic Places Trust; The Devonport Borough Council; Wellington and Dunedin City Councils; Denise Moore of the Auckland School of Architecture; The University of Auckland photographic laboratory; and Bruce Jarvis of *Prism*.

Professor Peter Bartlett; Mrs Ulva Belsham of the Wallace Museum; Dr Judith Binney; Christopher and Margaret Cochran; Dr Raewyn Dalziell; Mr Jack Diamond; Lady Aileen Fox; Tim Heath; Dr Barbara Kirstenblatt-Gimblett; Martin Hill; Alan la Roche; Dr Michael Linzey; Mrs Miriam McGregor; Mr Philip Muskett; Michael Pritchard; David Reynolds; Gerhard Rosenberg; Geoff and Deirdre Salmond; Narelle Scollay; Cheryl Sotheran; John Stacpoole; Geoffrey Thornton; Ash Spice; and John Wilson.

Irene Donovan and Judith Nelson who converted the text to a legible condition; Philip Ridge who knocked the spots off it; and hundreds of obliging house owners. I have made use of many photographs and illustrations from libraries and museums throughout the country. Each has been acknowledged in full or where appropriate with the following abbreviations: ATL (Alexander Turnbull Library); AIM (Auckland Institute and Museum); APL (Auckland Public Library); HPT (Historic Places Trust). All other illustrations are my own work or have been taken from early publications.

A work such as this is never complete. I hope others will trouble to point out to me the errors and omissions and I thank them in advance.

Lastly and best of all, I thank my beloved Anne who believes in miracles.

INTRODUCTION

Old houses in a New Zealand landscape

In the past ten years or so, old houses in New Zealand have been celebrated as never before. Painters and printmakers have placed them in their two-dimensional landscapes — Robin White's portraits of old houses, Peter Siddell's urban hillsides, Don Binney's "Colonial Bird" hovering over a two-storey villa. Photographers such as Robin Morrison have preserved them in calendars and glossy art books; and countless pen-and-ink sketches fill local histories, cover placemats, and sit on the wall in framed sets of four.

Old houses have been assembled in circuses at Kelburn and Parnell, where they entertain the public with their fretwork, finials, and flights of balusters; and brand new colonial villages have appeared in urban shopping centres to coin capital out of this architectural nostalgia. For many people, New Zealand's old houses have become icons — visual metaphors which evoke and capture an historic European presence in this land.

It has not always been this way, however. Attitudes to old houses have changed greatly since 1900, when this country's European past was less remote and less romantically perceived. These changes can perhaps best be understood by looking at what has been written about ordinary houses in New Zealand since they first became objects of self-conscious attention.

The first critical descriptions of New Zealand houses were by British-trained architects writing in British journals at the beginning of this century — W. Hurst Seager[1] and F. de J. Clere.[2] Neither could be described as architecturally nationalistic. Seager began by saying:

> I can but regret that it is impossible for me truly to entitle [the article] the Architectural Art of New Zealand. . . . Unfortunately . . . we have no style, no distinctive forms of art . . . all our methods are those of the Old World . . . our cities are made up of architectural quotations.[3]

Seager and Clere had in common a guarded respect for the earliest cottages, and were appreciative of their simplicity and lack of pretension. They echoed comments by J.E. Fitzgerald who referred to "those small unpretending tenements . . . built by the early colonists; some of them not ungraceful in their proportions; all of them possessing the beauty of simplicity and truth."[4] The reason for this approval is probably to be found in the British ancestry of both the buildings and the observers. Many of the cottages had a Georgian symmetry even in their simplest form, and some of the earliest were brought prefabricated from England, while others were built to plans drawn up in the old country.

Clere described the early cottages with their "plain gables and simple outlines as immeasurably preferable to what followed when the people were better off before the advent of outside influences".[5]

The "outside influences" were heralded in New Zealand by the appearance of American publications such as *Woodward's National Architecture*, with their ideas for decoration by attaching "features" to the simple box-shaped house. These opportunities were eagerly adopted by builders, so that before long:

> bay windows and other excrescences were carted from the mills and attached to the fronts; classical porticoes, with cleverly built and glued-up columns, marked the wealth of the building owner; while ruby and bright green glass appeared in the vestibule and other doorways, and for some years vulgarity reigned supreme.[6]

So Clere dismisses the whole period of villa building in New Zealand.

It is clear that the New Zealand villa style never appealed to architects trained in the English tradition. While many made use of the mass-produced features portrayed in the merchants' lavish catalogues, architects as a group resented the challenge to their position as arbiters of taste in building. The new leaders of popular housing fashion became those whom Clere referred to as the "enterprising carpenter-architects", catering to the newly affluent second generation New Zealanders and recent immigrants, all anxious to show off their prosperity.

After World War I, still no one had anything good to say about the villa. Its form was that of a "packing case structure", poorly planned, with "the passage acting as an efficient funnel for the conveyance of cold winds and clouds of dust: providing a cold home in the winter and a dusty one in the summer."[7]

While the villa's popularity lay in the doldrums of architectural fashion, new housing forms appeared and flourished in quick succession. Each new style of house had its inspiration in imported models, reaching New Zealand in the wake of large population shifts and growing international trade. More often than not, however, they simply dressed up the same old plans. As the new ideas were taken up they were adapted to local conditions and materials. Some, like the Californian bungalow, became part of an emerging national architectural character, although others such as the various "Spanish" styles were discarded to await later fashionable revival. Generally, such "foreign" influences did not meet the approval of the architectural profession. The prevailing sentiment was that "New Zealand being a British colony, the people should endeavour to hold onto the English tradition left by

the pioneers and not be led away by the dazzling prettiness of some American modern architectural craze".[8]

It was not until the end of the 1930s that a new generation of New Zealand-bred architects could view the evolution of the country's housing with some detachment. The first, and for many years the most important review of New Zealand housing, was by Paul Pascoe, published in 1940.[9] Pascoe's writing, as well as his work, showed the influence of the Modern Movement in twentieth century architecture, with its austere morality echoing the material austerity of the early houses. He expressed a hope for a national style that would develop in a simple common sense way, and he argued for a break with the tradition of preconceived form and decoration, as the colonists had broken with the elaborate aesthetic conventions of their time.

Like many commentators, Pascoe concentrated on the construction of the very early slab, cob, and sod huts. A brief look at the simple early timber houses was followed by an equally brief comment on the Victorian taste for ostentatious decoration and the use of wood to imitate masonry construction. The characteristic ingredient of the later Victorian pot pourri was the bay villa which Pascoe placed alongside an eclectic mix of other styles flooding into the country from abroad — the Spanish Mission style, the English Arts and Crafts house, the Californian bungalow.

From this mixture the Californian bungalow emerged as the dominant influence on the ordinary New Zealand house of the 1920s and 1930s, and for an architect of that period Pascoe was remarkably tolerant of the results. His delight, however, lay in the buildings of the Modern Movement which he and some contemporaries were adapting to New Zealand conditions. These were not to be confused with houses in the "moderne" style, where "a freakishly 'modernistic' exterior disguise[d] an unchanged interior plan".[10] Here instead was a model which combined a rational approach to planning, materials, and climate, and offered just the break with tradition which Pascoe and others were seeking. The early Modern Movement houses in New Zealand, as seen in the work of Vernon Brown for instance, contained the essential ingredients of the post-war private and state houses.

Paul Pascoe was the first to claim for New Zealand a "degree of maturity" in architecture, yet his approach still sought its inspiration from abroad. Just as Seager, Clere and Binney looked to England for their architectural standards, so Pascoe and his generation borrowed an ideology as well as a vocabulary from Europe and America. All examined the home-grown housing stock and found it either unworthy, or (ironically) tainted by foreign — i.e. not English — influences. The important difference in 1940 was a readiness to discard past mistakes and set about creating an indigenous architecture. Like the young writers and poets of that time, the architects had become "dissatisfied with the colonial-English traditions in which they had been schooled. The pakeha settlements had matured into a subtly different way of life that could not be expressed by the outlook and style of Englishmen in the beautiful but forever foreign country. Yet these were the confusing terms of that generation's background and education. Culturally speaking, England was home: 'You were English and not English. It took time to realise that England was far away'."[11]

The next period was one of cool evaluation. The Second World War slowed down many domestic activities in New Zealand, including house building, and its effects lasted for several years after. Housing became more strictly regulated and was modelled closely on the development of the state house. Young architects continued the quest for "the New Zealand House", largely uninspired by the pre-war stock, and when discussion of older houses began again, it was preoccupied with dating houses so that they could be valued as commodities on the property market. As new motorways spread grey fingers across the older parts of the cities, and local authorities were caught up in the international fad for wholesale redevelopment, great swathes were cut through housing areas that had become rundown, and were inhabited by the poor, the old, students, and immigrant minorities. There was undeniable interest in these old houses, but it did not lie in their intrinsic qualities. Old houses were now part of an expanding development market, and it had become important to be able to assess their depreciated value so that when they were destroyed, appropriate compensation could be paid.

In 1970, however, the Commission of Inquiry into Housing convened to look at the "housing needs of the people of New Zealand".[12] Among other matters it considered the existing housing stock, its conservation, rehabilitation, and redevelopment. In its 1971 report, the commission spoke of the "incipient problem of ageing houses" and the fact that "not enough positive information was available on the type, nature and use of older urban dwellings".[13] These concerns were summarised in recommendations which included proposals for a national housing authority, and the conservation of old houses through local body projects and systems of improvement grants. The commission's report marked the end of an era of public indifference to old houses, and the beginnings of a popular love affair.

With the publication of the commission's report, a literature of appreciation of old houses began to emerge. In 1972 Charles Fearnley and John Stacpoole wrote articles for the *New Zealand's Heritage* series,[14] and Stacpoole with Peter Beaven reviewed the country's architecture since 1820 in their book *Architecture 1820-1970*. In 1976 Stacpoole published the most comprehensive account so far of New Zealand's colonial architecture.[15] Nevertheless, this literature has focused on "finer" buildings — architect-designed, and patronised by the wealthy, the influential, and the institutions; and New Zealand still lacks an architectural history which gives fair recognition to the popular taste in housng. Australia, by comparison, is well served with scholarly works by J.M. Freeland, Robin Boyd, and others. Well-researched restoration manuals also exist such as Tanner and Cox's *Restoring Old Australian Houses and Buildings*, which also includes a detailed classification of housing styles.

Practical manuals have begun to appear in New Zealand. The best of these is Christopher Cochran's *Restoring a New Zealand House*,[16] which approaches the subject in an advisory way, referring mainly to nineteenth century houses. This book was published for the New Zealand Historic Places Trust, which has already produced a two-volume survey of historic New Zealand buildings, and has systematically catalogued and recorded buildings of all descriptions since its Buildings Classifications Committee was set up in 1969-70.

The most remarkable expression of this fascination with old houses are the "new-old" houses produced by the speculative housing industry (always sensitive to public taste), which has channelled some of its resources into reproduction buildings. Some are architect-designed, some are literal copies, others are free interpretations almost always of mid nineteenth century houses. At the same time an industry has grown up which caters especially to the rehabilitation market, and produces mouldings, turnings, hardware, wallpapers, and furniture in period designs. After years in the wilderness, the demolition yards have also come into their own and are now busy and profitable concerns.

This cottage industry has also produced some eccentric stylistic muddles. Just as in the 1920s and 1930s when the Californian bungalow was in its heyday and many of the older villas were modernised, so now in the excitement of the old house revival many bungalows are receiving similar treatment. Today, the "bungled" villas of the 1920s and 1930s must compete with the "villa-fied" bungalows of the 1970s and the colonial confectionery of the 1980s. There has also been a strong mood of nostalgia in the work of some New Zealand architects, who have seized on such elements as the bay window, steep-pitched roofs, finials, dormer windows, and the verandah to recreate the forms of the colonial house.

Why is the villa in particular so endearing to a younger generation of New Zealanders? The answer may be that it represents an early example of independent thinking in this country — independent, that is, of England. The New Zealand villa did not obey the rules of taste dictated by English-trained architects. Instead, it followed the inclinations of the "carpenter architects" who liberally re-interpreted ideas circulating around the colonial countries of the Pacific Basin. They took the simple "Georgian" cottage and added American gothic bargeboards, the Anglo-Indian verandah, Australian cast iron or its wooden equivalent, Welsh slates, French tiles, and classical stone details reproduced in timber. From this exotic mixture they produced the first mass-built New Zealand houses.

The early architects in New Zealand maligned the villa because it wasn't architecture and it wasn't English. For the colonials, these may have been its chief virtues; they may not have known much about architecture, but they knew what they liked.

As for th'architects . . . most of 'em don't know where to set a chimney so as it shan't be quarrelling with a door. My notion is, a practical builder that's got a bit o' taste makes the best architect for common things; and I've ten times the pleasure i' seeing after the work when I've made the plan myself. [17]

The research

"In many ways the poor man's house is the most important of all, for it is more interesting to know how ordinary folk were lodged than how kings and lords built castles and fortresses."

— NATHANIEL LLOYD, *The History of the English House* (1931).

Detailed research for this book began about 1977 with a project to record good examples of ordinary old New Zealand houses, and where possible to establish their ages. This has involved extensive photography on field trips to many parts of the country in both the North and South Islands. About 2000 photographs were taken and many of these have been enlarged for inclusion in a "New Zealand Houses Index". This index was devised to record as many details about each house as possible, including its location, age, legal description, original owner, builder, designer, construction, and structural history. The purpose of the index was to record the houses (some have since been demolished or altered), and to build up a large dated sample of old New Zealand houses, which would

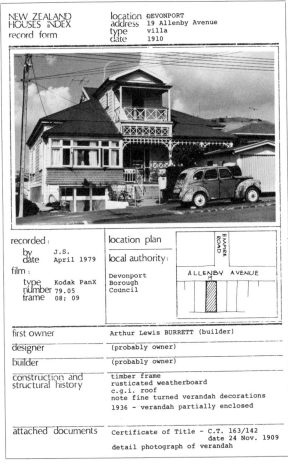

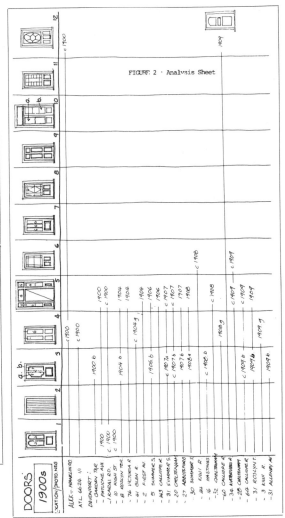

1. (above) New Zealand Houses Index — a typical entry.

2. (right) Research analysis — a typical sheet of door types.

reveal their stylistic and formal development over time and in different parts of the country.

To give more depth to this survey, a particular study was made of Devonport, an Auckland borough established in the 1860s. Some 300 houses were photographed there, and their histories researched in council records and the Auckland Land Registry Office. A large number of old photographs of Devonport were collected to give a time series portrait of the borough from the 1880s. Records of house plans in Devonport (as in most local authorities) do not extend beyond a certain date — in this instance 1908 — and the ages of houses built before then had to be deduced from information about mortgages contained in the certificate of title. This approach was tested against some later buildings whose ages were positively known, and proved to be quite reliable. Similar surveys in local authority records in Wellington and Dunedin gave a useful comparison between buildings of identical age in three well-separated parts of the country.

The research also made use of a number of national and local archives:

* the measured drawings collection at the Auckland University School of Architecture;
* the regional house files and photographs from the New Zealand Historic Places Trust in Wellington;
* the photograph collections of the Alexander Turnbull Library, the Auckland Public Library, and the Auckland Institute and Museum.

From all this information an extensive sample of dated New Zealand houses was assembled in a "style file" — ordered by decade, and within each decade, by region. Details of these houses were recorded on analysis sheets, which systematically described their walling materials, roof forms, bay windows, dormer types, doors, windows and bay ends — over time, and in different parts of the country.

Finally, extensive library research was carried out in New Zealand and overseas for each period of housing covered in this study. For the first period (up to 1860), the main sources were emigrants' handbooks and guides, letters, early eyewitness accounts and recollections, newspapers, local histories, early sketches and drawings and architectural texts. For the second period (1860-1910), the most useful sources were local histories, manufacturers' catalogues (where these could be located), newspapers, technical books, journals and articles, early photographs, and local body records and plans. Sadly, there were relatively few of those vividly descriptive accounts of housebuilding which were a feature of the pioneers' diaries and letters of the first period. For the third period (1910-1940) technical journals were valuable, as were plan books and trade catalogues. A survey was also made of the general literature on vernacular buildings in New Zealand, Britain, the United States and Australia.

The overall aim of this study has been to produce a well-founded account of old New Zealand houses, which does justice to the complexity of their histories and the richness of their forms.

PART I

THE FIRST HOUSES
1800 — 1860

Settling New Zealand

MAORI HOUSES 800-1769

The first settlers of Aotearoa were the East Polynesian ancestors of the Maori, who arrived by canoe at about A.D. 800. Little is known about their houses because only postholes, fireplaces, and drains usually survive for archaeological inspection, *and the very earliest settlements have not yet been found. Probably they were not very different from those houses built by their eighteenth century descendants,[1] and described by those aboard the *Endeavour* when it visited this country in 1769. Anaura Bay on the East Coast was the first place where Cook and his men could freely wander about onshore, and there Monkhouse, the ship's surgeon, saw:

> ... up the hills on the South side of the bay ...
> a single house pleasantly situated. Here was a
> man, his wife, two sons; an old woman and a
> younger who acted as servants. . . . A little chest
> with Cord hinges, stood close within the door of
> the house. [The man] was unwilling we should
> go within; and indeed it is no desireable
> business, the doorway hardly exceeding two feet
> in either direction; over the doorway was a
> carved board. This house was well made, the
> wall made of reed about four inches thick — the
> roof a thatch of course grass with a covering of
> bark, and a net over all to prevent its being
> effected materially by the wind. It was very neat
> within, and had a matt on the floor . . .[2]

This must have been a fairly good smaller house, and although its size was not given it does not seem to have been a chief's house.

Size was one distinction between the houses of ordinary people and those of chiefs. Ordinary sleeping houses (wharepuni) were commonly 3 to 4.5 metres long by 2 to 2.5 metres or more wide, while a chief's house could measure from 6 to 13

metres long by 3 to 6 metres wide. As well, a chief's house often featured carving, which was itself chiefly work and an indication of his personal mana and tapu. Because the chief was a tapu person this was reflected in the tapu of his house, especially the roof. In 1814 Marsden described the banishment of a rooster and hen for persistently perching on the roof of a chief's house in spite of being forbidden to do so.[3]

Within the house there was a clear social organisation of space which allocated the left or junior side (looking in) to the hosts, women, children, and slaves, and on the right or senior side to guests and men, with the most important position nearest the window. This appears to have been an ancient pattern of use.[4]

The construction of houses varied in different areas but a description from the French officer Roux in 1772 illustrates the range of materials and techniques used by pre-European Maori builders:

> ... their houses prompted our admiration, so
> skilfully were they made. They were rectangular
> in shape and varied in size according to need.
> The sides were stakes set a short distance from
> one another and strengthened by switches
> which were interlaced across them. They were
> coated on the outside with a layer of moss thick
> enough to prevent water and wind from getting
> in and this layer was held up by a well-
> constructed little lattice. The interior was woven
> with a matting of sword-grass [flax] on which
> there were at intervals, by way of ornament as
> well as to support the roof, little poles or, more
> accurately, planks, two to three inches thick and
> rather well carved. In the middle of the house
> there was also a big carved pole which
> supported the weight of the roof (together with
> two others at the two ends). What surprised us
> still further was that the whole construction was
> mortised and very strongly bound together with
> their swordgrass ropes.
> ... Each house had a sliding door, so low that
> we had virtually to lie down to enter. Above it
> there were two little windows and a very fine

---

* An exception here is Mangakaware, a swamp pa excavated by Bellwood in the Waikato, where uprights, some of the principal roof timbers, and bedding materials were preserved in the peat.

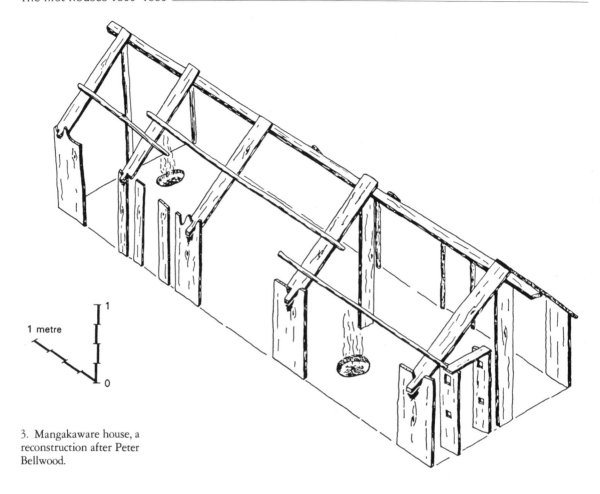

1 metre

3. Mangakaware house, a
reconstruction after Peter
Bellwood.

lattice. Running right round the outside was a
little ditch for water to flow in. These houses
are roofed with reeds;

. . . In front of each door three stones were to be
seen, forming a sort of hearth where they would
make a fire . . . It seemed to me extraordinary
that anyone could do such work without tools
such as ours : however, nowhere did we find
traces of any metals.[5]

These observations have been well corroborated
by archaeological work, as well as by the reports of
other early explorers, missionaries, and travellers.

The typical form of these houses was a pitched
roof, low to the ground with wide overhanging
eaves to shed water into the perimeter drain. Often
a raised mound under the eaves, or sometimes a
wall of stones, gave wind protection. Alternatively,
the floor was sunk into the ground for warmth.
Other roof shapes which allowed more head room
included ridged houses with rafters curved

upwards, or even "barrel-vaulted" roofs — like the
roof of a covered wagon.

The simplest construction was a ridge pole supported by pitched rafters set into the ground on
each side, with or without a verandah in the gable
end. Larger houses had walls and made use of
central posts in the end walls and within the house
itself. Early visitors were astonished at the techniques used, such as mortise and tenon joints, and
the squaring of many of the timbers.

The sleeping houses were only part of a cluster
of small buildings which together served the needs
of a family group, just as a single dwelling does for a
European family. Each building in the cluster had
its own particular use. As well as the sleeping house
there was a cooking house or shelter, store houses,
an adjacent open space (often communal), and
further away latrines and middens.

This separation of functions was of the greatest
importance. In particular the main house was tapu

4. A cluster of houses in
Queen Charlotte Sound.
British Museum.

5. "Titari's House and
Cooking Place at Taiamai"
— from a pencil drawing
by Rev. Richard Taylor,
1841. *ATL.*

1842 Kainga no pihi Kaivahanga manga

6. "Mangakahia" — Pataka (storehouse), from a pencil drawing by Rev. Richard Taylor, 1842. *ATL.*

and reserved solely for sleeping and casual talking; food was never eaten inside, and the sick were taken outside to recover. Food was prepared in the open or in a special shelter (kauta). It was cooked in earth ovens (hangi) or over an open fire, and eaten in the open air or under a shelter — sometimes attached to the house, sometimes in a separate enclosure.

Each family had its own storage, either on stages or in special houses raised off the ground (pataka or whata) or in pits in the ground. There were two main kinds of pit : shallow rectangular excavations with drainage and a pitched roof overhead, and circular bell-shaped hollows accessible from above or by a tunnel from one side.

The open space (marae), while sometimes part of a family cluster, was often communal, especially in a confined pa site, and it survives today in the modern marae. Early visitors were impressed with

the cleanliness of the marae, and of the settlements in general. Banks, in particular, was much struck to find that "every house or small knot of 3 or 4 has a regular necessary house where everyone repairs and consequently the neighbourhood is kept clean . . .[6] The latrine, which was extremely tapu, usually consisted of a flat timber squatting board at the edge of a high bank or cliff, with a horizontal pole for a handgrip. Banks also noted the existence of rubbish heaps where food scraps and other rubbish were thrown.

There were two types of settlement, whose form was largely determined by the expectation of attack. Where attack was probable, highly organised pa sites were created in places where access was difficult and defensible. In these locations, space was often limited, and greater use was made of communal facilities — marae, storage houses, and pits. A fortified pa site was often associated with an otherwise undefended village, or individual family clusters dotted among cultivated gardens.

Apart from these base settlements, it was customary for whole sub-tribes to make seasonal visits to other areas such as the coast for food gathering. Here temporary shelters (wharau) would be erected very quickly. Captain Cook watched one such group at Queen Charlotte Sound put up more than twenty wharau within an hour of landing on shore in their canoes.[7]

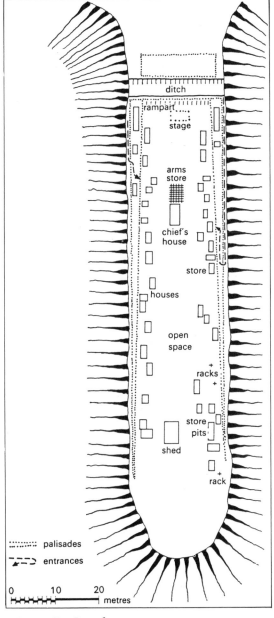

7. Paeroa Pa, Bay of Islands. *Aileen Fox*

FIRST EUROPEAN ARRIVALS
1792-1840

Cook described New Zealand's harbours and resources for people back in England, and in the eighteenth century the first European migrants began to arrive. Some of the first European-style houses were prefabricated in England or Australia, but the great majority were improvised from materials at hand — sometimes using the services of immigrant tradesmen, very often with the help of Maori labour, but probably mostly by unskilled settlers working with one eye on a colonist's handbook.

The earliest record of a house erected by Europeans in this country dates from 1792 (twenty-three years after Cook), when men from the whaling ship *Britannia* were left at Dusky Bay to collect seal skins for the Chinese market. No details of this building are given beyond its size: 13 metres long, 5.5 metres wide, 4.5 metres high.[8]

In 1806 the first prefabricated house came to New Zealand, a gift from Governor King of New South Wales to the Maori chief Te Pahi when he returned home from a visit to Port Jackson:

All Tip-pa hee's treasures which he had from hence were safely landed; and the house sent in frame by the Lady Nelson was erected by Lieutenant Symonds on an island in the Bay of Islands.[9]

This house was later burned by whalers in retribution for the attack on the *Boyd*.

The first European settlers in New Zealand were whalers and sealers, who depended heavily on Maori people for shelter and food, and commonly took Maori wives both for their own comfort and for the protection afforded by their wives' relations. In return they brought iron tools, trade, and many technical skills such as carpentry, as well as European vices. In time they formed their own settlements, usually close to the village of their Maori patrons. One such settlement was at Te Awaiti in Queen Charlotte Sound, where Wakefield described the houses in detail:

After prayers on board we landed and visited

8. Thom's Whaling Station
near Porirua, 1847 — an
engraving after an original
by S.C. Brees. *ATL.*

the whaling town of Te Awa-iti. Dicky Barrett's
house was on a knoll at the far end of it, and
overlooked the whole settlement and anchorage.
There were about twenty houses presented to
our view; . . . Dicky Barrett's house, or whare as
it is called . . . was a very superior edifice, built
of sawn timber, floored and lined inside, and
sheltered in front by an ample verandah. . . .

[An ordinary] whaler's house is generally
built by the natives. It is either entirely composed of reeds and rushes woven over a wooden
frame — or else the walls consist of a wattled
hurdle made of supple-jack [kareao] covered
inside and out with clay, and the roof is
thatched. A huge chimney nearly fills one end
of the houses. . . . Bunks with neat curtains line
the greater part of the sides of the house. A
large deal table and two long benches stand in
the middle of the hard earthen floor . . . Two
square holes in the wall serve as windows, with
wooden shutters for the night. The harness-cask
[for salt-meat], flour-keg, and water-butt, stand
on one side, and a neat dresser, shining with
bright tin dishes and a few glasses and articles
of crockery, [are] on the other side of the door.
. . . The great cleanliness and neatness which
prevail in the house . . . reminds one of a Dutch
coaster; this is evidently a point on which the
whaler is exceedingly particular.[10]

Not all the whalers were so domesticated. Kororareka in the Bay of Islands had a deserved reputa-
tion as having "a greater number of rogues than
any other spot of equal size in the universe",[11] and
some of its houses served equally as grog shops,
gambling dens, and brothels. But by 1840 when W.
Wakefield visited the Bay, whaling had declined,
and respectability had overcome the town, which
was well kept with neat wood cottages and a
hotel.[12]

The activity of the whalers and sealers soon
attracted a small land-based service industry. Europeans established chandleries and bought whale oil
and seal skins at better rates than in Australia, and
by attaching themselves to a local tribe developed
important trading links between Maori and Pakeha. The earliest surviving plan of a trader's house
in New Zealand is that of Oakes at Kohukohu,
recorded in Edward Markham's journal in 1834 as
a little boarded cottage without linings or glass. A
major part of this trade was the cutting of timber
and ships' spars for export to the Australian
market. This work was usually done by groups of
itinerant sawyers, but in places such as Horeke,
permanent yards were set up and quite large ships
built to carry the timber. Typical of their cottages
were those visited by Markham up the Maungam-
uka River: "mostly Weatherboarded and lined.
Some of them very nice and their saw pits sheded

9. Kororareka, Bay of
Islands, 1836 — an
engraving after an original
by J.S. Polack. *ATL.*

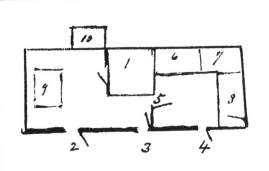

1 Pantry   2 and 4 Windows
3 Door into the House
5 Door of the bed room
6, 7, and 8 standing bed
places one over another.
9 Table.   10 Fire place
put up after.

10. Oakes' Cottage,
Kohukohu, 1834 — from a
sketch by Edward
Markham.

over, and Thatched and convenient for Water
carriage."[13]

At this time, the established settlements were
whaling camps, with some permanent inhabitants,
but highly seasonal and looking to the sea for
income. There were also scattered trading posts
dealing in timber, flax, pork and potatoes. These
settlers were wholly reliant on adopted Maori
tribes for the produce of the land — indeed, Markham felt it was not safe to live in the country
without a chief's daughter for protection.[14]
Although individual traders had acquired land and
had begun to work it, the first attempts to set up
more or less self-reliant communities were made
by missionaries of the Church Missionary Society
following Marsden's arrival in 1814. By 1838 there
were ten CMS mission stations from Tauranga to
the Bay of Islands. These included a mission store
at Kerikeri built of local stone with Sydney sandstone dressings, as well as a weatherboard house
(now the oldest timber building in New Zealand);
and the farm settlement at Waimate North, which
was to supply food for the northern stations.[15]

The mission stations took on the appearance of
English villages, with houses set in fragrant
gardens "all ablaze with flowers. Honey-suckle,
and passion-flowers and cluster-roses hung

in masses all over the verandah".[16] At Waimate there were three large houses, stables, workshops, barns, cottages, a mill, and a large chapel. Nor was this large community the unaided work of the "mechanic" missionaries who founded and laid it out. Under the direction of a gunsmith, a farrier and a flax dresser, Maori workmen — whose traditional tools had been stone and wood — worked to bring the rough land under cultivation and prepared and assembled the materials for the buildings, using European tools and techniques. Their achievement was catalogued by William Yate:

> By the natives . . . upwards of fifty thousand bricks have been made and burnt, most of which were used in building chimneys; upwards of seven hundred thousand feet of timber have been felled, and sawn up into plank, board, scantling, &c.; and more than two hundred thousand shingles have been split, and made use of. Three substantial weather-board dwelling-houses, forty feet by twenty, with skilling at the back, and returned at the ends, have been erected; likewise stables . . . stores, carpenters' shops, blacksmiths' shops, out-houses, eight or ten weather-board cottages, twenty feet by fifteen, and a spacious Chapel.[17]

While Waimate was a large undertaking for its time, Maori co-operation with Europeans was by no means uncommon and had become a feature of the pattern of settlement in New Zealand. From the very first contact with explorers and whalers, manufactured articles had been bartered for food and artifacts, and traditional skills had begun to change. Iron nails given by Cook and others were sharpened to become chisels which transformed the qualities and scale of carving; iron axes and adzes simplified the tasks of felling trees and shaping timber. As a result, Maori houses — though still of raupo construction — were often built larger with greater use of timber and carving.

Young Maori sailors learned the skills of carpentry and smithing from the whalers (as well as seamanship), and in their camps helped to construct houses which mixed Maori forms of construction with such techniques as pisé, wattle and daub, and eventually weatherboarding.

Individual Maoris travelled to Australia, America, and England, often returning to New Zealand with material gifts, and minds filled with European ideas. The chief Ruatara explained to Marsden in 1814 his plan for a town laid out "with regular streets to be built after the European mode."[18] Another much-travelled young Maori, while in England in 1816, learned "the first principles of drawing and perspective, [did] several of the first problems in Euclid, and [drew] various plans and elevations for building of houses."[19]

In 1820 the Hokianga chief Witi "expressed his intention of . . . building himself a house as much like the Europeans as he could and of living in their manner. He . . . often remarked 'that New Zealand would one day be the white men's country'."[20] In 1824 Earle recalled the house of one chief which was "really a very comfortable dwelling. It has a high door, which we would enter without stooping, and in a separate room was constructed a bed, after the pattern of one on ship-board."[21]

Maori houses began to be built, therefore, with features borrowed from the English, including higher walls, hinged doors, glazed windows, timber floors and partitions, and were furnished with beds, tables and chairs. Using the same construction methods, chiefs' houses grew in size to match the mission chapels, and with the elaboration of carving gradually developed into the modern meeting house. The new ideas were not accepted by all Maori leaders, however; many who were successful in their own world were cautious of the changes taking place and held fast to tradition, so that raupo houses continued to be built and lived in well into the twentieth century.

11. Tuhawaiki's House, Ruapuke, 1844. *ATL, J.J.G. Barnicoat*

SETTLEMENT 1840-60

"I have a house and garden of my own, and I never intend to be an English slave more."

LETTER FROM NEW PLYMOUTH,
2 March 1842.

In January 1840 the first of a stream of British settlers arrived in this country to establish the New Zealand Company's colonies at Port Nicholson (later to be named Wellington) and Wanganui. Within two years a third colony was installed at New Plymouth and a fourth at Nelson. In co-operation with the Free Presbyterian Church of Scotland and the Church of England, further settlements were founded at Dunedin in 1848 and Christchurch in 1850. By contrast, Auckland was established by proclamation in 1840 when Hobson moved the seat of government from the ill-starred Russell at Okiato near Kororareka. In the same year, the French established a colony at Akaroa, the first of a number of national minority settlements in the country. By the end of the decade there were nearly 26,000 Europeans in New Zealand.[22]

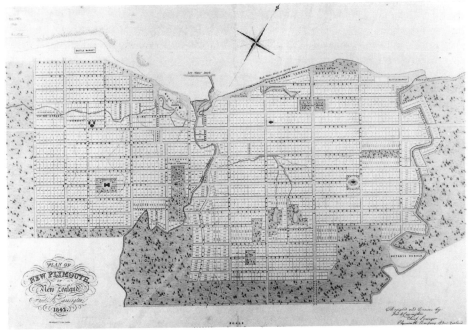

12. New Plymouth — The plan, 1842. *ATL*

13. New Plymouth — The reality, 1843. *ATL*

25

In most of the embryo towns, order was quickly established — on paper. Surveyors moved in, often with settlers hard on their heels, and grand avenues, squares, and "sections" were pegged out over scrub, forest, and swamp. In New Zealand Company colonies, the immigrants were unloaded from the ships and deposited with their belongings on the beaches. Wakefield vividly described the scene at Port Nicholson in 1840:

> the sand-hummocks at the back of the long beach were dotted over with tents of all shapes and sizes, native-built huts in various stages of construction, and heaps of goods of various kinds, which lay about anywhere between high-water mark and the houses. Thus ploughs, hundreds of bricks, millstones, tent-poles, saucepans, crockery, iron, pot-hooks, and triangles, casks of all sizes and bales of all sorts, were distributed about. . . . They pitched their tents and piled up their goods in rude order, while the natives, equally pleased and excited, sang Maori songs to them from the tops of the ware or huts where they sat tying the rafters and thatch together with flaxen bands.[23]

Not that Maoris necessarily remained pleased with the new arrivals. After several shiploads had landed in Port Nicholson, one local chief lamented, "They are all well armed; and they are strong of heart, for they have begun to build their houses without talking. They will be too strong for us: my heart is dark."[24]

The most immediate problem for new settlers was shelter. Those who could afford to brought prefabricated houses with them, but these could not be assembled until permanent sites were agreed upon. Others brought tents, such as Edgington's "Square Double Tents" (recommended in E.J. Wakefield's handbook),[25] but most of the new arrivals depended on the goodwill and skills of local Maoris, who quickly constructed raupo houses in return for small gifts. Later, the Company erected barracks for those arriving on succeeding ships, and some of these places were noted for their corrupt administration and the misery inflicted on their inhabitants.[26]

When the surveys were completed, the settlers selected their town, suburban, and country sections, and began to put up more permanent shelters.

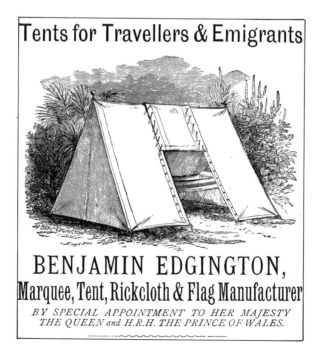

14. Edgington's Tents —advertisement from the *Yearbook of New Zealand,* 1885.

Houses for settlers
1840-1860

IMPORTED TECHNOLOGY

"I would say, take your house with you, or at least the framework for it . . . [you] will pay in London from 40L to 120L for a wooden house complete, with windows, doors, and all ordinary fittings, according to its size, and the number of rooms [you] may require . . . all upon the ground floor . . . giving a free scope to tasteful designs in the erection. This house may be, in all cases, put up within two days, or, at a pinch, in one day" — GEORGE BUTLER EARP, *New Zealand: Its Emigration and Gold Fields*, 1852.

Emigration was an industry as well as a vocation, and the intending emigrants did not lack advice from the many handbooks published to inform and entice them to the New Zealand colonies. *The Handbook for New Zealand*,[27] *New Zealand: Its Emigration and Gold Fields*,[28] *New Zealand, the Britain of the South*,[29] and other titles compared the established settlements, offered advice on what to take to New Zealand and how to set up house on arrival. Edward Gibbon Wakefield's colonial philosophy depended on attracting a balance of capitalist and labouring classes to the new land, and the handbooks tailored their advice to suit all pockets.

For the wealthy, Wakefield's son Edward Jerningham suggested a look at iron houses made for export by Cottam and Hallem in Oxford Street, or Manning's wooden houses at 251 High Holborn.[30] In the 1840s Britain led the world in the manufacture of prefabricated buildings, from modest wooden or iron huts to elaborate cast-iron villas, churches, and hotels. Some houses were sent complete in all respects, but often just the framework came, to be covered later with locally available materials.[31]

Other firms known to have sent buildings to New Zealand included Middlemas's, Tippet Silk and Heywood, Samuel Hemming's and Ketcher's ("The Well-Known Stockholm Joiners"). Manning's manufactured the first Government House for Auckland, while the heart of the Waitangi Treaty House is a three-room building based on a plan by architect John Verge, and prefabricated in Australia for its owner James Busby. The parts for this house included: framing timber, the studs and plates all mortised and tenoned with matching marks in roman numerals; feathered-edge weatherboards; solid panelled doors; french casements and matching shutters for under the verandah;

15. "Hemming's Patent Improved Portable Houses" — 1860. *ANL, Nan Kivell Coll.*

16. Mr and Mrs Watts-Russel's imported house at Ilam 1856 — "Mr and Mrs Watts-Russel have brought two frame wood-houses, each of three rooms, and putting them together they get six rooms, besides lofts . . ." (Charlotte Godley 1851). *ATL.*

small-paned double-hung sashes for the rest of the building; laths for linings, shingles for the roof, bricks for the chimneys; elegantly turned columns to support the verandah; Sydney sandstone slabs for hearths and verandah paving.[32]

The imported houses were not always put up at once. Sometimes they did not arrive intact, or proved too difficult to assemble, or were simply unsuitable for local conditions. "It has been a source of great vexation and expense to me," wrote one disappointed owner. "The original cost of the house, and the putting it up, will stand me in less than £200, whereas I expect if I am compelled to take it down the materials will not yield more than £40."[33] Some settlers much preferred the Maori whare to the "trumpery wooden houses made in England".[34]

At Port Nicholson the sections had not been surveyed when the first colonists arrived, while at New Plymouth the available sites were sometimes inconvenient. The provision of houses depended very much on the materials at hand in each "colony", and timber sawmills powered by water or steam were very soon in production. Within the first year at Port Nicholson three colonists set up a twenty horsepower steam engine for sawing and flour milling.[35] This kind of enterprise was not unusual, and within a few years of the founding of Auckland, although English-built houses continued to arrive, prefabricated kauri houses were being built for export to the United States.

PORTABLE HOUSES. — A new article of indigenous manufacture is likely soon to be added to our list of exports in the shape of wooden houses for California, several of which are now being erected for shipment to that country. These are built very substantially, and quite portable for easy transmission, and being made of the kauri, one of the most valuable woods for building purposes, will doubtless prove acceptable to the crowds now without such comforts on the banks of the Sacramento. D.S.C., 27.7.1849.[36]

28

Not all the houses brought to New Zealand came from England, however. As well as Busby's house which came from Sydney, others were made in Tasmania. J.G. Gordon brought his house from India, and put it up at "Clifton" in Hawke's Bay. It is also thought that the Eteveneaux house at Akaroa was prefabricated in France.[37]

Even if an entire house was beyond their means, the colonists were urged in the handbooks to take certain materials with them. For example:

	£	s	d
— One front and four inner doors, half a dozen iron casement sashes, fitted in wooden frames, and a box of glass	11	4	0
— A small assortment of wrought-iron nails and spikes, door and gate hinges, bolts, locks, pegs, and latches	5	0	0
— The New Zealand Tool Chest	7	7	0
— Some corrugated iron roofing stuff, and iron rod and wire for porch or verandah. Hursthouse, 1861.[38]	6	0	0

The recommendation to take tools to New Zealand was echoed in the letters home from earlier immigrants, who perhaps wished they had had more foresight. And not only tools, but home comforts as well, although Vogel thought the immigrant would be astonished at the variety of uses to which packing-cases and boxes could be turned.[39] Fitton recommended that the lady who could not decide between a piano and a chest of drawers would get more satisfaction from the piano — the drawers could readily be made by any skilled colonial carpenter.[40]

Building skills were available in New Zealand. In fact, any tradesman in the building industry was sure of a job at first, and the handbooks gave detailed advice about wages and hours of work in each of the settlements. But most wage earners and small farmers could not afford to pay a carpenter or bricklayer, and the cost of sawn timber, bricks, and joinery for housing was prohibitive. Consequently, many of the earliest houses — and for years the houses of those who settled the hinterland — were improvised from what lay at hand, when the only cost was the labour of a man, and very often his wife.

Iron & Wooden Houses.

NOW LANDING, EX "INVINCIBLE,"

HEMMING'S

Patent Improved Portable Buildings,

CLIFT HOUSE, BRISTOL.

FOUR STORES, 25 x 37 x 12 feet,
    One   ditto,   25 x 36 x 12 feet.
Two SHOPS, 24 x 33 x 9 feet, with
    three Apartments behind, and with
    mahogany Counter and Shelves, complete,
Two HOUSES, 26 · 6 x 14 feet, with
    5 rooms each,
One HOUSE, 26 x 22 feet, with 4
    rooms, passage, closets, &c.

The Frame-work of the above Buildings consists of Iron and Timber, the Sills of Oak. The walls and roof are of galvanised corrugated Iron. The walls are lined with ½-inch boarding, covered with canvass, ready for papering, leaving a space of 4½ inches throughout the entire building between the iron and wood work, by which means a complete ventilation is effected, and the temperature in Summer much lessened, and increased in Winter. The doors have 4 pannels, with good locks and hinges, and the sashes are glazed with glass 21 ounces to the foot, with shutters and fastenings complete. The erections are entirely put together with Iron Screws and Bolts, and may be put up by any inexperienced person in a few hours.

Extract from London Paper :—

"The first idea that strikes a stranger, and it is one that interested parties, we are sorry to say, are not slow to encourage, is that these buildings must be both insufferably hot and miserably cold, and that however neat and tasty they may look in the builder's yard, after a little Australian sunshine, they will let in more light than comes through the windows. Now all this we conceive would most likely be the case with an Iron house put up by a common builder, but Mr. Hemming is not simply a builder ; and a residence in tropical climates has taught him both, what to provide for, and what to provide against. The shrinkage and warpage is prevented by subjecting all the timber, previous to use, to a seasoning apparatus on the premises ; while a clear space of several inches betwixt the Iron and Wood work of the buildings, and a wide space between the ceilings, of papered inodorous felt, and the Roof, secures an ample ventilation and equable temperature."
—*London Paper.*

Plans and Elevations may be seen on application to

C. PETSCHLER,
Field's Lane, Shortland-street.

17. "Hemming's Patent Improved Portable Buildings" —advertisement from the *Daily Southern Cross*, 1865.

29

LOCAL MATERIALS

"I wanted a kitchen but my husband could not leave his work to do it. He helped to mix up the mud before he went to work and I put the kitchen up, 20ft. long and 12ft. wide, with a chimney and a mud oven."
— SARAH HIGGINS of Nelson, 1850s.

With the New Zealand Company settlers came surveyors and men such as Dieffenbach, who set about methodically describing and cataloguing the country's flora, fauna, geography, and geology. At an early date, the potential building materials of New Zealand were located and tried; very detailed descriptions of native timbers were made by missionaries Yate and Taylor, and their uses assessed by sawyers and traders exporting them to Australia. The natural stones in each area were identified (Dieffenbach's journal is peppered with descriptions of these), and soil types were examined at the sites of potential colonies.

The prime requirements for a site were productive land and a sheltered anchorage, and the building methods adopted in each place resulted from a combination of local materials and the traditions of construction brought by each group of immigrants from their native districts in Britain.

At Auckland there were two fine harbours and an abundance of scoria rock and kauri timber. At New Plymouth there were sea moorings, good timber and sandstone, and immensely fertile land — the "garden of New Zealand". Nelson had some bush and a small anchorage; Canterbury had only its fertile plains and a harbour behind the hills at Lyttelton. By contrast, Otago was well wooded with rimu, had excellent building stones, and a good harbour. Everywhere there was raupo, toetoe, or tussock to thatch roofs, and the earths and clays necessary for those home-made houses of cob, pisé, and mud brick.

The traditional building methods brought from Britain fell into two main types: mass walling of earth, brick or stone; and framed construction where timber was freely available. For *mass construction,* rammed earth, bricks, or stones were raised up to form thick walls on which the roof was set. In East Anglia mud brick was common, and compacted earth techniques such as cob and pisé were found in the Scottish lowlands, parts of the Midlands, and the counties of Cornwall, Devon, and Dorset. Stone and brick construction were used throughout Britain.

In *framed construction* the roof was carried on a timber frame sitting directly on the ground or on a masonry foundation, and the gaps in the walls of this framework were filled in with panels of bricks,

18. Raupo whare near New Plymouth, c. 1860. *ATL.*

30

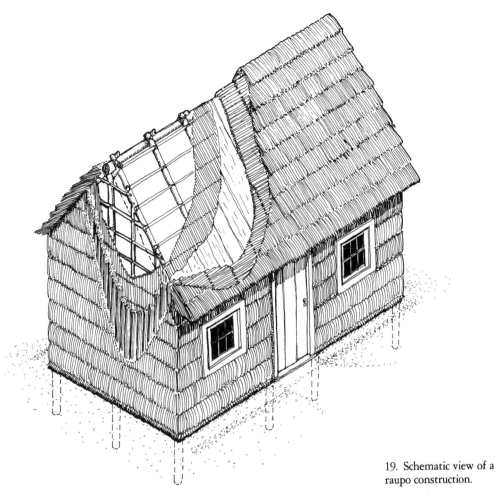

19. Schematic view of a raupo construction.

stones, or plastered basketwork (wattle and daub). Alternatively, the whole structure was covered with weatherboards, tiles, or plaster on laths. Buildings of this sort were common throughout southern England, the West Midlands, and in East Anglia.

In New Zealand these methods were adapted to build the first permanent cottages — usually single-storeyed and small, with one or two rooms to start with, and later perhaps an additional room and a verandah.

In New Plymouth settlers from Cornwall and Devon built cob cottages even though there was excellent timber available. In Canterbury cob and sod huts were built, simply because timber was so scarce. The Scottish settlers in Dunedin made cob, wattle and daub, and turf huts similar to the crofters' cottages back home. In Wellington timber milling and brick burning began in the first year of the colony, although bricks fell from grace after some early and devastating earthquakes.

There was no clear regional distribution of these methods in the early days of settlement, mainly because the immigrant population was so mixed, but also because the ubiquitous colonists' handbooks explained how to build in cob, pisé, turf, logs, timber slab, and masonry. These were the familiar cheap methods of building a first house in New Zealand; but to put them up took time, especially when a man had to earn a living, and for many immigrants it was the Maori *raupo* house that gave them their first shelter in the new land.

a. Raupo and timber

"Rapoo is a . . . Marsh Reed . . . it grows in Marshes and wet places, and makes a very warm hut or House."
— EDWARD MARKHAM, 1834.

The first colonists were surprised to find how comfortable a Maori whare could be, and how cheap — at first for the price of a few blankets and shirts, later for five or six pounds. The traditional

31

house had one room, with walls (if any) low to the ground, tiny openings, and earth floors. But European needs and expectations brought about a transformation of the traditional whare. Walls were made high enough to allow for sitting on a chair (or packing case) instead of the floor, partitions divided the space into separate rooms, floors were boarded over, and fireplaces added — at great risk to the thatched covering. Many were fitted with imported doors and windows which were later transferred to a more permanent house.

Construction of an ordinary raupo house was rapid. A warm and moderately weathertight hut could be erected in a day or two. Once the size of the house was determined, a series of stakes was driven into the ground around the perimeter and others were lashed horizontally to these to support thatching for the walls. In each end wall a pole with one forked end was set to support a ridge pole which in turn carrried the rafters, and stakes were laid across these for the thatched roof. This structure was very firmly lashed with flax. While this work was in progress, thatching materials — pref-

erably raupo — was dried in the sun so that it would be lighter to carry to the site, then tied in bundles and lashed to the framework.

There were many variations to this method. E.J. Wakefield described a fine large house erected for him at Taupo, 50 feet by 28 feet, with a framework of totara slabs at 5 feet intervals, and walls "nine feet high and six inches thick . . . composed of neatly packed bundles of *raupo* or bulrushes, lined inside with the glazed reed of the *tohe tohe* [toetoe], and outside with the *wiwi*, or fine grass . . . The roof, also 6 inches thick, was composed of four layers: the innermost, *tohe tohe* reeds, like the walls; the second, bark of the *totara*; the third, *raupo*; and the outside one, tufts of fine grass, put on like shingles, with the roots downwards."[41]

The Maoris lavished great skill on houses for white settlers and missionaries, and their work was often admired by men such as Dieffenbach, who described Chapman's house at Rotorua:

It was high, had glass windows, and several side apartments branching off from the middle room; it was built in the native style with these

20. Immigration barracks,
New Plymouth. *ATL.*

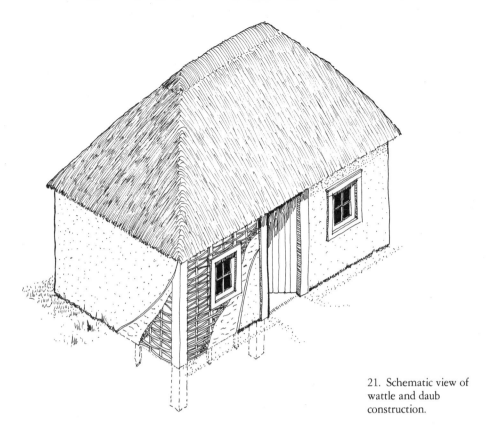

21. Schematic view of
wattle and daub
construction.

improvements . . . This house was in strength
and beauty equal to any in New Zealand on the
European plan; and, indeed, the natives are
excellent architects in any style.[42]

In the Company settlements Maoris were
employed to put up barracks for shiploads of
immigrants (rather like raupo motels), and the
value of the raupo hut continued to be recognised
as late as the 1880s — "with a rustic verandah they
are snug enough dwellings for three or four years,
and cost from 20L to 30L".[43]

Raupo huts, however, were never intended by
their European owners to be permanent dwellings.
They were highly inflammable and were eventually forbidden in towns and taxed out of existence.[44]
For more durable structures, the colonists turned to
the traditions of Britain, and to their handbooks.

b. Timber and mud

"As for 'wattle and daub' I could
wish that it had never been
invented. The more it saves in
time and gains in space, the
greater and the more general is the
disaster that it may cause for it is
made to catch fire, like torches."
— VITRUVIUS, BOOK II, ch VIII.

A combination of timber and mud is one of the
most ancient ways of making shelter. It dates from
the earliest human communities and in Britain was
for centuries the typical self-help housing of the
poor. Mud and small branches were easily collected,
cost nothing, and required little skill to make into
walls. There were many different ways of combining them, and different names for each process.
The most widely used method in Britain was *wattle
and daub*, known variously as "raddle and dab" in
Cheshire, "rice and stower" in the North County,
or "stake and rice" in Scotland.[45]

In its simplest form, wattle and daub was a
basketweave lattice plastered with mud on both
sides. It was notoriously fragile, lightweight,
inflammable, and had virtually no weather resist-
ance, yet it continued to be used in parts of Britain
as late as the nineteenth century. There were also
related building methods such as "split and dab"
(plaster on lath), and "mud and stud", where mud
was packed between two rows of horizontal
saplings fixed to a frame — both methods being
used in New Zealand.

The wattle and daub buildings that still survive
in Britain today are not the cottages of the rural
poor, but rather the "half-timbered" houses of the
well-to-do yeomanry. These were built with a

33

heavy timber frame leaving open panels into which were set windows, doors, or plastered walling. Slender uprights called "staves" were sprung into prepared holes and grooves in the frame. Wands were then woven through these, and the lattice was plastered on each side with a mixture of clay, hair, and dung — sometimes called a "pug". Each panel was finished with a lime plaster for weather protection and colour washed, and in some areas the frame was painted black to give the picturesque "magpie" effect of the tourist brochures and calendars.

Mud and timber construction emigrated to the colonies travelling steerage. In the drier parts of Australia there are still timber-framed station buildings which have basketweave panels. There are also buildings constructed in "mud and stud" —known there as "sapling and mud" or "half-timbering". The Australian acacia became popularly known as the "wattle" because its branches were so useful for this work. In New Zealand the dense bush was a generous source of suitable materials — nikau stems for the structure, manuka or matipo for the uprights, kareao (supplejack) for the basketweave, and tussock or wiwi grass for the pug mixture.

In both Australia and New Zealand any timber and mud construction was loosely called "wattle and daub", but Ensign Best knew the real thing when he saw it in Wellington's first Government House:

> Govt House is a Mauri built dwelling of Wattle and dab and Wattle and dab is this. A number of stakes are driven into the ground and a species of bine worked in between them so as to form a wall of basketwork exactly like a Gabion. This big basket is then pelted with soft clay until all the interstices are completely filled up both inside and out and then the ragged bits are carefully smoothed off and when dry it makes a tolerably good wall.[46]

Some early mission houses were also wattled. Henry Williams describes his cottage at Paihia as having sides formed of "a sort of basketwork and covered with mud to a considerable thickness, the external surface being plaster."[47] Settlers in Otago, however, preferred variations on the "mud and stud" method:

> . . . a framework [of posts about three feet apart] being first put up, and a number of small poles tied horizontally both in the inside and

22. Mud and stud house at Makiri Station near Gisborne. *AIM.*

34

23. Mud and stud house at
Robin Hood Bay,
Marlborough:
(a) general view;
(b) wall detail showing
weatherboard cladding over
mud walls.

outside of the posts, varying from 6 inches to 1
foot apart; the space is then filled up with wet
clay by the hand, and smoothed inside and
outside, so as to hide both poles and posts, or
some fill the vacancies with dry pieces of clay or
mould, and then plaster it smooth.[48]

When the walls were dry they were draught-
proof, but they had an unfortunate habit of turning
back to mud in a heavy rain. The Otago solution
was to line the outside with planks,[49] and the same
was done by the French at Akaroa where "the
colonists [dwelt] in small houses with wooden
beams and clay walls. Some of them [were] covered
with planks, others with reeds and rushes."[50] Dr
Barker's Christchurch house was also like this,
except that he put up the weatherboards first,
nailed to young trees set in the ground, then
rammed in behind the boards a mixture of clay,
earth, and grass, over which laths were fixed.[51] A
variation on this solution in Canterbury was described by Paul Pascoe as "slab, cob, and ricker"

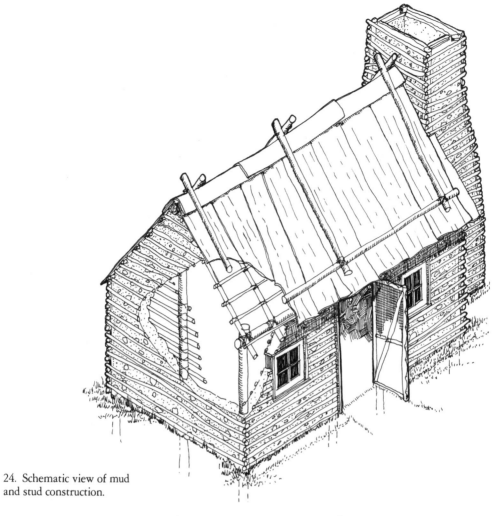

24. Schematic view of mud
and stud construction.

—rickers were the inner lattice of black birch
saplings, cob was the mixture of clay and chopped
tussock, and slabs of black birch replaced the outer
layer of saplings to make a completely weatherproof exterior.[52]

Another way of using a wooden lattice to support a mud mixture was plaster on lath, often
known in England as "split and dab", and found in
the gable walls of cob cottages or on both sides of
entire walls as in Essex. There are not many known
uses of this technique in New Zealand, but a
Dunedin house was described in 1849 as an
"Elizabethan mansion" finished with lath and plaster,[53] and Petre's house in Wellington was built of
lath and plaster, and roughcast like a farmhouse in
his native county of Essex. The last known building
of wattle and daub construction in New Zealand
was Jenkin's Cottage, built at Otaki in 1869. After
15 years' ineffectual negotiation with the Historic
Places Trust, this unique structure was bulldozed in
1985.

c. Earth

Mud or earth was not only used in combination
with timber, but as a construction material in its
own right. Regional tradition in Britain determined the form in which earth-built houses could
be raised, and five distinct methods can be identified, all of which were used in New Zealand. These
are: turf or sod, cob, pisé or *pisé-de-terre*, unburnt
brick or adobe, and burnt brick. Of these, the most
readily prepared and most primitive was turf.

i. Turf

> "a poor man, a wisket-maker,
> made a cot of stickes and turffes."
> — RECORD OF 1604.

Turf was widely used in Britain as a walling material (especially in the north), as roofing, and as a
fuel. It was an ancient right of the poor in Britain to
cut turfs for walls and fuel, and it was still used as a
building material in the early twentieth century.

25. Jenkin's cottage, Otaki, showing wattle and daub construction — until recently the only surviving example in New Zealand. *HPT.*

In building walls, turfs were cut in blocks about 150 mm deep and 900 mm long by 600 mm or so wide, ideally from close-cropped grass, and laid in rough courses on stones to make thick (up to 2.5 metres) irregular walls which were then pared with a hay knife to get a uniform surface.[54] Sometimes timber was used at corners or along the top of the walls as part of the roof structure.

In some areas the layers of turf alternated with layers of stones, and in other areas walls were constructed of two rows of turfs with stones in the middle to take roof water — as with the "black houses" of Lewis in Scotland. In these houses the roof was also turf, laid over a frame of timber and a thatch of bracken, strong enough to support a few sheep grazing on the living grass. Turf building was well known in Europe, and with the growth of the new colonies it travelled to the Americas and Australasia where it became known as "sod". In the United States sod houses were raised to a high art, in Nebraska for example, where Belgian settlers built very large two-storey houses, or "soddies".

The Australian sod houses are not well recorded, but in New Zealand sods were a valuable building material where timber was scarce, especially in Canterbury and parts of Otago. Fitton recommended sod buildings with a wooden frame and plaster as being warm and cheap — the only cost being a sharp spade and the owner's labour.

Excellent tough sods may be obtained almost everywhere, as the surface of the ground which has never before been broken up is densely matted with roots and fibres, and when cut like peat into blocks dries into firm compact masses.[55]

The sods were cut at an angle, sometimes with a special wide spade which produced pieces about 500 mm wide. In some places long strips were cut, rolled into cylinders, and carried to the building site. There were two kinds of construction: walls could be built of two rows of small sods with rammed earth between (not unlike the black houses of Lewis);[56] or a single thick wall was made with sods laid at an angle in layers, the slope in each layer opposite that in the next layer. This gave the finished wall a characteristic "herringbone" appearance, until it was covered with a clay plaster weathercoat.[57]

In 1851 Mrs Godley visited a Lyttelton house "of sods with a boarded roof, thirty feet long, and divided into two rooms",[58] and one of Samuel Butler's well-known houses at Mesopotamia in Canterbury was made of sod.

Sod houses did not last long, however. They were usually deserted once the fleas got in, or a more permanent house had been built, and they crumbled after a few years in the weather. But the technique has survived, and "soddies" are still occasionally built as temporary buildings in New Zealand. There are sod walls still standing in South Canterbury, and a "restored" sod house at Mt Pleasant in Christchurch reveals some of the original

sods under walls restored in cob and plastered in cement.

ii. Cob

Cob was really a kind of concrete: a wet mix was made of clay, tempered with chopped straw and cow dung, which set hard as it dried. Like wattle and daub, and turf, the materials were free, and the method very old. In Britain it had different regional names — cob in the West Country, witchit or wychert in Buckinghamshire, clob or clom in Lancashire, and others — words all meaning "clay" or the act of plastering.

This was a more sophisticated form of building with unbaked earth and although still a method used by the poor, houses made of cob were known to last for as long as 200 years. The great areas of cob building in England were the West Country, Hampshire, Leicestershire, Wiltshire, and part of Buckinghamshire.

26. Sod hut, Waipori, Otago — The Rev. A. Don visiting Chinese miners on the goldfields. *ATL, McNeur Coll.*

Walls were formed in layers without moulds or formwork, over a base of brick or stone about 600 mm to 1 metre high (but less in New Zealand — about 200 mm) and topped with a well-thatched overhanging roof. The great enemy of cob was damp, and it was said in Devon that "all cob wants is a good hat and a good pair of shoes".[59] If this rule was disregarded, the cob walls collapsed, or, as with the Richmond family's cottage in Taranaki, the chimney collapsed:

> . . . these cob chimneys are clay towers against the house side with an opening next the house, the wall of the tower above the opening rests on a beam and in the wet one end of this beam crushed down the wall it rested on: so before breakfast, it was 6½ when it fell, we had to dig our chimney out and make a fire in the open air and rain . . .[60]

The cob mixture was made at the site, and forked onto the wall at the feet of the "cob mason", who trampled each layer to a thickness of about 600 mm at first, but less for each new layer. Walls started at about 600 mm wide and tapered slightly as they rose, with the corners being rounded to stop them from cracking as the mixture dried. Construction was rather slow as the drying time for each layer was usually at least a week, although in Dumfries and Galloway cob houses were raised in one day at a "daubing" or community working bee.[61] For windows and doors, a timber lintel beam was laid in the wall and the openings cut out later when the cob was dry. Walls were "tinkered" (smoothed off) with an iron "cob-parer" — the only tool needed apart from a dungfork and spade. The finished work was then plastered to make it waterproof.

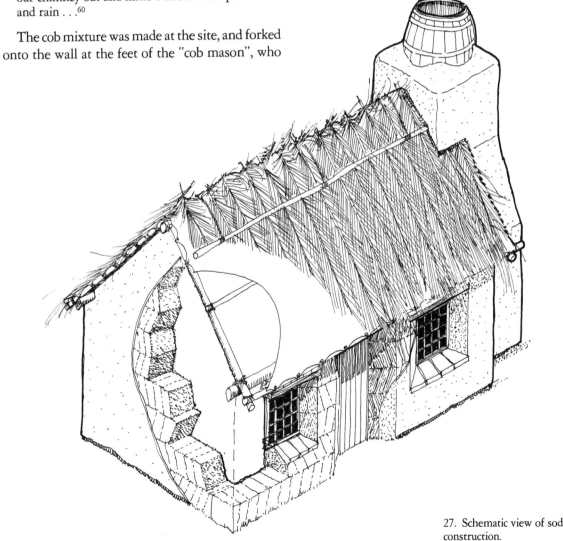

27. Schematic view of sod construction.

In New Zealand cob construction was common, and several of the colonists' handbooks recommended it for its simplicity — "any two farm-labourers with an eye sufficiently practised to form a good wheat or haystack, can build the house."[62] Herries Beattie quoted an extract from a diary kept at Puketoi Station in Otago, recording the progress of a cob house under construction in 1859:

[Feb] 15th: Puddled up clay and cleared a place for a house. 16th: Built up 18 inches of wall of house. 17th: Put layer on hut. 18th: Ditto. 19th: Ditto. 21st: Ditto. 23rd: Finished walls of hut. 24th: Put wall plates on hut. 28th: Pulled thatch for hut. March 1: Ditto. 3rd: Put battens on roof of hut. 4th: Commenced thatching. 10th: Thatched roof and built up chimney. 11th: Finished thatching. 14th: Tinkered up hut. 15th: Built up gable ends. 16th: Timbered up chimney. 18th: Put floor on hut. J. Murison made door. 21st: Clay hut and put dogs in chimney. 23rd: First occupation of the new hut.[63]

An 1851 house was built of cob by contract in Canterbury, with the framework supplied by a carpenter. It had three small rooms on the ground floor and two rooms upstairs under the roof, and was built so that more rooms could be added later.[64] At £150, this was an expensive production. Hursthouse in his handbook claimed that cob houses could be built at two-thirds the price,[65] and New Plymouth settlers valued their cob houses at around £40 in 1843.

In Nelson, New Plymouth, and elsewhere, cob was popular with settlers from Dorset, Cornwall, and Devon. In thinly wooded Canterbury there were many of these houses, including Butler's second hut at Mesopotamia. Pascoe described how the clay was "puddled" to make the cob mixture, "the puddler being the packhorse of many parts. He was tethered to a centre post by a radial cord and constrained to walk round a circular trench into which clay, chopped tussock and water were alter-

28. Cob farmhouse, Otago.
Otago Early Settlers Museum.

29. Cob cottage still standing at Brightwater near Nelson:
(a) general view;

(b) wall detail showing distinct layers of cob and remains of plaster weathercoat.

natively fed to the mixer."[66] He also described houses built of "boxed" cob, where the tempered clay was placed in a timber formwork or box to produce walls much straighter and more even than could be made with the usual open method.

In these Canterbury houses, the typical form was two rooms with a door in the centre of one long wall — the prototype of thousands of early cottages throughout New Zealand. Many of these houses still survive, more probably than is realised. These include Bloor's cottage at Allandale near Lyttelton, the large house "Broadgreen" at Nelson, and the Riverlands cottage near Blenheim which has been restored by the Marlborough Historic Society. There are other smaller houses in Nelson, Canterbury, and Otago, but few are adequately protected except by the good will and care of their owners.

iii. Pisé

Pisé is earth rammed into moulds. The name pisé comes from the ramming tool — or *pisoir* — used

41

30. Schematic view of cob construction.

to consolidate the earth in the mould. The system has Roman origins and is very well documented, particularly in France and Italy where it was widely used. Pisé was introduced into England in the late eighteenth century by Henry Holland, an architect who translated the most important French account of the method by Cointeraux. There was enthusiasm for the system among literate and professional people, and some housing was built of pisé by philanthropists, but it was seldom used by ordinary people except in parts of Southern England.

Pisé differed from cob in three important respects: rather than clay, screened earth was used and mixed with small pebbles about the size of hazelnuts; the mix was used dry, apart from a light moistening; and the tempered earth was placed in

removable timber moulds and rammed hard with the pisoir. The method is difficult to describe simply, and a more detailed account may be found in Lewis' book *Victorian Primitive*.[67]

Briefly, the mould was made to be taken apart and reused. Prepared battens called *putlocks* were laid across the wall, and large boards — approximately 4 metres long and 300 mm wide — were set on edge over these to contain the earth. The boards were kept apart by the earth and small struts at the top. They were kept from falling out by uprights wedged into holes in each end of the putlocks and bound above the boards with twisted ropes.

Earth was then built up in rammed layers about 100 m thick finishing at the open end of the mould in a steep slope. When the mould had been filled and rammed solid with the pisoir, it was taken down and the putlocks were pulled out of the wall, leaving a characteristic pattern of small rectangular holes. Each moulded layer was started from the end where the previous layer finished so that the soil slope in the open end of the mould lay in the opposite direction. The wall tapered from about 600 mm thick at the bottom, reducing by 15 mm in each course. Walls formed by this method were very hard and durable, and once plastered could be expected to last as long as cob. Like cob, pisé had to be kept dry, so a stone or brick base was essential. Both sides had to be plastered once the wall was dry to keep out the rain and to stop insects that otherwise burrowed in and riddled the walls.

Strangely enough, although cob houses were common in New Zealand and rare in Australia, the reverse seems to be true of pisé. There are a large number of well-preserved pisé buildings in Australia while in New Zealand it is not certain if any survive apart from the well-known Pompallier House at Russell.

31. Pisé construction — an illustration from C. Tomlinson, _Illustrations of Useful Arts and Manufactures_, 1858.

32. Pompallier House at Russell, Bay of Islands —the only known pisé building surviving in New Zealand.

People may have been discouraged by the extra cost of the formwork and the tools needed for the work, although these could be improvised, as missionary Richard Taylor did in 1848 when he showed Maori converts how to make pisé walls for a church. The Maoris adzed ten boards from 3 to 6 metres long, 900 mm wide and 75 mm thick. They are also recorded as having made their own wheelbarrow.[68]

Later, European settlers built pisé houses, possibly working from one of the handbooks which described the system — Earp, Burn, or Peter Nicholson. Wilson's 1949 survey recorded a Canterbury example from 1850,[69] and Charlotte Godley recalled a one-room pisé house bought by J.E. Fitzgerald from a squatter that same year. In Nelson the Redwood family built "Stafford Place" in 1842 of "peasy" — a mixture of clay and gravel.[70] William Pratt had two attempts at his pisé house in Christchurch, the first being destroyed when driving rain softened the completed walls.[71]

The best known and oldest surviving pisé building in New Zealand is Pompallier House, built in 1842 by Marist priests from the Lyons region of France under the supervision of the French architect Louis Perret. This building has a base of 600 mm thick walls and a first floor of 150 mm timber framing with pisé *between* the studs and all plastered over — a system known as "panelled" construction.[72]

Pisé was reckoned to be a fast method of construction as there was no need to wait for each layer to dry out. It is interesting, therefore, that Pompallier House took many months to erect. Perret was not a very practical man, the fathers were strictly amateurs, and they found the local soils difficult to work with. Father Gavin revealed some of their frustrations in a letter:

> . . . we can build in *pizet* without money, but with some difficulty and time! Still, we can supply the latter. Well, good, let it be in *pizet!* Brothers, Fathers, all get to work, but what a job it is making these walls emerge from the soil. Finally they do appear. Now they rise on their foundations. But as Father Epalle often says: "This *pizet* splits and cracks in all directions; the principles of Rondelet are not based on the soil of the antipodes, a soil which one thinks is quite good is found to be quite bad" . . . while waiting, we say: "Little by little the bird builds its nest".[73]

33. Detail of mud brick wall, North Canterbury.

iv. Mud brick

"Then the officers of the children of Israel came and cried unto Pharaoh, saying wherefore dealest thou thus with thy servants? There is no straw given unto thy servants, and they say, Make brick."
— EXODUS V;15,16.

Mud brick construction is well known in America as *adobe,* and in England as *clay lump.* In New Zealand, mud brick buildings can still be found in Central Otago and parts of Canterbury. It is just as likely that the technique came with the rush of gold diggers from the American west, as from the small part of East Anglia where clay lump construction was common. But the method was the same and the forms were those common to most early cottages — the simple gable roof, the chimney at one end, perhaps a verandah.

Mud bricks were shaped in bottomless wooden moulds — as burnt bricks once were — from a cob mixture of clay and straw, turned out and left to dry in the air (but not the sun) for a month or two. The bricks were larger than those made for burning, but there was no uniform size and it was just a matter of what was convenient — accordingly they varied from about 300 x 150 x 125 mm to 450 x 225 x 150 mm or more. Small bricks could be laid in the same bonds as burnt bricks, but more common were walls of one brick thickness, laid in stretcher bond.

The bricks were laid fairly roughly in lime mortar or clay slurry, to give a good "key" for the weatherproof plaster coat. Once bricks had been prepared, actual construction was much faster than for cob or pisé, and though the walls were thinner, their insulation was just as effective as that of other mud houses. Adobe was also considered drier than walls of burnt brick, but as with all mud walls, it still needed a stone or brick base to stop rising damp.

Many mud brick buildings survive in the Ranfurly area of Central Otago near the Kyeburn gold diggings, and some appear to be in remarkably good condition, including a group at Patearoa, and others at Oturehua. North of Balclutha a small cottage has been restored, and others may be found intact as far north as mid Canterbury.

34. Mud brick (adobe) buildings, Central Otago. *Tim Heath.*

v. Burnt brick

"By and by, as you grow richer, you may burn bricks at your leisure, and eventually build a brick house. At first, however, you must rough it."
— SAMUEL BUTLER, 1860.

Brick is the most sophisticated of the earth-based building materials. By the mid-nineteenth century brickmaking had become an exact science in Britain and bricklaying a high art, and for middle- and upper-class people, brick or stone were the only proper materials for building. It was not surprising then that brick-burning was one of the first industries established in the new settlements. At Wellington two colonists, Sinclair and Miller, had begun to make bricks by May 1840, and at the end

35. Hand-making bricks
—from C. Tomlinson,
*Illustrations of Useful Arts
and Manufactures*, 1858.

157. BRICKFIELD, MOULDER'S BENCH, KILN, &c.

of that year a large kiln was operating at Kaiwharawhara.[74]

In Auckland in 1841 William Mason called for tenders to supply 300,000 bricks and lime for the new St Paul's Church.[75] In 1842 bricks were being burnt at Nelson (almost certainly by Sinclair), and at New Plymouth, although not always successfully. There was the problem of finding good clays; one letter writer from New Plymouth thought the local clay was too sandy, and that a pugmill was needed, as well as an experienced brickmaker.[76]

The earliest New Zealand-made bricks, along with those brought as ballast from England, must have gone into chimneys, and it was not until mid 1842 that an immigrant bricklayer claimed to have built Wellington's first brick house — two years after bricks were first fired.[77] By this time, "bricks were . . . plentifully supplied from several rival kilns; and many buildings were being erected of that material."[78] In Dunedin, after one year only the "best houses" had brick chimneys, others making do with chimneys of clay and wattles.[79]

These early bricks were made using traditional English methods. Clay was dug and tempered — in England using a pugmill — in New Zealand at first by being turned over with spades and wetted, or by being trampled underfoot by animals. The tempered clay was then given in lumps to the brick "moulder" who threw it into a wooden mould, scraped off the excess, and turned out the "green" brick to be stacked for drying in the air.

There were no kilns for the first firings, so bricks were burnt in *clamps*, about 20,000 at a time. A clamp was a stack of bricks which were set out in layers with enough space between each brick for heat to circulate. As the stack was built up, brushwood was packed in between the bricks and between each layer. The whole stack was covered with turfs or cinders, a fire was lit on one side, and during the twenty or thirty days needed to complete firing, the fire was moved progressively around the kiln. It was a wasteful method, and Heaphy commented that the first bricks burned in Wellington "did not prove good" because the clay had not been well worked and the firing had been poor,[80] and in Dunedin the first bricks were described as "nothing but lumps of half-burnt sand".[81] People who settled away from the towns had to make their own bricks using the same methods. According to Hardwicke Knight:

> . . . the farmer could find clay somewhere on his section, dig it, and inform the brickmaker when he was ready. The brickmaker would then turn up with moulds and the farmer would puddle the clay by walking his horse round and round in it. The brickmaker would then mould and fire the bricks after which all would be cleared away and no evidence of the activity left except the bricks.[82]

If they could not hire a brickmaker, settlers had to depend on handbooks such as *The Colonist's and Emigrant's Handbook of the Mechanical Arts*.[83] At

36. Clamp kiln. *Jack Diamond Coll.*

Waimate North, over 50,000 bricks were made and laid by Maoris, and these bricks have the characteristic thumb print in the corner, where the wet clay was pressed into the mould. In 1844 Mrs Greenwood described her Motueka house, and wrote that "bricks are now [being made] on our own ground at the very moderate rate of 15 shillings per 1000, and before next winter we hope to have a nice stack of chimneys, comprising two (for the parlour and kitchen) rising in the middle of the house."[84]

As important as the bricks was the mortar in which they were laid, and which held them together. The essential ingredient for mortar was lime which gave it adhesive strength, and which had to be manufactured. Traditionally, lime was made by burning limestone in a kiln to remove carbonic acids and reduce the stone to a powder. The burnt lime was then *slaked* by mixing it with water, and in this form it was again wetted and combined with sand to make the mortar.

At first in New Zealand, lime came from sea shells which had to be collected and burnt in very large quantities. This made rather indifferent mortars, but by 1843 lime kilns were working in Nelson, and others followed in Otago and near Auckland in the early 1850s.

Bricks were in great demand in Wellington following a disastrous fire in 1842 when more than 40 raupo and timber houses were destroyed.[85] In Auckland in 1843 Thomas Henderson hinted at the dangers of building wooden houses when he advertised:

"Bricks! Bricks! Bricks! The undersigned congratulates the public of Auckland on the happy decline of the vile practice of building Town Houses with wood. That he may do his part towards so desirable an object, he has established a Brick walk, and has now the pleasure to announce that he is ready to deliver Bricks of a better quality than have usually been offered to the Auckland public.[86]

Wellington people soon learned, however, that brickwork was a poor risk in an earthquake — especially when the mortar was only sand and clay

— indeed, humble cob was considered safer than brick.[87] There were earthquakes as early as 1842 in the settlement, and at first it was thought that these would not damage a well-built brick house. However, in a major earthquake six years later, "almost all the brick edifices went . . . and as almost all the chimneys [were] of brick, they too nearly all either came down or cracked."[88]

In spite of this and later earthquakes, bricks continued to be made throughout New Zealand, and there can have been few small communities that did not in time have at least one brickyard. All the same, brickwork never became the basic building material in New Zealand that it was in Britain, partly because of its cost, and also because of the earthquake risk. Only the grand buildings — churches, commercial premises and public institutions — followed the English tradition of building in bricks and mortar or stone.

37. (a) Building known as Dacre Cottage near Auckland, built of hand-made bricks. (Since reconstructed in modern metric bricks.) *David Reynolds.*
(b) hand-made bricks from Dacre Cottage.

d. Stone

Stone is another ancient building material. It has long been used for important buildings, yet in England its wide use in ordinary houses dates only from about the seventeenth century. Within 200 years stone became an important vernacular material in Britain, especially in Scotland and Wales, the north and southwest of England, and in a long swathe from Yorkshire down through the Midlands to the Dorset coast.[89]

Special techniques were developed to build stone walls for both houses and fences, and although there are many kinds of building stone, there are only two main methods of constructing stone walls: *ashlar*, where quarried stone is sawn to particular sizes and laid in courses with fine joints; and *rubble*, where rough stones are used as they are found, or only roughly shaped, and laid with wide joints. Because of its cost, ashlar work was used in the buildings of the gentry or their institutions, and ordinary folk made do with one of the various forms of rubble work for their houses.

Some of these walls were laid dry — that is without mortar — and even when a mortar was used it was more often just clay to fill the gaps between stones, so that the strength of the wall still depended on how the stones were fitted together. Lime mortars were rare, and the lime often leached away in time.

There are three main kinds of stone: igneous, sedimentary, and metamorphic. The igneous group is formed when molten lava (magma) solidifies, and in New Zealand this includes Auckland's scoria, South Islands "bluestones", and granites from the Coromandel and Southland. In the sedimentary group are the limestones and sandstones, most of which are easily cut and worked. Oamaru stone is the most-used New Zealand limestone, but there are also some fine marbles, in Nelson for example. Of the metamorphic rocks, the most significant is the Central Otago schist, the only stone that was important for building ordinary cottages in this country, although slate from North Otago later became a common roofing material.

The earliest stone building in New Zealand was

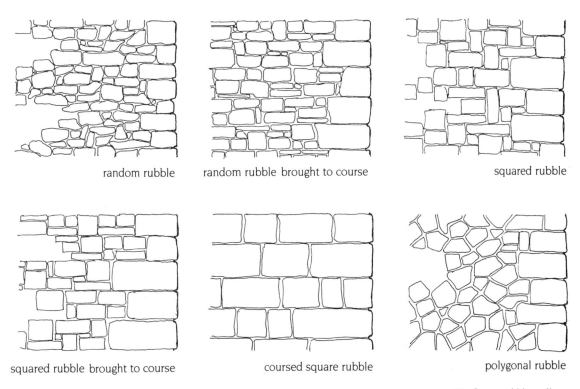

random rubble random rubble brought to course squared rubble

squared rubble brought to course coursed square rubble polygonal rubble

38. Stone rubble wall construction.

39. Stone cottage,
Benmore, North Otago.
ATL, Middleton Coll.

the Kerikeri Stone Store, built by a Sydney mason for the Church Missionary Society in 1832-6. He took shattered basalt from the nearby riverbed and laid it as coursed rubble, with the openings and corners edged with sandstone brought from Sydney and sawn on the site.

Other stone buildings were built for missionaries in the 1840s and 1850s — Te Henui Parsonage at New Plymouth, using the local sandstone; and at Auckland the Deanery at Parnell, the Melanesian Mission and St John's collge at Meadowbank, all in the local scoria. A number of expensive private houses of this period were also built of stone — Hulme Court and the Kinder House in Auckland; Richmond Cottage at New Plymouth; and in Canterbury Purau Homestead, "Harlston", and later the Lyttelton Vicarage and Potts House.

Less well recorded, or protected, are the simple stone cottages of Central Otago. This area was poor in timber, but schist stone was freely available and proved ideal for wall-building. Many of the schist huts and houses still survive in a crescent stretching from Dunback, over the Pigroot to Alexandra, and out to the Taieri Plains near Waihola.

These were not the only simple stone cottages in New Zealand. In Hawke's Bay pumice was squared into blocks to make a house for the McKain and Villers families;[90] in New Plymouth stone was first brought from further south then worked locally; and Canterbury has many stone buildings, some crumbling through neglect, but many still in use.

There was plenty of information about building stones for the early colonists. Dieffenbach's journal, which had been published in 1843, exhaustively described the country's geology and rock formations, and in 1885 *The Yearbook of New Zealand* reviewed the main building stones accessible to the settlements. Like brickwork, stone was expensive and vulnerable to earthquakes, yet many believed it would replace timber — "the little wooden houses . . . are not very sumptuous places of abode; but they do well as the first covering. No

40. Squared rubble brought to course in a derelict cottage, North Canterbury (see fig. 38).

doubt, when people grow richer, they will be replaced by stone buildings."[91] Despite these hopes, stone is mainly used in New Zealand today as road metal and concrete aggregates.

e. Timber

> "Wooden house with shingle roof,
> neither wind nor waterproof."
> — CANTERBURY SKETCHES, 1879.

One of the most difficult things for British settlers in New Zealand to realise was that they had to exchange the reassuring mass of a solid masonry house — of cob, brick, or stone — for a "poor, flimsy, band-box sort of dwelling" made of wood.[92]

The weatherboard house seemed just another way of building short-term shelter until it was possible to buy or build something more permanent. Letters from early New Zealand repeatedly expressed surprise at the number of wooden buildings here, even though the country was heavily wooded with many species of high quality timber trees.

The characteristics of the major native timbers, and many of the lesser varieties, were well known when the colonists arrived. Very detailed descriptions of the species had been made in their journals by Yate, Taylor, Polack, Dieffenbach, and Heaphy. Sawyers from Australia had been working here for years, exporting huge quanitites of kauri to Melbourne and Sydney, where Marjoribanks had seen

"the most beautiful floors laid with it in some of the more fashionable houses".[93] Yate's account was especially valuable to settlers for its discussion of how each timber could best be used in buildings, boats, and furniture.

Yate described the puriri as easy to split and work, and resistant to rot, which made it useful for shipbuilding and as foundations for houses. Although the wood polished well, it was of little use for furniture because it was riddled with the holes of the mokoroa grub which infested the living tree — a cause of complaint in the first mission church at Waimate, where the wind whistled through the grub holes in the puriri walls.

Tawa, though likely to rot if allowed to get damp, Yate considered valuable as a lining for houses. Tanekaha was recommended for posts, verandah floors, and decking for ships. Kahikatea (or white pine) was considered soft and spongy and liable to rot. Yate said little about totara or rimu (red pine) except that their qualities were not sufficiently known for them to be much sought after.[94]

The kauri, however, Yate described as the "monarch of the forest" and the most useful of all New Zealand timbers. He was particularly impressed with its use in buildings: "the whole superstructure, with all the furnishings, inside and outside, [might] be supplied with advantage from the mighty trunk of this valuable pine."[95]

The uses made of the apparently limitless supply of timber ranged from fuel for cooking fires

41. Ponga log cottage,
Heathfield settlement.
ATL.

and palings for fences, through rough frames of branches for thatched roofs and walls, to houses built entirely of timber sawn from the trunks of large trees. Not all wooden houses were made of sawn timber; sawing was laborious work needing at least two men to cut a log into *scantlings* (framing timber) and boards, and a man on his own could more readily make a house from logs or slabs split from the felled tree. It was not even always necessary to cut the trees down:

> On my leasehold there was a clump of maple trees, but before cutting them down, I stretched a line through them for the ground plan of the house: trees which coincided with this line *I left standing,* merely cutting off the tops, and those which were out of the line were cut down and put in the line by digging holes. By this novel plan the walls were made strong and substantial in one day . . . There was a difference of two feet in the breadth of the gables, but as no one could see the four corners of the house at once, it was never known to any one but myself.[96]

The ponga (treefern) was popular for framed log houses, particularly in Southland and Otago. Typical of this type of house was one built in Dunedin in 1849. A frame of posts about 900 mm apart was made, with a wall plate to carry the roof. Fern trees were then set on end between the posts and tied with flax to small horizontal saplings at the top and bottom, with spaces being left for doors and windows. The ends and gables were made of "pales" set in the ground, touching each other, and tied to a cross rail, and the finished walls were plastered with clay on both sides.[97]

Charlotte Godley described such a house at Dunedin, built of split tree ferns by the Carter brothers and plastered inside and papered. This house had bow windows, red and white "pine" woodwork, and a well-oiled parquet floor.[98]

Surprisingly, the North American or northern European log cabin, where logs are laid horizontally and notched together at corners, does not seem to have been popular here, although it was common in Australia. There were, however, odd examples — in Westland for example — and the technique was explained by Robert Scott Burn in his handbook.[99] This was also true of the "drop-log" method, where logs with tapered ends (or slabs) were laid between uprights with sides grooved to hold them in place. Apart from the

Waihi redoubt, which had massive squared logs or slabs set between uprights, the nearest local equivalents were ponga houses where trunks of treefern were laid horizontally within a timber frame.

Slab houses, on the other hand, were quite common, although their construction was a little more elaborate and required logs to be split into pieces about 70 mm thick using wedges. Many of the native timbers were excellent for this purpose, and the method was well documented in *Brett's Colonists' Guide*. The following letter to the *New Zealander* also described the method:

> Mr Editor, — A little practical experience will be worth a deal of theorising. I will therefore give my own case in the building of a *"cheap habitation for a family."* Although not a newcomer, I am comparatively a new settler in the Bush. I have for two years lived (not existed merely) in a *split slab house*, which cost me 20L. and in this same cottage or hut — myself, wife, and family — in all six of us — have lived really comfortably.

Now, how to proceed: — Go into the Bush with your axes, maul, and wedges — fell a rimu, totara, kaikatea, or kauri, as the case may be —cross-cut it into lengths of seven feet. Then, with your wedges, *quarter* these lengths, and split them into slabs of about ten or twelve inches wide and two inches in thickness; cut some good posts for the corners, stringers, wallplates, and also ridge pole, rafters, and divisions. This is all the stuff you require, and up to this point, excepting your own labour, it has not cost you 1s. If you can get a few thousand shingles in the neighbourhood at 10s. or 12s. per thousand, do so — if not, thatch with nikau and rushes. A good slab chimney, six feet wide and four deep, is desirable: it should be, for about four feet high inside, piled up with stones. After a bit you can cut slabs, and put them down for the floor.

Now if you are not able to do this yourself, there are plenty of men who will do it for 15L. to 20L. and a week or ten days will suffice to ensconce you in a *snug* and *comfortable*, although not *showy* or *elegant* habitation . . .

OLD PRACTICAL. 100

42. Slab hut. *ATL, McAllister Collection.*

The construction details missing from Old Practical's letter were supplied in *Brett's Colonists' Guide*. Once the slabs had been split, hardwood posts 900 mm longer than the slabs were cut and set in holes at the corners of a plan marked out on the ground. Wall plates, squared from long straight poles, were fixed over the corner posts, and bottom plates fixed between, and to these the slabs were nailed. Rafters and ridge pole were cut from straight poles about 75 mm diameter and nailed in place. Split battens were then fixed over the rafters to support the roof shingles, which were about 300 mm long and 100 mm wide — although some were as large as 750 x 300 mm.[101]

Some of these houses survive from later periods of settlement. One such house is the *slab-hus* of the Scandinavian colony at Mauriceville in the Wairarapa, where slabs of totara were used to face rammed earth walls, not unlike the slab, cob, and ricker houses of Canterbury. Near Akaroa, there is a reconstructed slab house with a shingled roof in an open-air museum. Further south in Canterbury, Samuel Butler used a slab construction lined with mud plaster:

> This you will make of split wooden slabs set upright in the ground, and nailed onto a wall plate . . . on the inside of the slabs you will nail light rods of wood, and plaster them over with mud, having first, however, put up the roof and thatched it.[102]

This method was well known in Lancashire, where it was called "clam staff and daub".

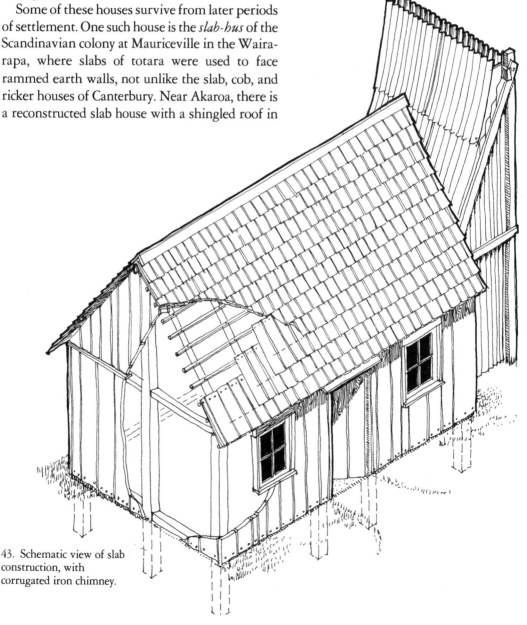

43. Schematic view of slab construction, with corrugated iron chimney.

44. Bush huts with paling roofs, Katikati. *ATL, Tudor Collins Collection.*

Another building material readily available in New Zealand was shingle or "shake", used to cover roofs and often walls. These were split from sawn blocks of totara or kauri with a hand-held knife called a "frow", which was struck with a mallet into the block. According to Hursthouse, cob houses were usually thatched, while stone, brick, or wood houses were shingled. Kauri, totara, and puriri were popular for this purpose because they split easily, but the wood became very dry in time and was easily ignited by flying sparks. In good houses the shingles were painted for preservation, and preparations were soon invented for fireproofing them. One such recipe, from a cutting stuck in the back of the Auckland Public Library's copy of Burn's handbook, suggested a wash of lime, salt, and fine sand or wood ash — with lamp black added if a darker colour was preferred.

Shingles were fixed so that only the bottom third of each shingle showed on the finished roof, and the joints in each row were offset from those in the rows above and below. This meant that at any point on the roof, there were three thicknesses of wood for weather protection. A New Zealand variation on the shingle was the use of palings — long boards laid in overlapping rows, each of double thickness with offset joints.

An alternative to shingles was bark, which was common in Dunedin where only the best houses had shingle roofs. Other houses had roofs covered with two or three overlapping layers of manuka bark, and a rough grass. One of the early settlers there described how neat the bark ceiling looked, and how in the firelight it was like some beautifully grained wood.[103] Bark sheets were also used in Southland on the roofs of saw-millers' houses.

45. Sawmiller's house with bark roof, Southland. *Wallace Museum.*

46. Pit sawing. *ATL, Godber Collection.*

These were held in place by a system of long horizontal poles supported from the ridge by "saddle poles", which prevented the sheets from curling up again into their natural shapes. This technique had been borrowed from the Aborigines by European settlers in Australia, and in New Zealand from established Maori practice.[104]

Wherever it was practical, timber was sawn for building. Sawn timbers were lighter, easier to handle and fix, wasted less wood, produced neater more weathertight buildings than slabs or logs, and were increasingly preferred as the new towns grew and forests gave way to farms. In the towns sawmills were soon established, and there were always immigrant carpenters and other tradesmen to build houses. However, in the bush or on the farms, and for those without ready cash, sawing had to be done laboriously by hand with the pit saw.

Sawing was probably New Zealand's first industry. From the early nineteenth century teams of itinerant sawyers had been felling and cutting up trees for the Australian market. Marsden brought sawyers with him to produce timber for the first mission stations, and pit-sawn timber was always the first available in the new settlements. Even when mills had been set up many immigrants could not afford to buy timber, and still had to saw their own to get boards and framing for a house. The advantage of handsawing was that the saw could be taken to the log, and only the usable timber had to be carried away. Moving logs was skilled and heavy work, and it was often easier to dig a pit where the tree lay, and saw it on the spot. Often a house would be built at or near the site of the felled tree and its pit.

It was not always necessary or possible to use a pit — on sloping ground it was more practicable to make a trestle from large branches to support the log. Sawing was arduous work and highly skilled. Two men worked the heavy, long (three metre) saw: one in the pit beneath the log pulled the saw down and was bathed with sawdust; the other

stood on the log taking the weight of the saw, and gauged the accuracy of the cut from an axed notch at the end of the log — because of this, he was known as the "top notcher". The men were highly paid, and in Wellington they could "earn enough in two days to remain idle and drunk the other five".[105]

The technique came from England with other carpentry skills, and was used there for cutting floorboards and other small timbers such as studs, rafters, and joists. In New Zealand all the timber for a house was cut in this way at first, and there are many houses still standing with boards that bear the straight saw marks of the pit saw.

The best quality timber came from logs which had been quartered, then sawn radially, producing close-grained boards which did not warp or cup. But this was wasteful of the wood and it was common practice to saw the whole log right through with each cut. It was the same at the

47. "Kai warra warra sawmill", 1843 —engraving after S.C. Brees. *ATL.*

48. English weatherboard cottage. *R.J. Brown.*

sawmills, except that the saws were circular, and driven by water or steam. The first water-powered mills were set up at Mercury Bay in 1838 and Ngunguru in Northland in 1840.[106] In his account, Wakefield noted several mills: one in Wellington in 1840 powered by steam, which also drove a flour mill; and another on the Manawatu River in 1842, where a twenty horse-power engine had been set up by the Kebbell brothers to saw logs rafted down the river. Yet another, on the Kaiwharawhara

River, was water powered with two or three circular saws in constant use.[107] In 1842 a steam sawmill was landed at Mill Bay in the Manukau Harbour, which had a Cornish Beam engine that drove frame and circular saws, a shingle cutter and a lathe.[108]

Timber used in houses was of two kinds: framing and boards (or as they were then known, *scantlings* and *deals*). Framing timbers have changed little since then, and common sizes were 75 x 50 mm, 100 x 50 mm, and up to 350 or 400 mm wide for studs, wall plates, rafters, and floor and ceiling joists. Boards were of luxurious dimensions by modern standards — often 225-350 mm wide and a full 25 or 32 mm thick, though also as thin as 8 or 10 mm. The thin boards were used for linings, and the thicker boards for floors, weatherboards and such fittings as stairs and doors.

A typical small cottage had two small rooms under a gable roof, with a frame of studs and plates — the studs mortised into the plates to reduce the

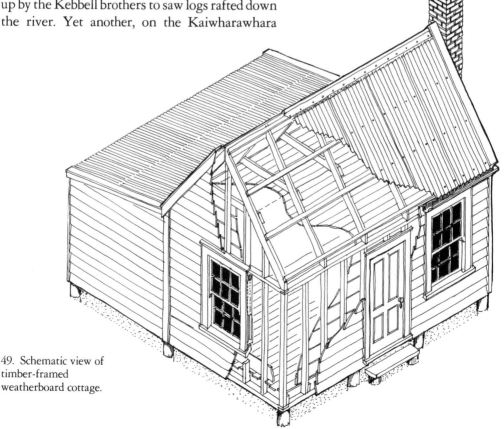

49. Schematic view of timber-framed weatherboard cottage.

need for nails which were still an expensive imported item. In the 1840s and 1850s many nails were still hand-made, although mass production had been possible since patents of 1810 in America and 1827 in England. In the past other fixings such as wooden pegs or even sheep's bones had been used, but the timber-framed and weatherboarded house of the 1840s onward depended on iron nails for its strength and ease of construction.

In eighteenth century England weatherboard houses were a novelty confined to the south eastern counties, although the technique had been used for farm buildings since about 1600. By the nineteenth century softwood weatherboards were common on cottages in Kent and Sussex. Whereas in England a brick or stone foundation was made for a wooden house, in New Zealand everything was wood including a ground plate of puriri on which the framed wall sat. In later houses, piles of puriri or totara were used — sections of round logs or branches about 600 mm long, set in holes with the bottom plate of the wall laid over them. Some imaginative builders used boulders, or even whale bones as foundation blocks instead.

The houses built directly on the ground suffered badly from decay as the untreated wood rotted because there was no ventilation to take away moisture. This was especially true with kahikatea, a timber also very susceptible to borer. Many settlers had been attracted by its clean grain and the ease with which it could be worked, only to find that it rapidly decayed in the wet. Damp and insects were the silent killers of the wooden building.

In these early houses the pattern of construction that shaped New Zealand housebuilding for a century was established. A simple frame of 100 x 75mm studs (uprights) was mortised into the bottom plate and a horizontal top plate, and fixed with timber pegs. Each wall was then braced with a diagonal board cut into the edges of the frame members. Openings were trimmed in the frame for doors, windows, and a fireplace. Then the outside was lined with weatherboards. These were most commonly fixed horizontally, each board overlapping the one beneath it, the usual size being 225 x 25 mm (9" x 1"). At first corners were made by stopping the boards against a solid vertical block.

50. "Long and short work" — timber construction made to resemble the quoins of masonry buildings, Springston, Canterbury.

There were other kinds of weatherboard. Houses with some pretensions to style often had large boards laid flat and close butting on the front elevation, and painted to resemble a stone wall. Sometimes there were extra boards at the corners, known as "long and short work", to resemble the stone quoins of masonry construction.

Much simpler were walls of board and batten, where wide boards (about 300 mm) were fixed vertically and each joint was covered with a narrow (75 mm) batten. In later houses this was used mainly on outbuildings, but the strong vertical lines were popular in early large houses in the "Carpenter Gothic" style of North America — two notable examples in New Zealand being "Oneida" near Wanganui, and "Highwic" in Auckland. Alex

51. Cottage showing part
of the framed construction,
linings, and weatherboards,
Wiri, Auckland.

Bowman noted an 1855 house in Lyttelton where the framed walls were lined with boards and the joints also covered with boards — rather than battens — and both walls and partitions were filled with a cob mixture between the framing.[109]

Interior linings were also made of timber, usually thin wide boards, close fitted or tongued and grooved to keep out draughts. These proved very necessary, as Charlotte Godley found during a good blow in Christchurch:

> . . . the wind rose suddenly, and in half-an-hour it was a violent gale, and the rooms, which are of single weather-board, unlined, became so full of dust that we could hardly open our eyes or draw a long breath, and all the remaining parties beat a quick retreat.[110]

The roofs too were all timber, with a simple frame of rafters, ridge board and spaced boards over the rafters, to which shingles were fixed. Sometimes even the roof was weatherboarded, but shingles were most common until the introduction of corrugated iron, slates, and tiles. Wooden floors were made of plain wide boards fixed to joists spanning between the walls, and in better houses the edges of the floor boards were tongued and grooved. In Petre's Wellington house, the boards did not fit very well, as Mrs Godley discovered during her stay there in 1850: "the light came through the floor of my room, which gave it a very ethereal look; but in cold damp weather made it far colder even than [our own] house."[111]

In 1858, of the 12,812 houses in New Zealand almost eighty per cent were built of wood, 2½ per cent of brick or stone, and the rest of other materials including earth, raupo, and canvas. Nearly half had only one or two rooms and a further quarter had three or four rooms.[112] By 1860 the small timber house had become established as the New Zealand vernacular dwelling, and from this little wooden cottage the forms of other ordinary New Zealand houses developed.

EARLY HOUSES IN GENERAL

In England rural housing was ranked on a hierarchy of size, and people were expected to live in houses whose scale reflected their station in life. The scale was finely divided, from the mansion or country seat of the landed aristocrat, to the villa —"a country house for the residence of an opulent person"[113] — and the cottages of the labouring poor. Even the cottages were graded by size, as Nicholson made clear in his *Encyclopaedia of Architecture:*

> . . . those of the smallest size for the common labourer; the second size for the labourer, who, by his frugality and industry, in earning more than ordinary wages, deserves a more comfortable dwelling than that of the most common labourer; the third size for the village shopkeeper, shoemaker, tailor, butcher, baker &c; the fourth size for the small farmer, maltster, alehouse, or other trades, requiring room; the fifth size for the large opulent farmer. Every cottage should have at least two apartments, and in many cases three, or even four.[114]

At first in New Zealand virtually any settler's house would have been a cottage on the English scale, and they were still graded according to size. The smallest dwellings were generally described as "cottages", the next size up were "superior cottages", and larger still were "houses", often qualified as "substantial" or "of more pretensions".[115]

The governing factor was cost. The poorest immigrants built their own cottages or rented them, and others bought ready-made as many rooms as they could afford — the cost of a wooden house depended on the number of rooms, and the quality of its "appointments". Hursthouse quoted a "substantial verandah cottage" of four rooms plus detached kitchen at £150 — "amply large enough for a family of half a dozen". By contrast, a cob cottage might cost a third less,[116] and "a snug four room cottage, built in wattle and daub fashion might be well finished off for £10 or £12".[117]

a. Siting and planning

In the planned settlements land was allocated for selection and purchase. In Dunedin the quota was a quarter acre or so in the town for each family, ten acres in the "suburbs", and fifty acres or more of rural land. In Wellington there was a town acre and 100 acres in the country. Those who could not afford to buy had to lease their land, but Vogel advised that "what the working classes are doing, and what new arrivals will find to be to their advantage to attend to as soon as possible, is, to secure each a section on which to build houses of their own".[118]

The land rapidly gained value as more people continued to arrive. Some of the first owners built two or even three houses on their town sections and made large profits from rent or resale to others. But the majority owned their own land, and the pattern of a single house on a quarter-acre section became a characteristic feature of the growth of New Zealand towns throughout the nineteenth century.

There is a popular belief that immigrants to this country built their houses as if they were still in England and faced them to the south, yet at least one handbook reminded them that in New Zealand:

> a northern or north-eastern aspect should . . . be chosen; the warmth of such a position is greater, and the light more abundant. The reader must recollect, that in New Zealand the sun is to the north, and not to the southward as in Europe.

Earp also advised the immigrant:

> to build on well-drained soils and not to be enamoured of the beauty of . . . streams as to place his cottage immediately on the bank of one.[119]

The sun, the wind, firewood, water, and a view were the main factors in siting the first houses in the bush and on the tussock; but in the towns, as soon as the surveyors' streets had been pegged out, the new cottages sprang into alignment and turned their faces to the road. The houses generally lay with the ridgeline parallel to the street, although on narrow sections in Wellington and elsewhere it was common for the gable end wall to be seen, a feature that Charlotte Godley noted in 1850.[120] Where this happened, a mild deception was sometimes practised by building up the gable wall with a large false wall of scantling and boards to conceal it.

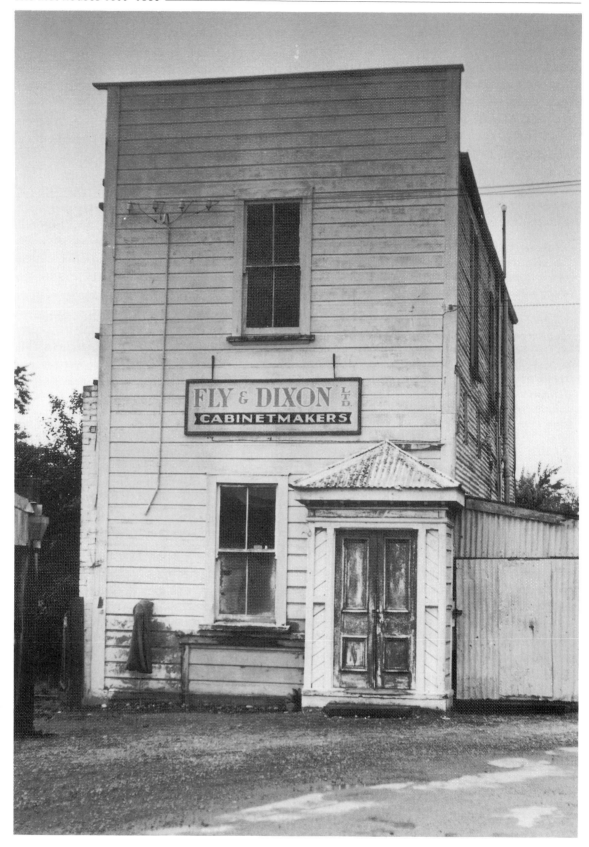

52. "A signboard, a hoarding stuck up in the air" (James Fitzgerald — 1868), Masterton.

53. Early fruits of the soil. *ATL.*

"Friend house, you are a complete humbug," said James Fitzgerald, deploring the practice, ". . . you are in a great measure not a house, but a signboard, a hoarding stuck up in the air . . . You are not a two storeyed house, but a cottage with one floor and cockloft; and as a work of art, you are everything that is odious and contemptible."[121]

In practice, then, it seems that people in the towns built their houses to line with the street (as in England), and in the country built them where it seemed fit: facing the sun, out of the wind, and close to a good supply of water and firewood.

Gardens flourished around the houses everywhere, and vegetables grew to mammoth proportions in places like the Hutt, South Otago, and New Plymouth. Mrs Godley observed:

It is rather characteristic in an *English* colony, that the gardens here are full of English plants and trees. We have in this garden (e.g.) quantities of fuchsias, roses (which don't seem to do very well), sweet briar, pinks, honeysuckle, daffodils (just now coming into flower) and so on and, besides the acacias, very few native things except one . . . There are grapes too, figs, nut bushes, and one oak, about eight feet high.[122]

English grasses were planted in the dust of the Canterbury Plains and the ashes of the bush, and English trees were planted and populated with English birds. Earp ended his chapter on the "Situation of the Dwelling" by saying:

. . . no English garden, however expensively kept up, can for a moment vie with the beauty of a cottager's garden in New Zealand in the beauty of its shrubs, to say nothing of the vines, melons, Cape gooseberries, peaches, all English and many tropical fruits, which will grow anywhere in the greatest luxuriance.[123]

54. Bush hut with nikau
roof. *ATL, Northwood Coll.*

b. Roofs, floors and chimneys

The roof gave a building its shape, as well as keeping out the weather. It also limited the size of a house (or at least the width) because with simple construction methods it was only possible to span up to about 5 metres — most cottages were only one room wide under a gable or hip roof, and additional rooms were built or added later under a *skillion* or lean-to. The preferred form was the gable because a ridge beam or pole could most easily be supported by the end wall, and the hipped roof was usually found only on thatched houses or those built by tradesmen.

Thatching in some form was common on the earliest houses. Every possible material was tried, including nikau, toetoe, reeds, tussock, or manuka twigs, and if many roofs needed a good haircut,

others were as neat and weathertight as any made in England. At Te Waimate in Canterbury:

> . . . the roofs were thatched with snow-grass or rushes, according to availability, the latter perhaps being the better of the two. The thatch was attached to round saplings of manuka or matipo, if procurable; the thatch ties were more easily pulled tight on round rafters than on split ones. If the eaves projected well over the walls, the rain was kept off, and the houses would last for years.[124]

It was not a job for the amateur though, as Butler found when he tried to thatch his cob house at Mesopotamia: "he put the top of each bundle of snow grass outside the bottom of the one above, so that all the rain ran inwards; . . . extraordinary for so clever a man".[125]

Apart from thatch, bark, or shingles (which have already been discussed in some detail), there was slate and the manufactured roofing materials which the settlers brought with them — canvas, tarred cloth, and corrugated iron. Canvas roofs were really permanent tents, often with wood, stone, or sod walls. (Later, sacking served the same purpose.) A good example was Dr Barker's "Studdingsail Hall", built at Christchurch in 1851 with a studdingsail from the ship *Charlotte Jane*. Tarred cloth was a woven felt impregnated with bitumen, and came in rolls which were draped over a roof of boards, or poles, and held in place with nailed battens or rows of tacks. Slates were for the

55. Bush hut with canvas roof. *ATL.*

56. "Studdingsail Hall", Christchurch — sketch by Dr. A.C. Barker, 1851. *Canterbury Museum.*

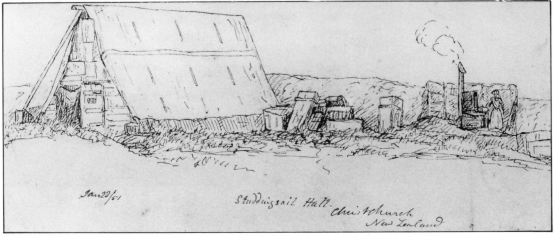

57. Bush hut with tarred felt roof. *ATL, Northwood Coll.*

wealthy, and at first were imported with bricks as ballast — but later discoveries in north Otago led to their wider use in the last part of the nineteenth century.

Corrugated iron was the other great New Zealand building material. It was first manufactured in this country in Dunedin by R. and T. Haworth in 1869, but before that, and for many years after, it was imported from England, and was available in the settlements from their beginnings. In his 1848 handbook, Wakefield suggested that "some *corrugated iron or zinc* will be found very handy for roofing houses or verandahs quickly".[126] In England corrugated iron was used for temporary buildings or for fencing, and many of the prefabricated houses were covered with it. In New Zealand it soon became popular as a quick and effective covering for roofs or chimneys. The sheets of 1800 x 600 mm up to 2400 x 900 mm were too unwieldy to cart about in the bush, and it was more likely to be used there for fireplaces and chimneys than for covering roofs.

58. Canvas hut with corrugated iron chimney. *ATL, Child Collection.*

59. House with cob chimney. *ATL, Marks Collection.*

During this period roofs of all materials were mostly steeply pitched, the aim being to shed water as quickly as possible, and to reduce the thrust on often flimsy walls. A pitch of 45 degrees or greater was common, and George Earp's advice in his 1853 handbook to use a low-pitched roof to reflect the sun was generally ignored.[127]

Floors were a simpler matter, and in most houses, mud or clay served very well at first. At Te Awaiti in 1839 Dieffenbach observed clay floors that had been compressed and beaten hard, so that they had a very smooth firm surface, and could be easily repaired if necessary by watering and sweeping.[128] There were recipes for more durable floors. For example, Burn suggested that a lime mortar floor might be laid, smoothed, and when dry (after about three weeks) oiled to resemble stone.[129] Nevertheless, the earth floor served well until a timber house could be built — or until a timber floor was laid in the original dwelling. These first timber floors were of split or sawn boards, perhaps planed on one side, and simply butted together as was common in English cottages. By 1860, how-

ever, new steam-powered machinery in the towns was producing floor boards that were planed, tongued, and grooved in one operation.

As for chimneys, the familial hearth was not so much the heart of the New Zealand cottage as an awkward appendage. Fire was always a danger in houses made of raupo, canvas, or wood, and at first many settlers did their cooking outside on an open fire. Where bricks were available, chimneys could be safely made and the only problem was earthquakes. Away from the towns however, it was necessary to improvise. Cob chimneys worked well, and sods made a reasonably serviceable fireplace, with perhaps a small barrel as a chimney pot. In one such chimney, the owner "had ingeniously arched it over about five feet from the ground, and inserted a bouilli soup tin (minus the bottom) in the clay, near the top of the back wall, at an angle of 45 degrees . . . It was facetiously called the one-gun battery."[130]

The only other solution was to keep the fire at a respectful distance from anything inflammable. The typical fireplace was a very large enclosure —

60. Brick cottage chimney,
Wiri, Auckland.

say 1.8 metres square, or even greater —with a wall around it and its own roof, joined to the cottage at one end. The wall could be made of corrugated iron supported by a wooden framework on the outside, or wooden slabs or palings, with stones and clay piled up inside about 1.2 metres high. The roof sloped upwards away from the house, protecting the fire from the weather and helping it to draw well, and this gave the whole affair its characteristic shape. But houses still caught fire, and in a brisk breeze could be destroyed in minutes. As bricks became plentiful, at least one proper fireplace could be afforded. Later baking and roasting were made easier when the colonial oven was installed — a large iron box with a hinged door, over which the cooking fire was built. Some houses even had a bread oven built into the side of the kitchen fireplace.

c. Joinery

Windows and doors were imported at first. Fitton quoted an 1855 advertisement in Auckland for articles brought from Melbourne, including "a considerable number of panelled and sash doors and window sashes, which the present demand for building materials were readily taken".[131] British-trained carpenters were well able to make up their own joinery from sawn timber, but even in 1861 Hursthouse still recommended settlers to take with them "one front and four inner doors, half a dozen iron casement sashes, fitted in wooden frames, and a box of glass".[132] This imported joinery was often moved from house to house as the owner shifted from a first dwelling of raupo to perhaps a cob or slab hut, and ultimately to a timber house. The imported windows were hinged casements, but the typical window in houses from the 1850s on was the *double-hung sash*, although casements were kept for service rooms at the back.

The double-hung sash was made up of two roughly square sashes one above the other, arranged so that each could slide past the other. The weight of each sash was counter-balanced by cast iron weights concealed behind the window frame and attached to the sashes by cords running over pulleys at the top of the jambs. In the 1840s most double-hung windows were the "twelve-light" type — i.e. each sash had six small panes (three across and two down) — but by the 1850s, when larger sheets of glass reached New Zealand, the "four-light" window (two-over-two) began to replace the twelve-light.

Double-hung windows were normally used singly in main living or bed rooms, but a particular exception was occasionally found in larger cottages in the 1840s and 50s. This was the so-called "Chicago window", where an ordinary two-over-two window was flanked by two narrow windows of the same height. (The term is an anachronism as these windows did not appear in Chicago until the 1890s, and the inspiration was more probably late eighteenth century classical.)

The *bay window* also appeared infrequently in the 1840s and more often in the 1850s, again on larger cottages. Clearly modelled on British examples, the bay graced the best rooms as a well-lit

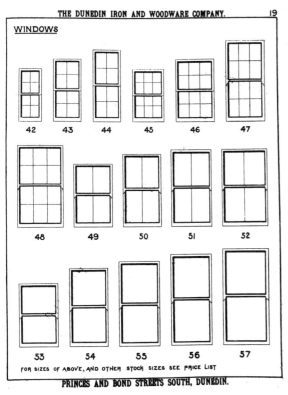

61. Stock windows from the Dunedin Iron and Woodware Company catalogue, 1880s. *Hocken Library.*

recess in the wall facing the view or the sun.

Glass for windows in this period was hand-made in England, expensive and only available in quite small sheets — the usual size of broad glass sheet was about 1200 x 800 mm, and for crown glass even smaller. Glass was difficult to transport and its cost in the colonies made it a luxury, although almost all the "good houses" in Wellington had conservatories.[133] Many people made do with substitutes such as wooden shutters which were opened or closed according to the weather. Also used was canvas or oiled calico, which at least let in some light while keeping out the wind, and could be fitted into a proper sash until such time as glass was obtained. Few of the early houses had two storeys, although many had loft space for storage or sleeping. Daylight for upper rooms came either from windows in the gable end wall — a practice common in Wellington, where houses were often sited with the gable facing the street — or from *dormer* windows in the roof, as in Dunedin, where houses commonly faced the street side-on. The typical shape of the dormer was a small box sticking out of the main roof with its own little gable roof (referred to in America as a "dog-house" dormer); or a hipped roof, as at the Waimate mission house; or a variation of this found in

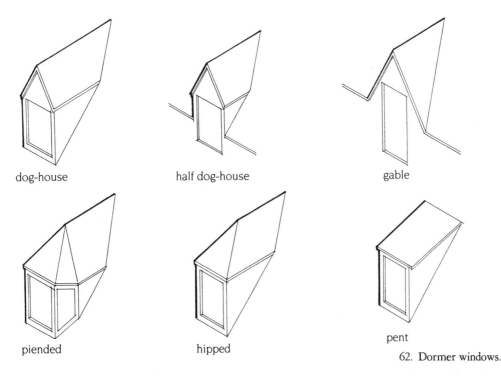

62. Dormer windows.

Dunedin, where the dormer was returned diagonally at the corners — a practice imported from Edinburgh.

Doors, like windows, continued British joinery practice, and the 1840s saw the last of the Georgian six-panel door. There were also doors with only two vertical panels, but for the remainder of the nineteenth century the standard was the four-panel door with panels set in "bed mouldings", and a variation with glazed upper panels arched at the top. French casements — narrow glazed double doors — were common in prefabricated houses, and their use in locally made houses steadily increased through the 1840s and 1850s. Each door usually had a moulded wooden bottom panel with divided glass panels above, three or four high and one or two wide, the vertical glazing bar sometimes offset towards the hinged side. Perhaps most common was the humble boarded door with horizontal "ledges" top and bottom, and a diagonal brace. This was easily made up from plain boards, with hinges improvised if necessary from leather strips or flax ties.

Access to sleeping lofts was simply by ladder — a stair used too much valuable floor space. Better-off colonists built larger houses of 1½ or two storeys with real staircases, properly made by a tradesman. Alternatively, the colonist could refer to a carpenter's handbook such as Peter Nicholson's *New Practical Builder*,[134] or a more elementary book such as Burn's *Colonist's and Emigrant's Handbook* which gave simple instructions for setting-out and making straight and dog-leg stairs.[135]

By 1866 local joinery manufacture was well under way. In Auckland the Union Steam Saw Moulding Sash and Door Company advertised:

> . . . sashes, doors and casements of every variety. Plain and sunk skirting, from six to twelve inches in width. Architraves . . . of very superior patterns . . . internal cornice, of elegant design, equal to Plaister. Tongued and grooved flooring and lining, Unequalled in the colonies.[136]

In Christchurch Frederick Jenkins had established his planing, moulding, and joinery works and steam saw mills, and other main centres had similar industries in full production.

d. Furniture and finishes

Assisted immigrants brought with them little more than their clothing, their tools-of-trade and their hopes, but the fare-paying colonists came determined to make themselves comfortable. The various handbooks matched their advice to both ends of the social order, so while Vogel extolled the many uses of packing cases,[137] Wakefield recommended that ladies should take their pianos by all means, and advised that "memorials of the Fine Arts of the old world" could be purchased from the British Museum and taken to the colony at little cost.[138]

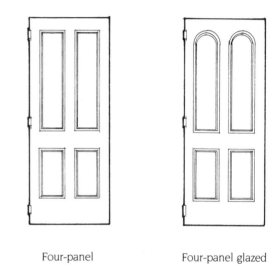

Four-panel   Four-panel glazed

63. Typical cottage doors.

There were few of life's luxuries that could not be bought once the main settlements were established and ships arrived regularly from England, Australia, and America, carrying everything from music boxes to tables and chairs, and four-poster beds. There was considerable wealth in the new colony, but those without ready cash or far from the towns still had to make many articles for themselves. In early Nelson, when there was no sawn timber, people split slabs for tables and chairs. Lady Martin recalled her life in Auckland of the 1840s when "furniture was not to be bought, but packing cases and empty boxes were plentiful. These made our dressing-tables, and washstands, and ottomans, and lounges. A little white muslin and pink calico, and chintz cushions stuffed with scraped flax, made a handsome show."[139]

Even earlier, before Auckland was settled, Logan Campbell created his own four-poster bed:

> A few saplings, the thickness of one's wrist, the forest supplied us with . . . and with some forty or fifty feet of supple-jack . . . and when we got clear of the forest some leaves of the flax-bush . . . Sharpening the saplings for the posts of our bed, we just drove them into the floor — mother earth — at the places we chose, each according to his fancy where his bed should be, then side and end pieces were notched and fitted into each other, and tied with strips of flax-leaf; then we interlaced the supple-jack

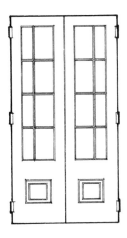 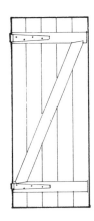

French casement   Ledged & braced

> with the flax-leaf for sacking, making the supple-jack go the long way of the bed, and the flax-leaf the cross way. In this simple manner we made a sort of hammock.[140]

In Canterbury bunks were made in the same way in huts on the remote hill stations.[141] The do-it-yourself tradition of New Zealand was born of necessity in the early days, and even in 1875 Vogel warned the immigrant that "he should not forget that a handyman in the colonies should be able to turn his hand to almost anything".[142]

The well-to-do colonists of the 1840s brought good furniture with them, and some households were virtual replicas of an English suburban villa.[143] Hursthouse advised families to take:

> Their plate, and the _best_ cutlery, glass, earthware, cooking utensils, and table linen; a _best_ table, set of chairs . . . a _best_ carpet . . . together with a _small_ selection of the best books, prints, chimney ornaments, and nick-nacks. Drowsy matrimonial four-posters give place, in Zealandia to elastic iron bedsteads and hair mattresses — but ladies can take their feather beds if they prefer.[144]

Inside their houses, many people put up wallpaper if they could get it, otherwise newspapers or magazine illustrations were popular. In timber houses the lining boards moved and ripped the paper, and the practice grew of sticking the paper to thin calico stretched over the boards.[145]

On the outside, many houses were untreated, although cob or pisé houses were usually white from their lime plaster weathercoat. Wooden houses turned silvery grey if left to weather, but some were painted — or whitewashed. Poor Dr Barker "was persuaded by an Ishmaelite of a fellow to daub [his house] over with tar and lime, which . . . made it hideously ugly".[146] Recipes for homemade paints contained horrifying amounts of toxic lead, which was used as a drying agent. Typical was Burn's formula for white oil paint which contained four per cent turpentine, nine per cent raw oil, nine per cent boiled oil and seventy-eight per cent white lead ground in oil. Colour was added by incorporating quantities of earth oxides, lamp-black, or verdigris.[147] To make a pale green paint, Brett's guide suggested a mixture of yellow ochre (1 cwt), wet blue (1 cwt), road dust (1½ cwt), blue-black (10 lbs), lime water (6 gals), fish oil (4 gals), "prepared residue" (7½ gals) and linseed oil (7½ gals).[148] Not an undertaking for the faint hearted!

e. Outbuildings and services

Most domestic chores were done in the house: cooking, washing up, and bathing in a tub before the kitchen fire or at a bedroom washstand. If there was a stream near the house, laundry was sometimes left overnight, weighted with stones, but otherwise it was washed in tubs of hot water at the back door, with harsh hand-made soap.

The water itself came from the stream, from barrels which collected rain from wooden roof gutters, or from wells drawn by hand or windlass or by force-pump. In towns, the wells risked pollution from unlined cesspits and buried night soil, and disease was common.

Every house had at least one outbuilding, known by a variety of euphemisms, and dedicated to that most personal of daily duties. Where timber was plentiful, a privy could easily be put up over a deep hole in the ground, and moved to a new location when necessary. A more primitive version was an enclosure of manuka or brushwood with a stout rail for a seat on two forked branches in the ground, and a back rail for support. Sod lavatories were also built, but these were not a good idea if stock were grazed nearby as cattle, especially bullocks, liked to rub against the sods, sometimes with disconcerting results.

The water closet had been re-invented in England in the eighteenth century with Joseph Bramah's patent of 1778, and was recommended by Burn in his colonists' handbook, where he showed how to improvise one out of boards. But for most it was a hole in the ground, or a bucket to be emptied somewhere in the garden.

Apart from the essential privy, other outbuildings were rare, except on farms where there might also be a stable, a dairy, and huts for pigs, hens and other livestock. The first temporary hut of slabs or sods often ended up being used for one of these purposes.

64. Slab hut and its weatherboard successor. *ATL, Northwood Coll.*

PLANNING AND FORM: Building with boxes

"I found that the houses of the majority of the inhabitants . . . were in a style of genuine simplicity — a long, narrow, but very large box: the sides fronting the street were about 8 feet in height and from 20 to 24 feet in length; they had a door in the middle, and a window about 5 ft. by 3 ft. on each side of the door. The house was divided into two rooms . . . and was frequently supplemented with the fashionable and useful *lean-to*, sometimes constructed at one end, but oftener in the rear of these truly convenient and comfortable colonial cottages."
— C.R. CARTER, *Life and Recollections of a New Zealand Colonist Vo.11, 1866.*

In colonial New Zealand wealth, not class, decided how people were housed. In Maskell's words: "You may meet a man at table who, by his conversation, you would imagine was some costermonger; he may be one of the richest men in the place, and, *therefore* one of the aristocracy." If so, he might also own the largest house in the district. Those who succeeded through their own efforts could buy a large house or simply increase the size of the one they already owned. Not everyone was so fortunate, however, and the little wooden cottage of one or two rooms, with a central door and a window either side of the door, remained the basic unit of ordinary house design throughout the nineteenth century. Not that all were made of wood — cob, stone, and brick houses used exactly the same form — yet most early houses can be seen to be made up from this basic unit according to quite simple rules of addition and arrangement.

Today it is most useful to group these first buildings according to their size and plan shape, and then by the form of the roof. Other factors such as the amount and quality of ornamentation, orientation, and the shape or size of windows are simply stylistic extras which have no effect on basic form. A simple classification based on arrangements of the basic boxlike cottage suggests that each of these

(I) the simple box cottage (rectangular plan)

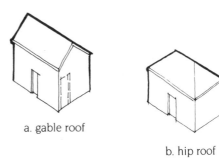

a. gable roof

b. hip roof

(II) the double box cottage (square plan)

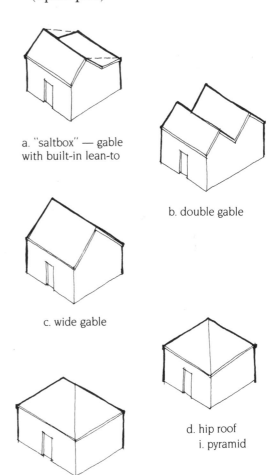

a. "saltbox" — gable with built-in lean-to

b. double gable

c. wide gable

d. hip roof
i. pyramid

ii. ridged

65. Cottage forms based on the repetition of simple basic units.

(III) combined boxes
(irregular plan — bay cottages)

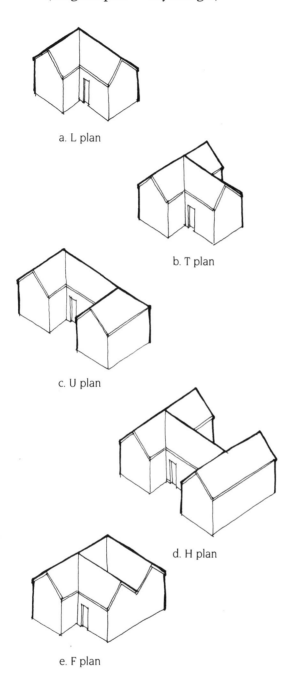

a. L plan

b. T plan

c. U plan

d. H plan

e. F plan

65. Cottage forms based on
the repetition of simple
basic units.

basic forms can always be modified in the following
ways — either singly or in combination:

(A) add a verandah

(B) add a lean-to (at one end, or at rear)
      a. built in
      b. built on[149]

(C) increase number of floors from:
      a. 1 storey
   to b. 1½ storeys
   or c. 2 storeys (or more on steep sites)

These simple formal possibilities produce as many
as 216 combinations, without taking account of
materials or stylistic features, and help account for
both the basic simplicity and the richness of variation in early New Zealand houses. A great virtue of
the earliest houses, especially those made of
timber, was their flexibility. It was possible to put
up the shell of a house and finish it inside when
money and time allowed. Alternatively, the house
could easily be enlarged by addition, and many were
designed with this in mind, "so that at any future
time more rooms could be added if desirable, without interfering with the parts already complete".[150]

Simple box cottages usually had one or two
rooms, a rectangular plan and a gabled or hipped
roof. A one-room cottage, for instance, served as
"Parlour, Kitchen, and — Everything",[151] but it
could also be divided by a partition or have a lean-to
added to the back, so that like the two-room cottage
there were day and sleeping rooms (by far the most
common arrangement) or two sleeping rooms, one
of which became a living room by day. Charlotte
Godley wrote of such a house:

> We have a wooden house with two
> rooms; one about ten feet square, which is
> bedroom for Powles, Arthur, and
> Elizabeth, and the other is for us,
> bedroom, sitting room, etc.; then we have
> a hired tent, which is servants' hall and
> kitchen, with a fire out of doors . . . Our
> sitting room is really quite a pretty room,
> with a high wooden roof . . . [and] our
> bed disappears, being rolled up under an
> opossum-skin rug.[152]

The kitchen was often a separate structure built of
sods or cob, and banished from the house because
of the risk of fire.

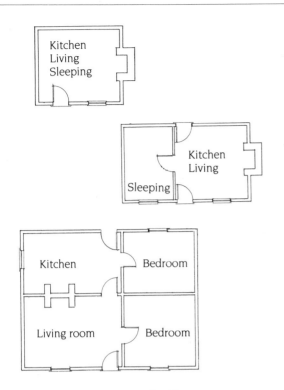

Double box cottages had three or four rooms and were roughly square in plan, with a hipped roof, or a wide gable, or two small gables, or a small gable with a built-in lean-to behind. Depending on family size, the rooms could serve more particular purposes — for example, two bedrooms, a kitchen, and a parlour. This four-square "box" could be enlarged by adding a lean-to, or the form could simply be expanded to become a square house of five or more rooms under a single roof. Another possibility was to take the simple two-room box and extend the ridge along a line to make a long house, as at "Avonhead" in Christchurch, or the many barracks built for new immigrants in the Company settlements.

The final set of formal possibilities was to combine simple boxes in various ways. In the L, T, U, H, and F plans, rooms were grouped about a passageway which linked all parts of the house, and in the U and H plans the rigorous symmetry of the simplest two-room cottage was preserved. These houses developed into the typical villas of the late nineteenth century and could afford space for rooms which might only be used occasionally. In

66. Typical cottage plans.

67. The one-room cottage — interior of Edenham Cottage, 1855. *Hawke's Bay Museum.*

68. Two- and four-room cottages with hip roofs: (a) Lawrence

69. Four-room cottages with gable roofs: (a) "catslide" roof, Waitotara

the larger houses rooms were set aside for servants, the study, a second parlour (or drawing room), the dining room, and even a bathroom, and the passage might be screened or widened at the front door to give an entrance hall. The room which projected forward at one end of the plan contained the front parlour or sitting room where visitors were received, and very often there was a bay window set in the end wall. In the H and U plans the best bedroom stepped forward in the same way on the other side of the house. In houses of 1½ or two storeys the bedrooms moved upstairs, leaving the ground floor free for living rooms and formal rooms. These basic forms endured for the remainder of the century, especially in the country and in provincial towns, where they served the

(b) Devonport

(c) Wellington.

(b) wide gable roof, Huntly

(c) gable and lean-to, Devonport.

immigrants who continued to arrive in circumstances little different from those of the 1840s.

The popular image of a New Zealand colonial house invariably includes a verandah, that classical colonial artifact which came to Britain from its colonies in Jamaica and India before being re-exported to other British-settled countries, including New Zealand. It first appeared in European houses here in the prefabricated buildings which were designed for any hot climate, and was quickly adopted in many houses built of local materials. It had the great virtue of sheltering walls from the weather, as well as providing extra living space at small cost. The verandah in New Zealand rarely attained the scale and magnificence of those on colonial Australian houses, but it became a feature

70. "Combined box"
cottages:
(a) L-plan, Napier;
(b) double gable plus lean-
to, Paeroa.

of any house with pretensions to style. It protected the front entrance and could be a pleasant outdoor room at the right time of the year. As Hursthouse observed:

> a snug peach and rose covered verandah, or porch, is a nice and easily obtained addition to a New Zealand cottage, and with a little framing and roofing-stuff at hand, any man worth his salt could easily put up something of this sort for his wife in his leisure hours after tea.[153]

The verandah often swept around the house on two or three sides, and when it found its way to the back door it sheltered boots, children at play, and the washing line in relative privacy. The verandah was originally an extension of the main roof —perhaps at a different slope — and as walls rose from 2½ or 3 metres to 3½ and 4 metres high, the verandah was tucked under the eaves to help keep the scale modest. With a growing interest in decoration, the verandah was enhanced by the addition of lavish cast-iron or fretted and turned wood, friezes, columns, and balustrades — but in most early houses, decoration if it existed was modest and elegant.

(a)

(b)

(c)

71. 1½ and two-storey cottages:
(a) 1½-storey, single gable, Napier;
(b) two-storey, hip, Devonport.
(c) 1½-storey, double gable, Kaukapakapa;

STYLE

a. Colonial styles

The small simple cottages of the immigrants had few pretensions to style, beyond perhaps the Georgian habit of symmetry. Even the larger houses of the colonists, the military, and the missionaries were built in a colonial style already well established in Australia, and described by Freeland as "stripped-down Georgian".[154] The earliest mission houses built around the Bay of Islands are typical wooden versions of contemporary brick houses in Australia, and built by missionary carpenters who had worked all their lives in the Georgian tradition. In time the *Mission style* they established in the North spread south to Tauranga, Waikato, and Hawke's Bay.

The basic form of the Mission style houses was a tall weatherboarded rectangular box with a hipped roof and a symmetrical front elevation. Roofs were shingled, with a slight eaves overhanging the walls and continued at the sides and rear to form a "skilling" or lean-to. Rooms on the upper floor were lit by dormers or by small windows under the eaves, and a verandah spread along the front and sometimes at the sides, supported by simple wooden posts. On the ground floor there was a central door with flanking windows or french casements evenly spaced on the front wall. Windows were small paned with two sliding sashes of six panes each (the twelve-light window) set in simple moulded architraves. Shutters were common.

The lasting impression of these houses is one of elegant simplicity. Surviving examples include: Kemp House, Kerikeri (1821); Mission House, Waimate North (1832); "The Retreat", Pakaraka; and "The Elms", Tauranga (1847).

Later, military colonists of the Fencible Regiment built houses in the same portable Georgian

72. Colonial Mission style
— "Stripped-down
Georgian", Waimate North,
1832.

73. Colonial Military style:
(a) fencible cottage,
Onehunga;
(b) Bell House, Pakuranga,
1851. *Alan la Roche.*

style in small villages around Auckland. The houses of the "other ranks" were simple cottages, but for officers houses similar (in appearance if not in plan) to Kemp House were built in the 1850s from designs prepared by the Army Ordinance Depot in England or Australia. Two of the surviving houses are well-proportioned two-storeyed structures, with hipped roof, a verandah on three sides, and extensive lean-to accommodation. Here too are the twelve-light windows under the eaves, french casements, and the symmetrical facade, with the added refinement of bay windows in the main ground-floor rooms. Two such houses still standing are: 7 Sale Street, Howick (1848); and Montressor Smith (Bell) House, Pakuranga (1851).

In the 1840s wealthier colonists in Auckland and Wellington built houses with some of the picturesque qualities associated with buildings of the English Regency. This was most apparent in the detailing of verandahs, where limbs of trees served as rustic posts — as in Colonel Wakefield's house in Wellington — a fashion established by Decimus Burton in his work at the London Zoo. Alternatively, the verandah supports were pairs of slender

74. Colonial Regency style:
(a) four-room cottage with
verandah; *ATL, W.J.*
Harding Coll.
(b) Hulme Court, Parnell,
Auckland, 1843. *ATL.*

posts with shaped timber brackets and trellis work between them — as at Hulme Court in Auckland (1843); and Terrace Station, Hororata (1853-4). This was a colonial version of the delicate wrought-iron balconies popular in England at the beginning of the nineteenth century. These houses shared many formal features with the earlier Mission houses, notably the hipped roof, the verandah tucked well under the eaves, and the "Union Jack"

balustrade. Windows were still twelve-light double hung sashes, and french casements were common, either side of a central door. Hulme Court in Auckland (1843) is a good surviving example of the type.

All the houses discussed so far have so much in common, that it is perhaps best to group them quite simply as *English Colonial* in style.

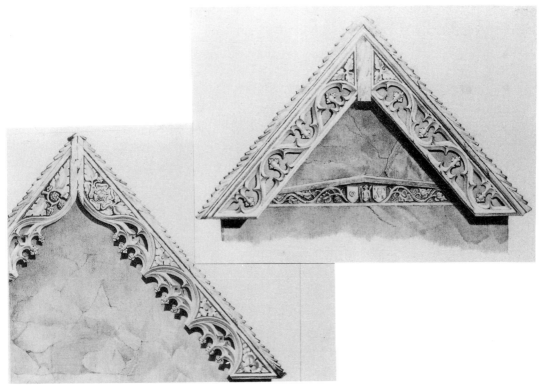

75. Bargeboard decorations
from *Pugin's Ornamental
Gables,* 1831.

Not all colonial houses were directly influenced by the fashions of England and Australia, however. In several places in New Zealand settlements were founded by other national groups — Danes, Irish, Bohemians, and in the 1840s the Germans at Nelson and the French at Akaroa. Some of the first houses erected at Akaroa by settlers of the Nanto-Bordelaise Society were quite unlike anything else in New Zealand, or as Charlotte Godley said, "somewhat different in pattern from our English wooden houses".[155] She particularly commented that they were larger, more pretentious, and less snug. However, there are not enough of these houses to define them as a particular style, except to group them as *French Colonial.* The Eteveneaux House of 1843, for instance, with its steep scalloped and hipped roof, frieze board and mouldings, pilasters, and flat entablature over doors and windows, has been described as "French Empire Style".[156] By contrast, the Baurian House (1840) with its soaring hipped roof and dormers has more in common with early houses of the French Canadian provinces.

In Nelson there is an extraordinary group of houses of the 1840s and 1850s which show the first sign in New Zealand of another architectural fashion of the early nineteenth century. The Gothic Revival in England renewed interest in the gable as an architectural feature, and the opportunities it offered for ornamentation were thoroughly explored by A.W.N. Pugin in various publications, including *Pugin's Ornamental Gables* of 1831. These illustrations of old English buildings influenced many architects, including Andrew Jackson Downing in America, and quite probably William Beatson, an architect in early Nelson who established there a style of building contemporary with the *Carpenter Gothic* of America. Several of Beatson's houses were built of cob and were quite large, but all his houses have in common steep gables with elaborately decorated bargeboards, sawn by hand from solid timber in scalloped and sinuous patterns reminiscent of Gothic tracery. His more restrained designs were pierced with trefoils, or were lightly carved in relief.

Many houses in Nelson and elsewhere were

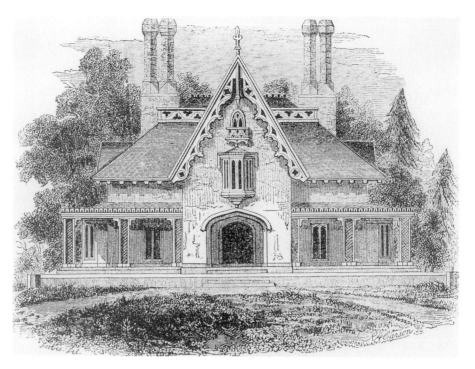

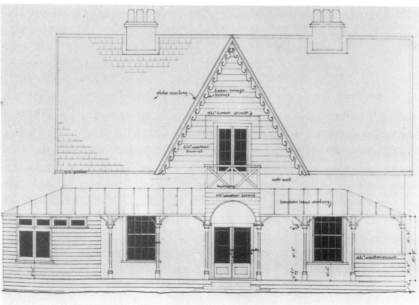

76. Gothic style:
(a) "Cottage-Villa in the rural Gothic style", from A.J. Downing, *The Architecture of Country Houses*, 1850;
(b) Woodstock, Nelson —William Beatson architect, 1856.

clearly influenced by this New Zealand Carpenter Gothic style, and it gave new significance to the gable roofs of the smaller cottages that made up the bulk of this country's housing. Some of the finer houses in this style are: Stead House, Stoke, Nelson, 1841 (cob); Stafford Place, Waimea, 1842 (pisé?); Woodstock, Nelson, 1856 (cob): Broadgreen, Nelson, 1857 (cob); and Te Makiri, Helensville, 1866 (timber frame); Netherdale, Wanganui, 1867 (timber frame).

The gable also appeared in simpler form on larger houses in other parts of the country, and several later houses in the Bay of Islands and Hokianga sprouted gable roofs and large gabled dormers but without the exuberant tracery of those in Nelson. Some of these houses are: Pouerua, Pakaraka; Choat House, Puketona (c.1860); Te Wahapu, near Russell (c.1860); and Clendon House, Rawene (1868).

77. Northland houses:
(a) Cottage in the Kaipara
district; *Matakohe Museum.*
(b) Bedggood Cottage,
Waimate North. *HPT.*

b. The beginnings of a New Zealand vernacular

A vernacular style grows gradually over many generations and adapts to place as well as social needs. In New Zealand the English Colonial houses were an important link with the past, and were not suddenly replaced by a distinctive local style. New houses continued to recall familiar forms, but because the materials were unfamiliar (or at least, unexpected), the expression of familiar ideas was transformed.

Thus the foundations of a New Zealand vernacular house style were laid with the first houses built of locally sawn timbers. The simplest formal proto-type — the two-room gabled wooden cottage — was the basis for many later houses that belong uniquely to this country. Up until about 1860 all houses built here fall into one of two categories suggested by Amos Rapoport. He distinguishes *primitive* construction where a few building types, with little variation, are built by everyone, from what he calls *pre-industrial vernacular*, where there are more building types, more individual variations, and the houses are built mainly by tradesmen.[157] In New Zealand the "primitive" period was relatively brief, persisting from about 1810 to about 1850 in the towns and until about 1870 in remote areas. The "pre-industrial vernacular" period was shorter still, from about 1850 to about 1870 in the towns.

During the pre-industrial phase, however, the first steps were taken towards a more distinctive local style by breaking out of the confines of the rectangular plan, timidly at first and then more confidently, to produce less formal and more complex buildings. The lean-to was one way of increasing the size of a simple building, but a more emphatic formal solution was the *cross gable* or *return bay*, in which the main roof line turned through 90 degrees at one or both ends of the house to produce the L, T, U, or H plan types.

The cross gable was a common enough device in many British cottages, but in New Zealand it became more important than it had ever been in Britain. (The bay cottage was certainly the direct ancestor of that thoroughly New Zealand house, the bay villa.) Houses with the "return bay" appeared in Auckland in 1845, and in some Wellington farmhouses of the 1850s. By 1860 this had become a fairly standard solution to the problem of making a larger house out of the short-span gable roof. In other respects the formula was unchanged: steep shingled roofs stopped abruptly at the eaves sometimes with "dog-house" dormers rising from the front wall; twelve-light windows (or increasingly, four-light sashes) were set symmetrically in weatherboard walls; and on the end of the projecting bay a three-sided bay window added a grace note to the houses of the more prosperous. The glass-panelled door sat discreetly in the angle of the front wall and the projecting bay, and in the same angle a verandah was set with corrugated or pan iron roof on plain posts, possibly with some delicate fretworked brackets. The gables of the bay, the main roof, and the dormers were often fretworked in the Carpenter Gothic style. Finally, the finial arrived — a further gothic reference which (as the old wives claimed) prevented witches from landing on the roof.

PART II

VICTORIAN
VILLAS AND COTTAGES
1860-1910

Introduction

New Zealand towns and cities contain an extraordinary collection of Victorian wooden houses built between 1860 and 1910. Each district has its own idioms and character: from the sweeping verandahed villas of Auckland to the up-and-down houses of Wellington on their close-packed windswept hilly sections; from Christchurch's orderly four-square houses in their grid-iron compartments, to the iron lace porches and bay windows of Dunedin's hills and valleys.

These cottages, villas, and mansions are an exact expression of their time, and of the lives that were lived in them. The Victorians were vigorous and inventive workers who made countless scientific and intellectual advances. They harnessed the power of steam, which brought railways, steamships and the large-scale mechanisation of industry to New Zealand. They also invented gas lighting, steel, photography, the telephone, electricity, the sewing machine, and the lawnmower. It was a time when one could advance oneself through education, "self-improvement", and sheer hard work. The middle-class morality which dominated society was high minded and demanded good manners, good works, good posture and, it was hoped, good fortune. Poverty was feared and despised — and great importance was attached to putting up a show.

Correspondingly, their houses were robust, exuberant and well built of fine materials, ingeniously worked by machine. The villa was the archetypal Victorian house in this country. It was brightly decorated and well ventilated, with big bay windows (which had to have curtains and blinds to cut down the daylight), and was set in generous gardens beside wide streets.

The Victorians turned their best face to the world in their houses. But implicit in these buildings was another face of the Victorian character —their relentless pursuit of comfort and material wealth. It is no accident that the events which marked the beginning of this period in New Zealand were the gold rushes of the 1860s and the land wars. As Maoris became less willing to sell their land, European settlers took large areas by occupation or by force, and in the towns traditional Maori houses were banned by law. Many of the settlers who arrived in the 1860s came in search of gold, and as the European population expanded (from 26,000 in 1850 to 80,000 in 1860, and 100,000 a year later), more houses were needed on more land, and more timber was needed for their construction. A seemingly endless supply of wood was stripped from the land, some of it simply burned where it stood to save the bother of clearing it away. By 1886 timber was being felled at the rate of several million feet a year:

> One of their chief industries is at present destructive . . . the kauri pine takes 800 years to grow. They are cutting it down and selling it as fast as axe and saw can work.[1]

Timber was the country's biggest industry. Steam-powered woodworking machinery was introduced in the 1860s, and during the last three decades of the century, thousands of houses were built by a highly mechanised timber industry which turned out an immense variety of components for villas and cottages in town and country.

Technology 1860-1910

WOODWORKING

The earliest wooden houses in New Zealand have often been admired for their unadorned simplicity. Timber for their construction was hard won from the bush, and laboriously worked and shaped by hand to make framing, weatherboards, floors, doors and windows of the plainest designs. Tradesmen worked with traditional hand-held tools such as chisels, saws, augers, straight and moulding planes, and a carpenter needed an elaborate kit of these to carry out even simple decorative work. Joints in timber were complex interlocking arrangements made with saw and chisel, often with concealed wedges and pegs. Hand planes of various kinds were needed to bring timber to its finished state: jack planes to take off a rough-sawn face; trying planes to straighten the surface; smoothing planes to give the final finish; shooting planes to obtain dead straight edges for joining pieces together; and a selection of moulding planes or "ploughs", each with its own shaped blade, to make up a moulded edge or surface. Where houses were decorated — as for example the Nelson houses in the Carpenter Gothic style — even this work was hand-done, with bargeboards sawn and drilled out of wide boards.

In the 1860s all of this changed. The Victorian vernacular in New Zealand was founded on a kitset of wooden parts, mass-produced by steam-powered machines which began to arrive here in the late 1850s. The country's European population trebled in the 1850s, again in the 1860s, and doubled in the 1870s* — and these machines helped the timber industry to meet the exploding demand for houses. Carpenters found themselves

*Vogel gives 26,707 for 1851 (Vogel, 1875, p.64)
Von Dadelszen gives 79,711 for 1860
248,400 for 1870
484,864 for 1880 (Von Dadelszen, 1906, table 1)

78. "Sheffield's best"
— the carpenter's tool kit.

putting up not only frames and boards from the sawmills, but also factory-produced doors, window sashes, and mouldings, and a profusion of decorative pieces chosen from the catalogues. The machinery used to manufacture these house parts came from Britain and the United States.

WOODWORKING MACHINERY IN N.Z.

New Zealand's experience of woodworking machinery began when the first water-driven sawmill was set up at Mercury Bay in 1838. Two years later the first steam-powered mill was oper-

79. Deal frame saw, reducing timber to boards. *ATL, Godber Collection.*

ating at Port Nicholson,[2] and from the 1840s sawmills were established almost every year all over New Zealand, powered increasingly by steam engines. The 1840s and 1850s were a period of rapid innovation in woodworking technology, and the new machines were brought to this country almost as soon as they were built. In 1842 a Cornish Beam steam engine was landed at Mill Bay on the Manukau Harbour, together with frame and circular saws, a shingle cutter and a lathe for turning — remarkable machinery for its time.

In 1851 the results of half a century of mechanical experimentation and improvement were displayed in London at the Great Exhibition, and at later exhibitions in Paris and Philadelphia. From then on, steam-powered woodworking machinery became widely used throughout Britain, America, and New Zealand. Bigger, faster, and more sophisticated machines were developed by the many manufacturers for planing and moulding, spindle moulding, mortising and tenoning, turning and carving, general joinery work, as well as grooving, recessing, dovetailing, and "therming" — shaping and moulding square, hexagonal, or octagonal table legs or balusters. All of these machines were quickly imported to New Zealand by enterprising businessmen.

In 1856, for instance, Auckland Steam Saw Mills

advertised their "newly erected Steam Saw Mills for Sawing and Planing, Grooving and Tonguing, &c."[3] As early as 1861 James Gilberd, "Steam Sash and Door Manufacturer", in Princes Street, Auckland, advertised "sashes, doors, mantlepieces, mouldings &c. always on hand or made to order".[4] By 1864 at least two other Auckland companies offered sashes and doors made by steam power — the infant Union Steam Saw Moulding Sash and Door Company Limited (USSM), and Eric Craig, carpenter and joiner.[5]

By 1883 Guthrie and Larnach's Dunedin Iron and Woodware Company employed 700 men and brought two million feet of kauri from Auckland's west coast forests for their "manufactory of woodware replete with the most improved American machinery".[6] In 1886 the Auckland Timber Company, under George Holdship, had:

> ... every possible kind of woodworking machinery of the latest and most improved English and American manufacture ... amongst which are Boult's carving and dovetailing

machine; Brown and Howe's gauge lathe; the Challenge scroll saw; the Eclipse perforator; the Variety wood-turning lathe; Howley and Hermane's new-style power mortiser with a speed of 800 strokes per minute &c.[7]

In 1865 Auckland sawmills were classed as "amongst the best in the world . . . fitted with the most approved machinery, not only for general conversion, but for the manufacture of doors, window-sashes &c . . . no expense is grudged to secure the most efficient appliances".[8]

There were several main classes of woodworking machines:

a. Saws

By 1860 sawmillers had three main types of saw to choose from:

(i) *reciprocating* — a blade which moved backwards and forwards like a handsaw, either

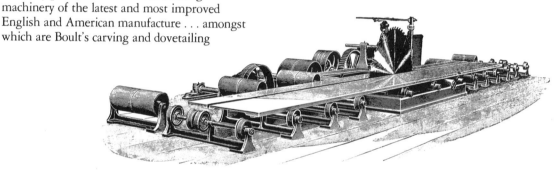

80. Circular log saw and moving table.

81. Horizontal bandsaw.

horizontally with one or two blades, or vertically with many blades held in a frame — the "log frame" or "deal frame" saw.

(ii) _circular_ — a rapidly spinning metal disc with a serrated edge, which split logs into balks rapidly, and resawed them into boards, or cut them into convenient lengths.

(iii) _band_ — a metal ribbon with a serrated edge, moving continuously in one direction. Re-invented as recently as 1849, these saws were valuable where very large or oddly-shaped logs had to be converted quickly, or in resawing work where they could cut out unusual shapes from the wood — the scroll, or "jobbing" saw.

b. Planing and moulding machines:

The moulding machine gave a particular shape to a piece of wood by forcing the wood at high speed past a set of rapidly spinning blocks which held the cutting irons or "knives" — small steel plates with shaped and sharpened edges which scooped pieces out of the wood, leaving behind the intended shape. The knives were ground and sharpened by the machinists from a drawing, or to match an existing shape. If straight cutting edges were fitted timber could be simply planed, and with shaped vertical knives at the sides, floorboards could be produced with a tongue on one edge and a groove on the other. The machines were arranged to take timber in sizes ranging from 75 x 50 mm up to 300 x 125 mm, at speeds as high as 300 metres per minute (18 km/h), moulding either one side only or four sides at once — as for example in a moulded handrail.

The spindle moulder operated rather differently with one or at most two vertical knives rotating above a table which allowed curved pieces to be moulded — something the large moulding machine could not do.

c. Mortising and tenoning machines

A _mortise_ is a shaped hole made in one piece of wood to take the _tenon_ or shaped end of another piece of wood in a firm tight joint. The mortise was traditionally cut by a chisel, and the first machine invented for the purpose mimicked the chiselling action with a series of vertical strokes. In later machines a hole was first bored with a power auger and then chiselled, or a hollow chisel made the mortise with a rotating auger inside it to take away waste wood.

In tenoning machines the piece of wood was clamped to a moving table, and fed to saws or cutters mounted horizontally and vertically on the machine. The cutters first of all cut the "shoulder" of the tenon (a cut right around the end of the wood), then cut away the sides — four cuts from

82. Ransome's four-sided planing and moulding machine.

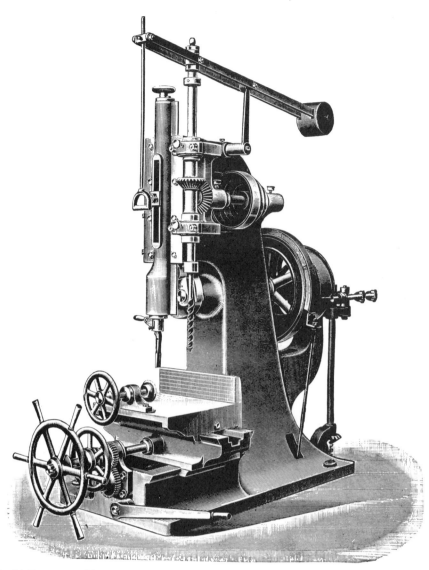

83. (a) Power mortising
machine.
(b) Tenoning machine.

(a)

84. (a) Ransome's
Complete Joiner.
(b) Work produced by the
Complete Joiner.

(b)

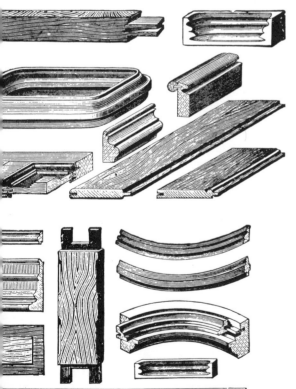

the end down to the shoulder. Tenoning machines
were also useful for other kinds of work such as
trenching and cross-cutting.

d. Lathes

Lathes were the first machines to be mechanised
because their rotary motion was quite easy to produce with a foot treadle; so, the belt drive from a
factory steam engine was a logical development in
the nineteenth century workshop. The greater
power also meant much higher turning speeds,
which led to better quality work, and enabled very
large pieces of timber to be turned up for columns,
stair posts and so on.

e. General joinery machines

These were known also as Universal Wood-
workers, Complete Joiners, or Variety Moulders,
and were useful in smaller workshops, or in large
workshops for small jobs which did not justify
setting up one of the larger single-purpose
machines. They were very versatile; the machine
illustrated here was designed for sawing and cross-
cutting, planing, tonguing, grooving, edging,
thicknessing and beading, straight moulding, circular moulding, tenoning, mortising, and boring.

95

THE COMPANIES

Although some of the first machines for planing, tonguing, and grooving, were imported by successful tradesmen,* the companies which owned and operated these machines were not small backyard industries. During the 1870s heavy public investment in joint stock companies and the amalgamation of smaller timber businesses led to large mills working in near boom conditions in Auckland, and the city soon became the timber capital of New Zealand.

By 1880 there were four giant timber companies in Auckland province, which between them owned most of the standing kauri and supplied most of the timber exported from the province to local and overseas markets, where they competed with timbers from the Baltic, Australia, and North America. These were the New Zealand Timber Company, the Auckland Timber Company, Logan Campbell's Te Kopuru Mill, and the Union Steam Saw Moulding Sash and Door Company. Their mills were large and elaborately equipped, and heavily capitalised.

But the prosperity of the mills was artifically sustained by heavy borrowing, and when the South Island markets collapsed in the depression of the 1880s (followed later by the Auckland market), and the Australian markets became uneconomic, the profitability of the timber giants evaporated. The bank moved in and sold up the Union Steam Saw Company in 1888, and the business of the other firms dwindled almost to a standstill.

From the wreckage of the Auckland timber industry rose another still larger giant — the Kauri Timber Company, formed in 1888, owned ironically enough by an Australian syndicate in partnership with George Holdship of the former Auckland Timber Company. The syndicate bought up twenty-four mills and the choicest standing timber in the province at rock bottom prices, but struggled for ten years before it showed a profit for the first time.[9]

*For example, Craig in 1864 and sawyers such as MacNab and Co. in 1865.

THE BUILDERS

In contrast with these concerns, the house builders were small groups of two or three men, boss and workers, who walked or cycled long distances to work six days a week, and who did all their work with hand tools. The carpenter was the main contractor, and a lot of his work came through the timber companies which supplied his materials. Bricklaying, plumbing, roofing and staircases were subcontracted to specialist tradesmen, but the carpenter was "the builder".

Materials were delivered to the job by horse-drawn carts and heavy drays, often over boggy unformed roads. According to a manuscript written by a builder of the period:

> Most builders made a point of getting all the timber on the job in the first fortnight. Scantlings [framing] were laid out in lengths. Weatherboards and flooring all stacked in racks to dry out. Builders' sheds were unthought of. With the first load of foundation timber came the 12" x 1" vertical boarding for the 5' x 3' W.C. which was erected that day and was the sole lockup until the house was well on. Later when a wash house was planned this also was apart from the house and gave a better lockup.
>
> Essential special tools for the carpenter at that time were a draw-knife, spokeshave, a German jack and a set of German bits and we were all content with the 2' rule which fitted better into the little leather nail pockets we wore.
>
> Scaffolding apart from the planks were widely built with kauri rikas, all held together with rope lashings. Men were very smart and tidy in the erection of them.[10]

The builders have left few written records, however; only the houses remain to judge them by.

CATALOGUE HOUSES:
The kit of parts

The timber companies produced an enormous range of products, not only the basic parts of a house — framing, weatherboards, doors, windows, linings, and mouldings — but entire houses, as well as gates and fences and furniture. In fact, anything for the house and section that could be made from timber was made. To convey this good news to the buying public, the companies advertised in newspapers and the annual almanacs and directories, but the most popular way of presenting their wares was that great nineteenth century institution, the company catalogue.

It is not clear when the first catalogues were issued in New Zealand. In the mid 1850s and throughout the 1860s, the public were courted by large advertisements which respectfully drew their attention to the quality of timber and workmanship, and the modest prices offered by different firms. However, in 1866 George Holdship kept priced samples of his mouldings "always at hand", which suggests that his firm produced no cata-logue. In 1867 the Union Steam Saw Moulding Sash and Door Company listed their entire range of wood products in a full-page advertisement in Stevens and Batholomew's *New Zealand Directory for 1866-67*. In 1874 Findlay and Company of Dunedin produced what may have been their first catalogue, which included plans and elevations for eight simple cottages, as well as windows, mouldings, fences, panelling and turned items. Another more elaborate catalogue from Guthrie and Larnach's Dunedin Iron and Woodware Company at about 1880 offered seventeen "Cottages", from two rooms to a two-storey ecclesiastical Gothic extravaganza; a variety of highly ornate specimen elevations; shop fronts; conservatories; windows in

85. Union Steam Saw Moulding, Sash and Door Company advertisement —Wellington, 1867.

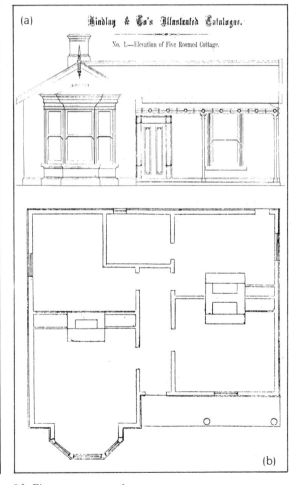

86. Five-room cottage from *Findlay and Company's Illustrated Catalogue*, 1874:
(a) elevation;
(b) plan. *ATL.*

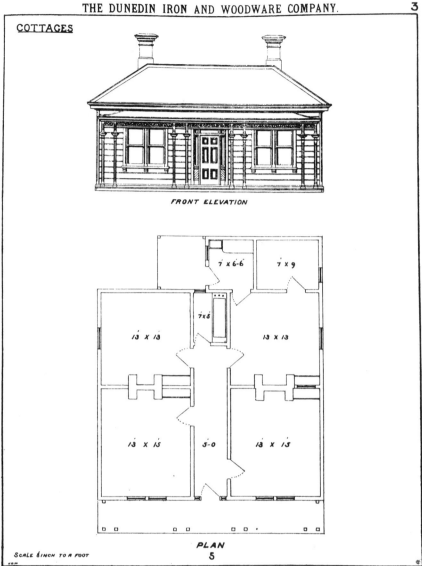

THE DUNEDIN IRON AND WOODWARE COMPANY. **3**

COTTAGES

FRONT ELEVATION

7 x 6·6   7 x 9

7 x 5

13 x 13   13 x 13

13 x 15   5·0   13 x 15

PLAN
5

SCALE 6 INCH TO A FOOT

PRINCES AND BOND STREETS SOUTH, DUNEDIN.

87. Five-room cottage from Dunedin Iron and Woodware Company catalogue, 1882. *Hocken Library.*

88. Pages from the Dunedin Iron and Woodware Company catalogue, c. 1882:
(a) gates;
(b) staircase details;
(c) fretwork;
(d) grindstone and washhouse equipment. *Hocken Library.*

every style; doors plain and ornate; gates domestic, rural and baronial; fences; stairs; fire surrounds; bargeboards and fretted frieze boards; ceiling roses; brackets; capitals and arches; finials; balusters; butter churns and washing machines; and a vast array of household furniture. This was the work of an expert draughtsman, and it must have done much for the company's turnover. Some of the drawings found their way into the catalogues of rival companies as far away as Feilding — a compliment of sorts.

The cottages offered to the public by the timber companies were "kitset" houses, where a basic plan supplied by the owner, the builder, or the catalogue, could be clothed in any of the optional extras illustrated (or produced to order) — the machinery made anything possible if the money was there to pay for it.

The towns and cities of New Zealand, therefore, expanded in quarter-acre increments along streets of houses which sprang from the pages of the catalogues. In this democratic architecture, owners of property could choose for themselves from a plethora of plans and parts, and then hire a builder to put the pieces together. The publication of catalogues continued unabated through the recession of

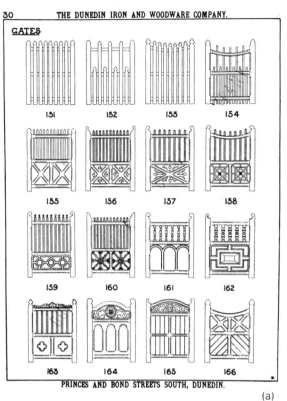

GATES

151 152 153 154
155 156 157 158
159 160 161 162
163 164 165 166

PRINCES AND BOND STREETS SOUTH, DUNEDIN.

(a)

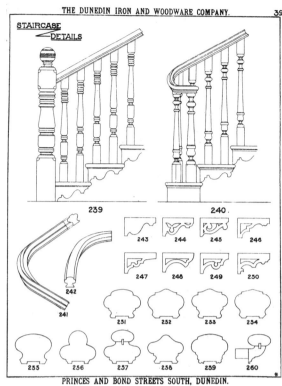

STAIRCASE
DETAILS

239 240
243 244 245 246
242 247 248 249 250
241 251 252 233 234
255 256 237 238 260

PRINCES AND BOND STREETS SOUTH, DUNEDIN.

(b)

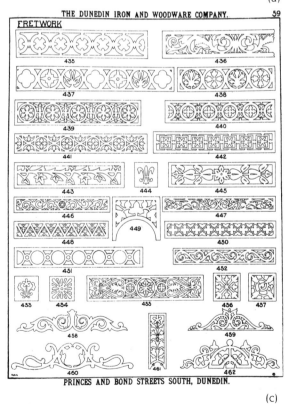

FRETWORK

433 436
437 438
439 440
441 442
443 444 445
446 447
448 449 450
451 452
453 454 455 456 457
458 459
460 461 462

PRINCES AND BOND STREETS SOUTH, DUNEDIN.

(c)

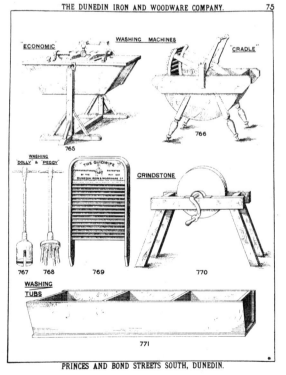

ECONOMIC WASHING MACHINES CRADLE
765 766
WASHING DOLLY & PEGGY
THE GUIDWIFE
GRINDSTONE
767 768 769 770
WASHING TUBS
771

PRINCES AND BOND STREETS SOUTH, DUNEDIN.

(d)

89. Kitset houses
—Koromiko Road,
Wanganui, 1907. *ATL,
Deuton Coll.*

the 1880s, but no longer included plans, and concentrated on timber mouldings, of which 200-300 might be illustrated. The Kauri Timber Company's catalogue of 1919 showed designs twenty years out of date, and even that company would have been hard pressed to find suitable timber for some of the items illustrated. By 1909 a new type of catalogue was appearing on the market, unconnected with the companies which produced the timber. These were the house plan books, the work of draughtsmen and architects who sold their design skills direct to the public. They marked the end of the Victorian villas and cottages, and the beginnings of the Californian bungalow in New Zealand.

BRICKMAKING

Bricks were being made in Wellington in the first year of settlement, and as the colony expanded every town or district supported at least one brickyard. The bricks and other earthenware products

were traditionally hand-made, and the first brickmaking equipment to be mechanised was the pugmill, which broke down the excavated clay to an even "plastic" consistency.

Brickmaking machines were more revolutionary. Some hand-powered models had been invented, but once steam engines were introduced two other methods were developed. In one, soft plastic clay was extruded as a continuous block through a metal die to be cut off with wires into bricks. Another system used ground clay in a nearly dry state, and this was described in the *Daily Southern Cross* of 10 January 1865 with a glowing account of new machinery installed at the Caledonian Brickworks by John Leckie:

We will perhaps give our readers an idea of what we saw by following the lead of Mr Leckie, and reproduce as nearly as we can the information which he gave us. You at first visit a very unpromising kind of bog or mud heap, which you are told is the raw clay, and men are busy wheeling barrows of it to what is called the cylinder, into which it is cast without the smallest ceremony . . . You would like to know where such ponderous mud could go to, or what could be done with it. Your guide informs you that it goes into a cylinder [pugmill]. You look down this cylinder which suggests the idea of a volcanic crater upon a small scale, for you see the mud, clay (call it what you will), or loam making extraordinary undulations. You look inquisitively, and are told that there are twelve knives placed upon a shaft at a particular angle . . . which cut, and cut, and cut through this mass of mud. You descend from the platform where you see this interesting operation going on, and find this mud coming out of two small apertures on to little pieces of square boards held by boys, seeming as if they were placed in moulds, so fine at the edges are they, so uniform in weight and shape, and stamped on them with all the distinctness of a wax impression, "Caledonian Brickworks, Richmond Bay". Your guide, the proprietor, tells you that

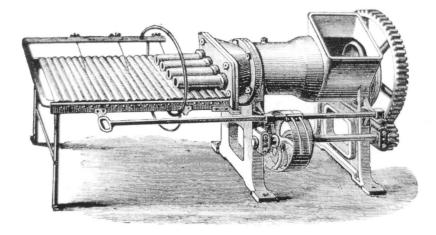

90. R.O. Clark's patent field tile-making machine. *Jack Diamond Coll.*

91. Moulders making soil-pipe traps. *ATL, Steffano Webb Coll.*

after the knives have done their work, the clay is cast out by an eccentric movement; that in the process it is subject to a pressure of upwards of fifteen tons weight, which effectively excludes the water, and the subsequent stages of drying are performed at present in the usual way.[11]

Bricks made in this way were very precisely formed, and though hard on the outside, they were relatively soft inside and were inclined to be brittle. By 1862 the Laurie brothers had a steam brick and drainpipe works in Karangahape Road, Auckland, and in 1866, the Water of Leith brickworks in Dunedin operated:

> . . . patent machinery manufactured by Messrs Clayton and Co. of London and worked by a 10 horse horizontal steam engine. When driven at ordinary speed, this machine is capable of turning out 1100 "standard" or 1300 small bricks per hour — the small bricks, which are rather less in size than those used in England, being the favourites in Dunedin. Not only bricks, but paving and roof-tiles, drainage pipes, and various articles of pottery-ware are largely produced.[12]

92. Drury Pottery and Fireclay Works' display of products, 1906. *AIM.*

Most of these products were made by other brickworks, drainpipes especially, and many were finished with a "salt glaze". This was done by throwing salt into the kiln during firing, which covered the earthenware with a hard permanent glasslike surface. The Canterbury Pottery advertised corrugated and plain roofing tiles in 1862,[13] although clay tiles were not widely used in New Zealand until Marseilles tiles were introduced via Sydney in about 1901.

Hand-made bricks were fired in the clamp kilns described on p. 46, and these kilns continued to be made throughout the nineteenth century in remote areas, or where small quantities of bricks were needed. Larger manufacturers built permanent kilns made from fired brick, usually a rectangular enclosing wall, with fire openings at the sides or below the floor. These "Scotch" kilns operated on the "updraught" principle (i.e. that hot air rises), but they were inefficient and produced bricks of uneven quality. A major advance was the Hoffman kiln, invented in 1858, which worked on the "downdraught" principle, and drew heat from a

fire built above the kiln down through the bricks, resulting in a more even and efficient firing. One type of Hoffman kiln was the "circular" kiln, in which a series of firing compartments were arranged around a tall central chimney, with connecting openings which could be closed or opened as required. "Green" bricks were loaded into one compartment as fired bricks were unloaded from the next, while on the opposite side of the kiln there were bricks at the height of their firing. From this cycle of gradual heating, burning, and slow cooling, a steady supply of bricks of reliable quality was produced. Hoffman kilns were in use in New Zealand by the 1870s,[14] and were still working until quite recently.

METALWORKING

Corrugated iron was brought to New Zealand in the early days as a temporary material. It was cheap, light, strong, fireproof, and easy to fix over a simple framed roof. Along with weatherboard walls, corrugated iron roofs became a characteristic feature of nineteenth century New Zealand houses.

93. Wellington house with a corrugated iron side wall.

94. House with a "sparrow iron" verandah roof, Dunedin.

95. Cottage with "pan iron" roof, Nelson. *Chris Cochran.*

If the roof was unlined beneath the iron, the house became an oven in the sun, a drum in the rain, and a percussion band in a hailstorm, but lined ceilings softened these effects and many New Zealanders raised in an old house still find the rattle of rain on an iron roof a pleasant and comforting sound. Corrugated iron came to be valued in towns as a fire resistant material, and many of Wellington's close-packed inner-city houses contrast a rusticated wooden street facade with a corrugated side wall. A particular form of corrugated iron, used mainly for verandahs, was known as "baby iron" or "sparrow iron" because of its small corrugations.

Iron was also used in flat sheets, known as "pan iron", laid over a boarded (sarked) roof for support, in small overlapping sheets. Vertical edges were

96. Nail-making; from Tomlinson's *Illustrations of Useful Arts and Manufactures,* 1858.

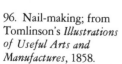

426. NAIL-FORGE.

turned up and folded over a wooden dowell or batten fixed to the sarking, and this gave the roof a ribbed appearance. The firm of Morewood and Rogers in England exported these sheets as "Morewood tiles" from 1843 — 900 x 600 mm galvanised sheets with two fluted edges.[15] Pan iron was more common on verandah roofs and bay windows than the main roof of a house, as the sarking added to the overall cost of construction.

The iron sheet imported to New Zealand was "plain", "black", and "galvanised" (or more accurately zinc-dipped) to prevent rusting. With the sheets came ridging and spouting of the same material, sometimes of pure zinc, but by 1875 all these items were being manufactured in Dunedin by R. & T. Haworth.[16] Once rolling machinery was available here, it became possible to form curves in corrugated sheets — verandah roofs could be made concave, convex, ogee, or bull-nosed, and corrugated iron rainwater tanks could be made.

On roofs, sheets were fixed by nailing through the ridges of the corrugations into a timber purlin underneath with flat-headed "clouts" or "rose-clench" nails which had a small diamond-shaped washer under the head. Later, the lead-head nail was developed with a flat head nail cast in a small hemisphere of lead which bent to the shape of the iron when it was hammered home.

Nail-making was another handcraft that was transformed by mechanisation. A machine for making nails was invented in Britain in 1790 by John Clifford, which converted iron rod into a "string" of nails which were then snipped off. In the United States, where wooden houses were common, a nail-making machine was developed in 1810 to cut and head nails in one operation at the rate of over 100 per minute. These nails, which were punched out of rolled iron plate in interlocking rows, were a third the cost of those made by hand and could be driven into wood without splitting it and without first having to drill a hole. Later, machines were perfected for cutting nails from steel wire, and cheap disposable nails appeared on the New Zealand market.

It is not clear when nail-making machinery first reached this country. In 1862 G.R. Burnett, "Ship Smith, Chain and Nail Maker", advertised his services in in the *New Zealand Almanac,* but his nails may well have been hand wrought. In 1873 J. & J. Dickey in Auckland were selling "Ewbank's and Cut Nails, French Wire Nails, 1 in. to 3 in., American Finishing Nails, ½ in. to 2½ in."[17] — and it is probable that nails were being manufactured in local foundries by this time.

An alternative use of iron in buildings was in the form of castings. Cast iron was a strong but brittle product of the smelting process and was developed for buildings as a fireproof structural material. Since it was moulded, cast iron could combine a structural *form* with a decorative *shape,* and these ornamental possibilities were quickly exploited in classical columns, gothic arches, and simulated stonework. Cast iron was the poor man's wrought iron, and at first, designs were copied from the expensive hand-made work. The Victorians loved decoration for its own sake, and in the iron makers' catalogues page after page of elaborate cast iron ware was displayed for use in every conceivable part of a building — roof ornaments at ridge and gutter lines, rainwater gutters, heads, and down-

427. PREPARING STRIPS.   428. MOUNTED STRIP.   429. CUTTING NAILS.

(a)

(b)

(c)

(d)

97. Iron gates:
(a) cast posts and wrought
gates, Dunedin;
(b) cast posts, wrought and
cast gate, Wellington;
(c) wooden posts, wrought
gate, Auckland;
(d) plastered brick posts,
wrought gate, Dunedin.

106

GLASSMAKING

pipes; windows; balconies and verandahs; stairs; conservatories; and gates and railings. Entire buildings were made of cast iron, from MacFarlane's "patent ordure closets" to gothic churches and office buildings.

Iron buildings were prefabricated for immigrants to the colonies by firms such as Cottam and Hallem in London,[18] and it is probable that some of their decorative work was brought here as well. Cast iron had reached Australia in the 1840s, and by 1848 a local foundry had produced castings from Australian ore.[19] It reached New Zealand some time later — a house of 1868 in Oxford, Canterbury, still has its cast verandah frieze — and when men from the Victorian goldfields migrated to those of Otago in the early 1860s, it is probable that Melbourne castings found their way to Dunedin.

Eventually, New Zealand foundries produced a wide range of cast iron products. By 1866 Frazer and Tinne in Auckland were advertising "Builders' Work (Wrought and Cast) . . . and Ornamental Iron Work",[20] and many foundries manufactured coal and wood stoves such as the "Orion", "Atlas", "Orb", "Zealandia", "Champion", and "Enterprise" — as well as grates, gates, and railings, with patterns based on local flora.

Glassmaking is an ancient art which was rediscovered in Europe in the Middle Ages. The material is a compound of many elements — silica, alkalis, and "earthy bases", fused together in a furnace to form silicates. The main kinds of glass used in windows, distinguished by their method of manufacture, were crown glass (or German sheet), cylinder (or "broad" or common window glass) and plate (or cast) glass. The first two were formed by hand, and the last by semi-mechanical methods.

Crown glass was made of better quality materials than cylinder glass, and was formed by blowing the molten "metal" into a globe which, when spun rapidly close to the heat of the furnace, flew open into a large disc "with a noise like that produced by opening a wet umbrella".[21] This disc was laid on a flat surface and then annealed (cooled slowly) to make it less brittle. A sheet of about 1.2 metres diameter could be produced by this method, with an inconvenient thick "blob" at the centre, so that the largest obtainable piece of clear glass was only from about 1000 x 300 mm to about 600 x 500 mm. Windows were, therefore, made up of small square panes of glass in divided wooden sashes, or

98. Making crown glass, from *A Diderot Encyclopaedia*.

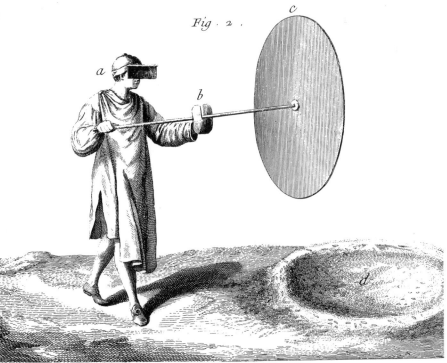

281. BLOWING AND SWINGING CYLINDER GLASS.

99. Making cylinder, or broad glass, from Tomlinson's *Illustrations of Useful Arts and Manufactures*, 1858:
(a) glass-blowers swinging the cylinder;
(b) stages in the cylinder glass process.

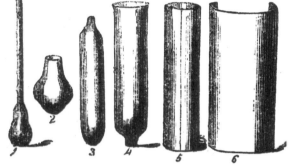

282. STAGES OF CYLINDER GLASS.

diamond shaped pieces held by lead rods with grooved edges called "cames". The leftover blob (the "crown") was sold cheaply and often ended up as windows in the cottages of the poor. The early importation of crown glass into New Zealand explains the wide use of the small-paned twelve-light double-hung sash until the 1870s, when broad glass became more common.

Cylinder glass was made from cheaper alakalis, and was formed from a long cylindrical globe blown by the glass maker. The ends of the cylinder were cut off, then it was cut open, and allowed to lie flat while still hot. The glass was slightly uneven, but larger sheets could be made with this method, and the process was later mechanised in America in 1896, using a hot metal cylinder as a mould. The whole of the Crystal Palace at the Great Exhibition of 1851 was covered by 300,000 panes of cylinder glass, produced in about two months by hand blowing.[22] The cylinder method also produced the glass dust covers so popular in Victorian living rooms. In New Zealand cylinder glass was used for ordinary house windows from about 1870 to the 1920s, and although quite large sheets could be made, the standard sheet of about 1 metre x 450 mm accounts for the wide use of four-light double-hung sashes.

Coloured glass became popular in the nineteenth century with the renewed interest in ecclesiastical glass of the Gothic Revival. Research and experiment produced clear brilliantly coloured broad glass by adding small quantities of various oxides to the glass mixture: cobalt oxide made blue, copper protoxide in small quantities made yellow and in larger amounts it made ruby-red. Red-brown glass was made with oxides of manganese and iron, and green by adding many elements including nitrate, arsenic, iron oxide and copper oxide. In a further refinement "flash" glass was produced by dipping hot clear glass into molten coloured glass, and then blowing this into a cylinder in the normal way to make sheet glass with a thin layer of colour bonded to it. This glass was cut into pieces and the coloured layer was ground away in delicate patterns of rosettes, stars, or repeating motifs. Flash glass was very popular in New Zealand houses of the 1870s and 1880s, when "ruby and bright green glass appeared in the vestibule . . . and doorways . . . and vulgarity reigned supreme."[23]

Etched glass was another form of decorative glass, often used together with flash glass. This was made by coating sheet glass with wax, then scraping some of the wax away in a pattern, and pouring acid onto the exposed glass to give it a frosted surface. Later, sand-blasting achieved similar results. Etched glass was popular in New Zealand as a centrepiece in ornamental windows or in glazed doors. The patterns were sometimes symmetrical stylised floral designs, and there was a wide variety of repeating patterns based on such things as butterflies, or simple geometric motifs, etched on very thin glass sheets.

Plate glass was an expensive product, first made in Britain in 1773. Molten glass was poured onto a cold metal table with a metal rim, then rolled flat and allowed to cool slowly for two weeks, after which it was ground and polished by hand, although later, steam machines did this work. Very

large sheets of glass could be made in this way (in 1871 in Lancashire, a single piece of 100 square feet was poured). An important form of plate glass, usually referred to as "cast" glass, was made by pouring the molten glass onto a *hot* metal table with a pattern stamped on its bed, so that the pattern was moulded into one surface of the sheet. Polished plate glass was used to make mirrors, and coloured cast glass became popular in New Zealand for doors and verandahs in the 1890s and 1900s.

"Stained" glass became popular in New Zealand after 1900. In this technique, formal geometric and symmetrical designs (often with an *art nouveau* inspiration), were created from coloured and painted glass set in lead "cames", which were bent to the shape of the cut pieces.

All glass used in New Zealand until the 1930s was imported from England or America, and although there was a small glassworks in Auckland in the 1880s, its products were "usually lamp glasses and chimneys, and water bottles and jugs". In 1862 James Gilbert simply offered "Window Glass, from 10 by 8 to 44 x 30",[24] but by 1879 Stewart and Co. in Wellington had stocks of "Plate, Rolled Plate, Ground, Ornamental, and colored [sic]" glass.[25]

100. Etched glass.

101. Cast glass enclosing the verandah, Ponsonby.

Villas and cottages

SITING AND PLANNING

The prototypical villas and cottages were rural dwellings, but they served equally well in the towns, where at first circumstances were not so very different. As long as town sections were large — quarter, half, or one acre, or more — siting depended mainly on the direction of the road, and less on what neighbours were doing on their land.

By the 1860s, however, town centres were becoming congested, and the earliest houses had to compete with two- and even three-storeyed wooden commercial buildings which ran right up to their side boundaries. New houses for labourers

sprang up on small sections as close as possible to the commercial centre — shank's pony was still the only way a worker could get to work. But the middle and upper-middle classes fled in their horses and traps to the outskirts, and new suburbs began to appear along the roads leaving town. All of these houses faced the road, and ignored such details as the sun and the prevailing wind.

Private property out in the suburbs was marked off with hedges of hawthorn, gorse and blackberry, or fences of stones, post-and-rail, and split palings. This was a practical measure at first when farmland was never far away, to keep meandering stock out of the gardens. For the street boundary, joinery

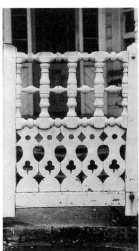

102 Wooden fences and gates:
(a) posts and pickets, Devonport;
(b) pickets and dowels, Gisborne;
(c) gate, Devonport.

(a)

(b)

(c)

shops turned out neat machine-made palings with fancy ends, and wide gates with massive posts to be set deep in the ground. The foundries joined in with ornate cast-iron railings, gates, and posts, and around 1900 "Cyclone" wire fences were introduced.

On a small or moderately-sized section, the front gate was carefully placed opposite the front door, and joined to it by a broad straight path of sea shells or gravel, kept in place by stout boards of jarrah or totara set in the ground, or by glazed earthenware edging tiles. The tilemakers also made a wide choice of garden ornaments such as bird baths, planting troughs, and decorative urns.

For larger Victorian houses, a wide curving driveway swept through an imposing double gate up to the front entrance where it ended in a turning circle. When the front path reached the front verandah or the steps leading up to it, a detour directed tradesmen to the rear through a gate in a trellis fence at the side of the house, separating the mundane affairs of the household from society.

GATES

103. double gates:
(a) from the Dunedin Iron and Woodware Company catalogue, *Hocken Library*
(b) wooden gates, Wellington.

104. House and garden, Devonport, 1911. *APL.*

The trellis was an ideal spot for cherished English climbers such as jasmine, rambling rose, and convolvulus, and front gardens were planted out with other treasures from the old country. Annuals and perennial borders edged the paths, with standard roses and ornamental shrubs crowding behind. By the 1870s nurserymen such as C.T. Wren in Auckland and Henry Budden in Nelson offered daffodils, crocuses, hyacinths and many other bulbs for planting under trees, along the drive, or on grassy banks.[26] Lawns were laboriously kept with scythe and handshears until the 1880s, when the spiral-blade lawnmower (invented in 1869) transformed grass from a lumpy surface to a smoothly textured sward.

The backyard was usually larger than the front, with space set aside for clotheslines, a wood pile, a well-stocked orchard and vegetable garden; and in a discreet position as far out of sight as possible, the privy, screened perhaps by the fragrant "lavatory tree" *(datura)*. For small town properties, few outbuildings were needed apart from the privy: a washhouse, of course, and a coal shed, and perhaps a small garden shed or even a glasshouse. Only the wealthy owned stables and horses, and only they could afford a detached kitchen behind the house, to keep cooking smells and noise out of the best rooms.

CONSTRUCTION

From 1860 to 1910 there were few changes in the way wooden houses were put together in New Zealand. Although more materials were factory produced, and machine-made nails simplified the work, the recipe remained basically the same as it had been for the first wooden houses: a timber skeleton propped up on piles and covered with boards, and its roof covered with slates, tiles, or iron. Its openings were now filled with factory-made standard windows and doors, however, and its edges and corners were decorated inside and out with a selection of mouldings, brackets, and fretwork or iron lace from the catalogues.

a. Foundations and floors

Houses were supported above the ground by rough *piles* of puriri or totara, although after 1900 square sawn totara blocks were common, or brick piers, and after about 1905 there were octagonal glazed earthenware blocks in some areas.[27] The piles were set out in rows, and over these in one direction wooden *bearers* were laid, joined where necessary over one of the piles, and in the other direction (over the bearers) floor *joists* were spaced about 450 mm apart — the floor boards were laid later after the outside had been covered. Wooden piles

105. Wooden house blocks, Devonport.

(a)

(b)

106. Framed construction
details:
(a) junction of wall and
floor;
(b) stud mortised into
bottom plate.

were the weak spot in these otherwise well-built houses, because in time they invariably settled into the ground.

b. Timber walls

Outer walls and those walls holding up the roof were put up first, the frames made up on the ground then propped up in one piece. In the early houses the bearer was part of the wall frame, and because nails were still expensive, it was mortised to receive the tenoned ends of the studs, and the joint was secured with two nails. The top *plate* was also mortised over the *studs*, and floor joists were laid over the bearers after the wall frame had been put up.

From about 1890 two things changed: studs were no longer mortised into the plates (the joints were butted and nailed); and the wall frame was set up *after* the floor joists with a separate bottom plate (often referred to as a "vermin plate"), which sealed off the wall cavity and kept mice and rats out

of the house. Walls were usually 3 to 3.5 metres high, but in larger houses could reach 4.5 metres. Interior walls (*partitions*) which did not carry roof loads were often put up after the floors had been laid. All load-bearing inside walls and the outer walls were braced to keep the frame square and to stop the house falling over. The *braces* were long boards recessed into the outside of the framework.

In 1½-storeyed houses, the American "balloon frame" was sometimes used. Invented in 1833 this had studs running full height in the walls, and first-floor joists fixed to the sides of the studs. But most two-storeyed houses were built with the "platform frame" in which the walls for each floor were framed separately above and below the first-floor joists.

Corners in the frame were formed with 100 x 100 mm studs at first, then two 100 x 50 mm studs arranged so that linings inside and out could be fixed together.

The walls were weatherboarded. The most

common form was the plain board, showing the marks of the circular saw, and overlapping the board below. Later, the boards were supplied planed and bevelled on the back, and some companies such as Prouse Lumber Limited of Wellington ran boards with weather baffles, and a fine groove on the face to mark the overlap. At corners, the boards were butted against solid *angle stops*, until the 1870s when this detail was replaced with the *boxed corner* — two boards fixed to each other *over* the weatherboard and their edges masked

with *scribers* (thin battens cut out to the shape of the overlapping boards). In some houses the boxed corner was made from a single piece of wood — the "rebated saddle".

Another kind of weatherboard which became popular in the 1880s was the "rusticated" board, where the top edge was planed down to fit behind a rebate in the edge of the next board. The completed wall showed pronounced grooves which resembled channel-jointed stonework, and in more elaborate houses timber *quoins* at corners assisted the illu-

107. Cut-away view of a typical villa of 1900.

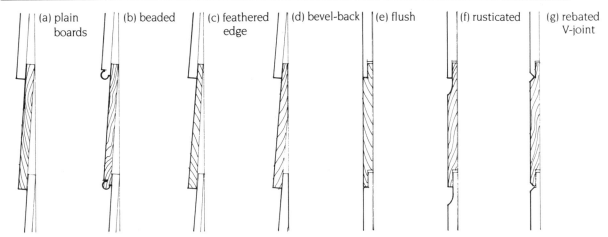

(a) plain boards (b) beaded (c) feathered edge (d) bevel-back (e) flush (f) rusticated (g) rebated V-joint

108. Common types of weatherboard.

109. Flush-boarded house, Wellington (note rusticated boards in porch recess).

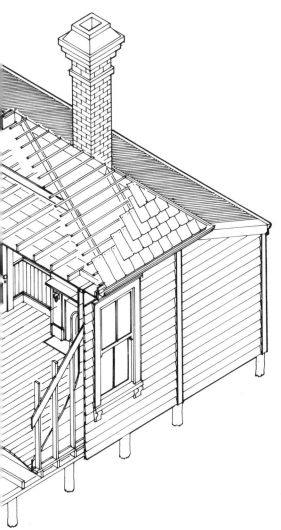

sion. The introduction of the rusticated board has been attributed to the Wellington architect Julius Toxward in the 1860s.[28]

In this period board and batten walls were considered suitable only for outhouses, or very cheap houses in newer areas, but there were the odd exceptions such as Ruatuna — the family home of Gordon Coates, built at Matakohe in 1877.

Inside, the frame of the house was still lined with boards, but these were wider and thinner than weatherboards, and rough sawn. These lining boards were fixed horizontally, and roughly butted together, stopping short of the floor where the skirting would cover them. In better houses, a common finish was lime plaster on timber laths, or else the outer walls were lined with tongued and grooved boards because plain boards with their wide gaps were so draughty. In the kitchen it was usual to find planed, tongued and grooved boards

115

(PT & G) on both walls and ceiling, or at least as a *dado* — wall panelling about 1.2 metres high. Sometimes, wider horizontal boards were used with a fine bead at the v-joint, and this type of wall covering was generally classed as *matched lining* (or "matchlining").

c. Masonry walls

Brick and stone houses were much less common in most parts of the country; they were more expensive than those made of timber, and the early experiences with earthquakes had not been forgotten. In 1888 there were more brick and stone houses in the Otago area than in the rest of New Zealand,[29] and although cut stone was too costly for all but the largest houses, there were many fine smaller houses of random or coursed rubble built during this period, especially in and around Dunedin.

Masonry walls needed a good foundation and they had to keep out water. Bearing and outer walls in brick houses were built at least 350 mm thick —more for a two-storey house — and below ground level, the wall stepped out on both sides until the bottom "course" (layer) of bricks was about twice the wall thickness, lying on a bed of well-rammed rock and lime concrete. Many bricks

110. Lime plaster over timber laths on interior walls, Southland.

(a)

(b)

111. Brick villas and
cottages:
(a) Dunedin;
    (opposite page)
(b) Dunedin;
(c) Dunedin;
(d) Auckland

(c)

(d)

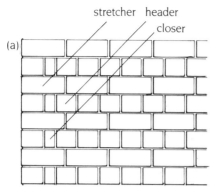

stretcher header
closer

(a)

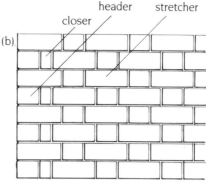

header stretcher
closer

(b)

112. Most common brick bonds:
(a) English bond —alternate courses of stretchers and headers;
(b) Flemish bond —courses of alternate stretchers and headers.

113. Local basalt with Oamaru stone facings on a large Southland house, Mandeville.

were very porous and could hold a lot of water, but rainwater usually only wetted the outer surface of a wall. However, rising damp — water sucked into the bricks from the ground — could make a house dank and uncomfortable, and could rapidly destroy finishes inside, crumbling plaster and rotting woodwork. The solution was a "damp proof course" of slate or asphalt laid between the bricks below the floor joists but above the ground.

Walls were built by arranging the bricks in particular patterns in courses to give the wall strength. This was known as bonding, and although there were many bonds, the most common were "English" bond (the strongest) and "Flemish" bond. In English bond, courses of brick laid *along* the wall ("stretchers") alternated with courses of bricks laid *across* the wall ("headers"). In Flemish bond, each course had alternate headers and stretchers with joints offset from those in adjacent courses. Over openings for doors and windows, bricks were usually laid on end or on edge, either straight across the span (on an iron bar) or arched. For window sills, a row of tilted bricks projected from the wall.

The chief aesthetic interest in brickwork was in its bonding, and the texture of the bricks, but in the 1880s and 1890s the fashion was for "polychromatic" brickwork which mixed bricks of different colours in contrasting bands, or patterns, or in combination, and around openings. Another

treatment for openings was to build up a plastered *architrave* or frame, often moulded and ornamented. On some houses, the entire wall was plastered — or "stuccoed" — with elaborate false classical details, including brackets, capitals, mouldings and quoins. Usually, very cheap rough brickwork was stuccoed, and sometimes the stucco itself was patterned to look like brickwork, giving the illusion of very accurate and true joints. This deceit was also practised by "tuck pointing", where a narrow straight groove was raked out of the flush joints, and repointed with a very fine bead of white mortar.

Ordinary stone houses were generally built of roughly squared quarry stone or field stones cleared from newly turned ground. There are many of these houses in Dunedin and other parts of Otago and Southland, built from local basalts for the walls, with Dunedin or Oamaru sandstones cut and shaped for corner quoins and around windows. These houses have a distinctive appearance due partly to the contrast of cream sandstone with the blue-grey basalt, and partly to the texture and evident thickness of the walls.

d. Roofs

In nineteenth century houses roofs were simple, and each span covered quite short distances. The basic *form* of the roof was a gable — two sides of equal slope meeting in the centre at the ridge — and the *shape* of the roof came from the way the roof finished at the outer wall, either as a gable end, or hipped, or a combination of the two.

The main structural members in the roof were the rafters, which met at the ridge board and were held together by a *collar tie* at about mid span. The rafters themselves sat on the top of the walls, and at first stopped short at the outer face of the wall frame, without any overhang. During the 1870s and 1880s, however, the *flush eaves* gave way to *boxed eaves* (which had long been common in larger houses), where the rafters sat on ceiling joists which extended beyond the wall frame. Boxed eaves grew to about 300 mm in the 1880s, and were lined underneath (the *soffit*). They were often decorated with shaped brackets chosen from the catalogues, and a *fascia* board was fixed to the ends of the rafters and ceiling joists to carry the gutter. Unlike the earlier wood houses, the roofline of the classic villa never had dormer windows. At outside corners, the roof (if not a gable end) was hipped — i.e. the two sloping planes met at an angle of 45 degrees. At inside corners, a *valley* was formed with wide flat boards each side of the angle, to support a valley gutter.

The shape of the roof is one key to the style of a nineteenth century villa. The problem of covering

114. Villa roofs:
(a) centre gutter — rear draining, Devonport;
(b) centre gutter — side draining, Wanganui;
(c) pyramidal, Devonport.

larger houses with a simple gable-form roof was solved in the "centre gutter" house, where the roof plan was U-shaped around an internal rainwater gutter that drained to the rear. From this type of roof with its uniform ridge height, the bay villa developed, and the number of bays could be increased without altering the basic roof layout.

The centre gutter solution dates from the 1860s and was the most common roof in the 1880s, but was virtually discarded after about 1909 because the internal gutters often failed and allowed water to leak onto ceilings and walls. Around 1900 the "pyramid" roof reappeared on the villas as a solution to this problem, and as one of the features of the "Queen Anne" style of house.

Where the roof was covered with corrugated iron, *purlins* were fixed across the rafters, the distance between them depending on the thickness, and therefore the strength of the iron. Short sheets were fixed with overlaps at the ends and sides. But whatever material covered the main roof, the low-pitched lean-to was invariably iron-clad.

If the roof was to be finished with shingles, it was first covered with rough boards (*sarking*) or narrow battens, which were also needed for Marseilles tiles and slates. Slating was another of the building arts brought from Britain, and slates were popular here as a "quality" roofing material. The craft had its own mysteries and special tools — the "zax", the "ripper", the slate hammer, and the iron straightedge. The slates themselves were ranked and named according to size: "smalls" were 300 x 150 mm, then there were "doubles", "ladies" (large), "countesses", "duchesses", "princesses", and "empresses" at 650 x 400 mm. The larger "imperials", "rags", and "queens" were rarely used here.[30] The overlapping slates were fixed to the tile battens with copper nails, and the joints were

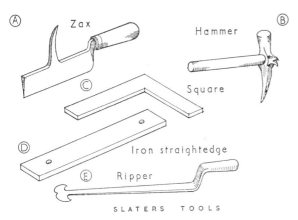

115. Slates:
(a) slate tools, from *Mitchell's Building Construction*;
(b) slate roof with variegated and shaped slates, Dunedin.

(a)

116. Marseilles tiles:
(a) part of a roof with
decorative ridge and
terminals, Devonport;
(b & c) Marseilles tile
construction.

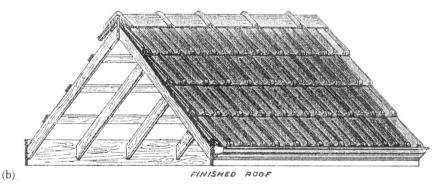

(b)

FINISHED ROOF

offset in alternate rows. Shaped or different
coloured slates could be used to make banded patterns along the roof. In New Zealand, ridges, valleys, and hips were usually formed in galvanised
iron or zinc sheet. Slate was found in Otago in
immense quantities, and in 1879 it was judged to be
at least as good as the best Welsh and Scottish
supplies.

When Marseilles tiles were introduced to New
Zealand in about 1901, roofs took on a new colour
and texture. The vivid terracotta-orange contrasted
strongly with the drab red-oxide paint of iron roofs
and the grey of slate. Furthermore, the silhouette of
the roof was marked like a dragon's back by specially shaped ridge tiles with spikes, holes, and
fleurs-de-lys, ending at the gable with a spiral ter-

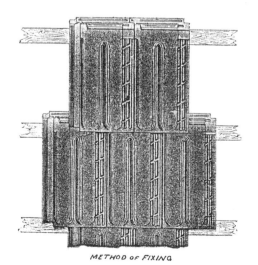

METHOD OF FIXING

(c)

122

minal. "Marseilles Roofing Tiles are a splendid investment" proclaimed the agents, Briscoes. "They make your residence superior to those covered with other roofing material. The tendency of the Marseilles Tile is to impart a brighter summer-like tinge."[31]

Water for the household was collected off the roof by iron gutters (or spouting), fixed to the fascia board; either half-round in the English pattern, or more commonly here, the "ogee" (or O.G.) pattern named for the classical ogee-curve of its side wall. This was made up from 2.4 metre lengths soldered together and supported by heavy iron brackets nailed to the fascia board. In the south, or wherever snow was likely, "snow straps" were screwed to the gutter bracket and nailed to the edge of the roof. In the best work gutters were fixed to the brackets with machine screws and nuts. At strategic intervals round iron drainpipes were fitted under the gutter to carry water to a storage tank at the side or rear of the house.

Pipes and chimneys stuck through the roof, and here elaborate measures were needed to stop water getting in. "Flashings" for these holes in the roof were part of the roofer's art, and the best material was lead sheet which could be cut with shears and beaten to the shape of the roof covering. Lead was best and neatest for flashing pipes and vents, but flat iron sheet was adequate around chimneys. Many iron roofs were crowned with a ventilator to let hot air escape from under the roof. Some were manufactured items such as "Tudehopes Patent Deodorising Ventilator",[32] others were the creation of the plumber on the job.

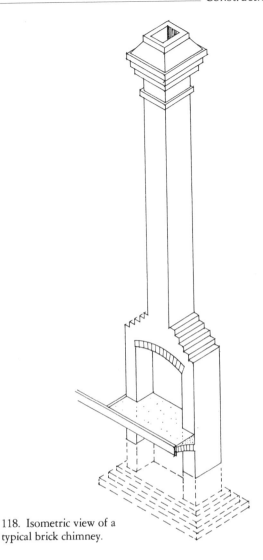

118. Isometric view of a typical brick chimney.

e. Chimneys

Every house had a fireplace, and all but the meanest had at least two — one in the kitchen and one in the parlour. The chimney might stand at the eaves, or on a gable wall, halfway up the roof slope, or (most commonly) through the ridge, and often the bricklayer adopted quite desperate measures to get his chimney to come through the roof at the ridge-line. The chimney began with a wide brick foundation in the ground and rose to the floor level where a brick "barrel vault" was made for the hearth, and the "firebox" was formed. Above the firebox a brick arch on an iron bar made from worn dray tyres supported the chimney breast, over which the chimney was built, usually two bricks each way with a clear opening for the flue inside.

117. Ridge ventilators:
(a) Gisborne;
(b) Auckland.

(a)

(b)

119. Brick chimneys.

For economy, fireplaces were arranged back-to-back in adjacent rooms, and the flues built together in one chimney. After 1900 it was fashionable for the fireplace to be in one corner of the room, and often the chimney was twisted through 45 degrees so that it emerged through the roof square with the framing. Above the roof, the chimney was a challenge to the bricklayer's art, and even modest houses sported chimneys with extravagant tops corbelled out, and out, and back again, often with specially shaped bricks. In some areas (notably Wellington), chimney pots were essential to ward off downdraughts, and even these strictly functional items were elaborately designed.

In the 1880s and 1890s, chimneys echoed the decorative style of the timber merchants' catalogues, with tops supported on shaped stone brackets, over a shaft of coloured bricks — pale cream at the corners, reds in the middle, or bands of different colours with moulded specials at every change of direction. But by 1900 red was the only acceptable colour, and chimney tops had become studies in complex geometries of rising pilasters and grooves, and cantilevered courses.

120. Chimney pots.

f. Verandahs

The first verandahs in New Zealand were simple lean-to affairs on plain posts, perhaps with a slender batten under the roof beam turned down against the posts, with tiny turned "droppers" near the ends, or a delicate fretworked bracket between posts and beam. If there was a handrail, it sat on a plain "union-jack" balustrade, made by the carpenter

121. Changes in wooden verandah decorations:
(a) Devonport;
(b) Dunedin;
(c) Devonport;
(d) Ponsonby;
(e) Wellington;
(f) Mt Eden.

(a)

(b)

(c)

(d)

(e)

(f)

(a)

(b)

122. Contrasts in verandah decoration:
(a) cast iron, Devonport;
(b) cast iron, Wanganui;
(c) cast iron, Parnell;
(d) wood, Dunedin;
(e) wood, Wanganui.

on the job. But from the 1870s the catalogues became irresistibly tempting, and decorative fretwork from the factories spread like vines under the roof beam from one post to the next. Brackets sprouted tendrils and leaves, flowered, and bore fruit, while others trailed a frieze of geometric and repeating patterns below the roof beam, often using gothic or classical motifs — quatrefoils, mazes, spirals, and medallions. Sometimes this frieze was an extension of the post brackets, but often it was a separate design carried above the brackets. Later, in the 1900s, the frieze was filled with turned spindles, and supported by strutted or fan-shaped spindle brackets at the posts.

Cast iron was an alternative decoration, fixed through prepared screwholes to posts and beams, and available in many complex lacelike patterns. Cast iron and wood competed to produce the most

(c)

(d)   (e)

123. Verandah posts and friezes:
(a) cast iron, Springston;

exotic patterns, and if cast iron was more intricate, the most breathtaking designs were in wood. Balustrades, too, were made up from cast iron panels, or turned wooden balusters; and later from plain boards with scroll-cut edges like unfolded paper cutouts. After 1900 the turned balusters were combined with plain sticks of wood in interlocking maze-like patterns (*chinoiserie*) to match the spindlework frieze. The posts too were decorated; at the very least the corners were stop-chamfered. Sometimes the faces were fluted, and beneath the brackets a "capital" was formed from mouldings fixed to each face of the posts. Sometimes the posts were true columns, turned out of large pieces of wood, with a capital in one of the classsical orders, or some new disorder.

Early verandah roofs were covered with boards and battens, or flat pan iron sheets. But once

(b)

(c)

(d)

(e)

123. Verandah posts and friezes:
(b) wood, Ponsonby
(c) wood, Ponsonby
(d) wood, Devonport
(e) wood, Devonport

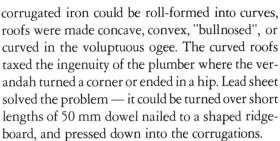

124. Verandah roof shapes:
(a) straight, Wellington;
(b) convex, Wanganui;
(c) concave, Waihi;
(d) bullnose, Gisborne;
(e) ogee, Wanganui.

corrugated iron could be roll-formed into curves, roofs were made concave, convex, "bullnosed", or curved in the voluptuous ogee. The curved roofs taxed the ingenuity of the plumber where the verandah turned a corner or ended in a hip. Lead sheet solved the problem — it could be turned over short lengths of 50 mm dowel nailed to a shaped ridge-board, and pressed down into the corrugations.

Verandahs were less common in colder areas —a wind-swept verandah was perhaps worse than none at all. Many houses had only a small porch at the front door, sandwiched like a lace hanky between buxom bay windows, or recessed at one corner. Even these porches were decorated, with posts crowding onto the top step, supporting generous arches, gables, trellis work, and wooden sunrises; and in some houses, porch and verandah combined to emphasise the position of the front door.

In towns women competed to have the cleanest, whitest verandah floors, and scoured them each week with sandsoap and a scrubbing brush.

(a)

(b)

(c)

(d)

(e)

131

(a)

125. Porches:
(a) Dunedin;
(b) Auckland;
(c) Wellington.

(b)

(c)

g. Joinery and mouldings

The standard front door of the 1860s was a robust piece of work, with four panels fixed in a solid frame by thick "bolection" mouldings, and finer "bed" mouldings inside. The top panels were often arched at the top and fitted with rough-cast glass, and this became the most common front door during the 1870s. At about the same time, the first doors with large single glass panels were introduced, some with rounded corners. These finally became the standard front door in houses of the 1910s.

Inside the house, the four-panel door was used everywhere for more than half a century, changing in size and thickness according to the quality of the house and the importance of each room — in descending order from front to back. In many houses the hall ended at a "half-glazed" door with coloured "margins" (edge panels), cut flash glass corners, and acid-etched centre panels. Occasionally, a heavier edition of this door appeared at the front, or opened from the dining room onto a side verandah.

French casements were popular, especially in the 1860s, and usually opened from a best room onto a verandah. But around the back, the outhouse doors were the cheap "ledged and braced" type with vertical boards on the outside, and in the privy the top of the door was cut into a serrated edge for ventilation.

"Sidelights" and "fanlights" were first added to the front door in the 1860s to brighten the hall, and to lend a little of the gaslight's glow to the street at night. Glass panels beside and above matched those in the door, and by 1880 were found in all but the simplest cottages. The colours changed from brilliant blues, reds, and oranges — often with cut patterns — in the 1870s and 1880s, to rose, puce, eau-de-nil, and lemon around 1900, and from smooth thin flash glass to thick crusty cast glass.

Windows scarcely changed from 1860 to 1910. The double-hung sash was the common type, and it answered every purpose. In the 1870s Findlays in Dunedin offered this window with four choices of glazing; twelve-light, four-light, and two-light, or with side and corner margins. The early twelve-light window persisted until about 1880, especially away from the towns, but the four-light double-

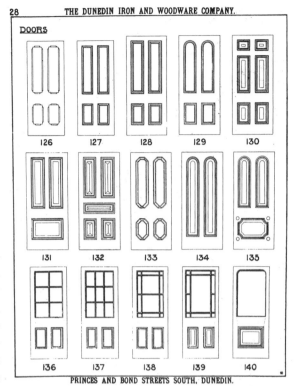

126. Doors from Dunedin Iron and Woodware Company catalogue — c. 1882. *Hocken Library*.

127. Italianate windows in a Gisborne house.

hung sash was most common from the 1850s onwards.

In Wellington especially, houses in the fashionable "Italianate" style of the 1880s featured windows with rounded tops on the upper sash, usually a flat arch (i.e. not a full semi-circle) cut out of a wide top rail, or in expensive work, a fully rounded top to the sash with a matching curved frame.

(a)

(b)

(c)

(d)

128. Combinations of
windows:
(a) single opening, Ponsonby;
(b) double opening, Christchurch;
(c) double opening, Gisborne;
(d) triple opening, Wellington.

129. Double-bay houses,
Wellington (above).

130. Double-bay houses,
Dunedin (below).

During the 1870s the "Chicago" window (see page 68) had a renaissance which lasted until after 1900. Similar combinations of two, three, and even four double-hung sashes satisfied the Victorian fondness for big windows, and lots of them. But the bay window was the perfect way to brighten a room, with three or sometimes four big windows which opened up the wall and gave a sense of space to houses built on tight urban sections, hard up against the street. In Wellington hundreds of otherwise unremarkable houses of the 1880s and 1890s were transformed into interesting, often elegant villas by a bay window on each side of the front porch, under a hipped, gabled, or flat extension of the main roof. In similar Dunedin houses, each bay had a separate gabled or hipped "rooflet" tucked under a large gable out of the main roof. In Auckland the classic bay villa began with a factory-produced bay window added to the end of a room projecting from the house. Some windows let in too much sunlight, so sunhoods were added — a further opportunity for decoration.

131. (Above) A typical factory-produced bay window, Devonport.

132. (Right) Sunhoods over windows:

(a) Devonport;
(b) Ponsonby;
(c) Gisborne;
(d) Wanganui.

Porches and verandahs were often partly enclosed by fixed windows for wind shelter. This was usually taken as an opportunity to use decorative glass, although some fixed windows were simply single sashes divided into nine or twelve panes. These windows matched the glass doors — flash and etched glass in the 1870s and 1880s, and in the 1890s and 1900s, cast glass in sashes divided into geometric patterns of squares and diamonds. Provincial centres borrowed freely from fashions in the main centres, often blending ideas from two directions in an original way, but lagging slightly in the introduction of new products and practices.

Every joint between materials or surfaces was covered with a moulding. Their designs were classical, and made full use of the classical rhetoric — ovolo, scotia, ogee, torus, and cavetto. In fact, the Kauri Timber Company's catalogue began with a

(c)

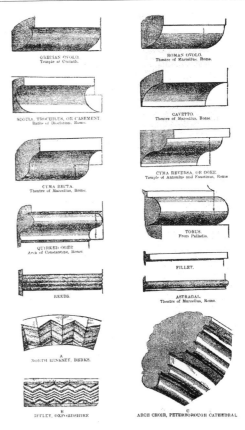

133. (Above) "Chapter on Mouldings" from the Kauri Timber Company Limited catalogue

(d)

"Chapter on Mouldings" which described their provenance in the historic architecture of Greece, Rome, and England. A typical merchant's catalogue pictured more than 200 mouldings, but most of these were rarely seen in or on ordinary houses.

Moulded architraves surrounded doors and windows, inside and out, covering the junctions with weatherboards and linings, and holding the window into the wall. They were carefully graded in size through the house, from the best rooms at the front to the mundane kitchen at the rear. Around each room a skirting board ran along the floor, and a scotia (or cornice) trimmed the ceiling — in the best rooms, these were made up of three or four separate mouldings. Battens were fixed over the joints between ceiling boards, with a ventilator at the centre of the room to let out hot air. The ventilator was a fretwork roundel, sometimes in

(a)

(b)

(c)

134. (Above) Ceiling
ventilator "roses":
(a) moulded plaster;
(b) fretworked timber;
(c) stamped metal.

135. (Right) Papier
mâché dado,
Devonport.

(b)

c)

(d)

two layers, and usually with a thick rolled "torus" collar. Later, the ventilator could be made from moulded plaster or perforated stamped metal. Some rooms had a dado on the wall, of vertical boards or embossed papier mâché, with a moulded trim along the top edge.

Outside, mouldings were sometimes fitted under the window sill between shaped brackets, or around wall panels beneath the sashes in a bay window. But mostly they were used to decorate the upper reaches of the wall — trimming the edge of a frieze board to which eaves brackets were fixed, or made up into patterns of chevrons and diamonds

136. Eaves brackets:
(a) machine relief carved, Devonport;
(b) fretsawn stencil, Wanganui;
(c) spindle fan and frieze, Gisborne;
(d) struts and knuckles, Gisborne.

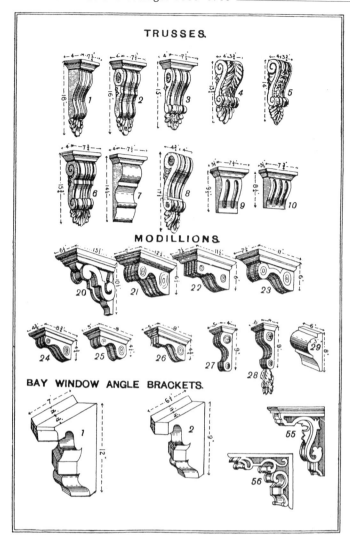

137. Moulded plaster truss supporting a hall arch, Christchurch.

138. Trusses, modillions and brackets from the Kauri Timber Company catalogue.

on the frieze itself, or on the bargeboard. Bay windows, verandahs, and gable ends were the most heavily moulded parts of the house, and even the spouting sat on a bed moulding attached to the fascia.

Eaves brackets were solid chunky pieces — 350 x 300 x 75 mm — band-sawn out of the best kauri plank, some with a turned "teardrop" hanging from the projecting end. In the 1880s the eaves overhang was a standard 300 or 350 mm wide, and under the "soffit" brackets went up by the hundreds, some rising under the overhang at the gable end. In the bay villa houses, the eaves over the angled windows of the bay sat on fretted, turned, or cast iron brackets matching those of the verandah, and in many houses the same patterns could be found under the gable bargeboards. There are many

local variations to the design of eaves brackets — knuckled braces, turned spindles radiating from one corner, stencilled panels, and combinations of wood and iron. The decorative bargeboards on the gable end floated clear of the wall, with patterns which echoed the tied rafters under the roof, and ended with a vertical finial post at the apex. Between the main members were ornamental panels of fretwork, stencilled cut-outs, sunrises in spindlework, and carved relief, rows of teardrops, and plain boards with fretted overlays or "blind fret".

Inside the house, carved brackets called "trusses" or "modillions" were used to support an arch in the hallway or to frame the opening for a bay window and in many later houses these were moulded in plaster. Trusses were a distinctive feature of chimneypieces up to about 1895, attached to wooden

140

pilasters on either side of a square or arched fire opening to support a wide mantel with a heavy moulded edge. Chimneypieces were at first based on respectable Georgian and Regency originals, and until the 1890s they were quite sober in design. But as the centrepiece of the parlour, the chimneypiece invited the worst excesses of Victorian taste, and by the following decade, the mantelpiece was festooned with brackets, turned spindles, deeply carved trusses and relief panels, shelves, recesses, fluting, and mirrors. Some rose nearly the full height of the wall, with immense over-mantels of shelves, knobs, and brackets around a large mirror with bevelled edges. On the floor a shining tile hearth was guarded by a brass and iron fender which sheltered the fire set — brush, tongs, poker and shovel. The only fitting to survive unscathed was the coal range mantelpiece, which remained

139. Chimneypiece and overmantel, Devonport.

140. "The centrepiece of the parlour" — 1890s. *ATL, Bothamley Coll.*

true to its simple prototype — but even then, draped with a lace or paper valance.

The joinery shops excelled in making staircases — the largest single item in the kit of parts, and often the most splendid. Most ordinary houses were single-storeyed, except perhaps in Wellington and parts of Dunedin. The two-storey villa usually marked a prosperous and successful owner, and in these houses the stair occupied a prominent spot in the hall, in full view of the front door. Every device of the carving and therming machines was called into play. Complex rising bends in the moulded handrail had to be worked by hand, and setting the stair out was a specialty in itself, but

machines produced the moulded edges on the treads, and housed the stringers to support them. They turned the balusters, and carved, turned, and moulded the astonishing newel post which stood like a sceptre on the bottom tread. Less elaborate stairs were made for more modest houses, and for the servants' stairs in big houses.

Mouldings were machined out of plain sawn pieces of timber, often of very large dimensions, and it was not unusual for the greater part of the wood to be left as chips on the shop floor. As one retired tradesman recalled, "the trade was most wasteful of timber and, looking back, we acknowledge that the extravagance was criminal".[33]

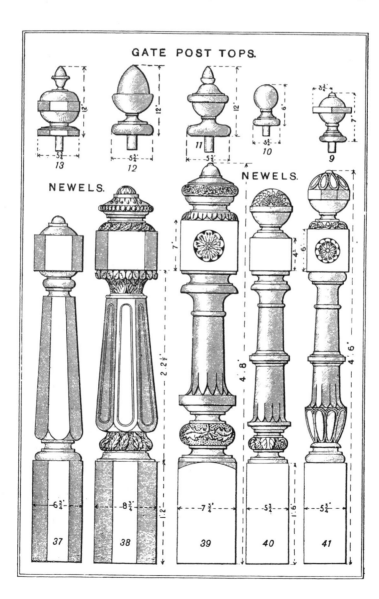

141. Newel posts for stairs from the Kauri Timber Company catalogue.

142. Bath tubs:
(a) James Hargreaves' "Ideel" No. 1 zinc bath;
(b) wooden bath tub (note porcelain w.c.). *HPT.*

h. Services

The main sources of water in nineteenth century New Zealand towns were wells, rainwater cisterns, and rainwater tanks — until public piped water supplies were constructed in the 1880s. Wells and cisterns were expensive, and there was no certainty that a well would strike water anyway. Even worse, seepage from cesspools and privies in built-up areas could leach into a water supply below the ground and contaminate it.

Wooden barrels, when they were obtainable, were used at first to collect rainwater in small quantities, but in the 1880s big corrugated iron tanks came on to the market which were cheap enough for most households, and large enough to store water for the biggest of families. The round corrugated iron tank became a characteristic of villa houses, sitting out the back on its high wooden stand, hard up under the eaves, so that water would flow naturally through the outlet pipe in the bottom to the house.

In an age when labour was cheap, and fetching and carrying was a normal part of everyday life, it was some time before water was piped into houses. In 1879 George T. Hall advertised his services in Wellington for laying on water supplies,[34] and in 1882 the Thames Galvanized Iron Works offered "30,000 feet Galvanized Water-Pipe from ½ to 2 inches".[35] Piped water in the house was a major innovation — even if at first it only went through the wall as far as the kitchen sink, and stopped there. Until the 1880s, when ranges with hot water boilers were introduced, water was heated over the kitchen fire, or in the laundry copper for washing clothes and for the children's weekly bath. The other members of the family washed themselves at the bedroom washstand with its ewer and basin, or in a tin bath hauled into the kitchen, and emptied, as it was filled, by bucket.

In the last two decades of the nineteenth century, however, the bathroom entered the house — a very small room to begin with, just large enough for a

BOTTOM & SIDES IN ONE PIECE.
(REGD DESIGN 536)
STOCKED BY ALL IRONMONGERS
"IDEEL" NO 1.
£2 · 4 · 0
PHONE 2536.
JAMES HARGREAVES AUCKLAND.

"IDEEL" A I. Same design as above, but made of No. 14 zinc. £2 15s. Please note this! The only bath made in 3 pieces. Zinc used, therefore no leaking or rusting.

tin bath and a basin of tin, enamel, or English porcelain on a wooden stand or cast iron brackets. Instead of a bucket to empty the bath there was the novelty of a waste pipe which took the water to a soak hole outside. Two things inspired the pursuit of cleanliness in middle-class homes: one was the death of the Prince of Wales from typhoid in 1871 (blamed on poor drainage); the other was the Victorian fascination with mechanical devices. Eminent "sanitarians" wrote earnest and detailed texts to demonstrate the workings of baths, water closets, sinks, and drains. Soon, British and American manufacturers began to produce genuinely hygienic fittings of glazed earthenware and porcelain, with splendid cast brass attachments.

No fixture received more attention than the water closet, but it was a long time before it was allowed inside the house. Nevertheless, by the 1890s the lavatory — whether earth or water closet — was built on to the end of the laundry outhouse, or at the end of the back verandah in some new houses. Others were still content to leave it at the farthest corner of the garden, with a little water tank on the roof and the tell-tale vent pipe.

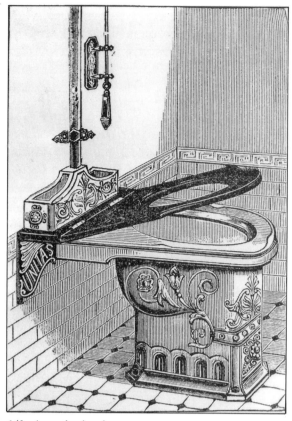

143. An early glazed earthenware water closet.

144. Moule's earth closet.

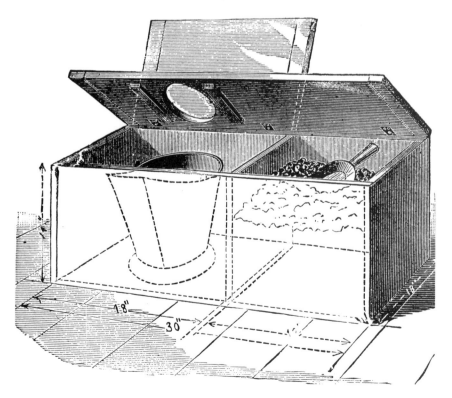

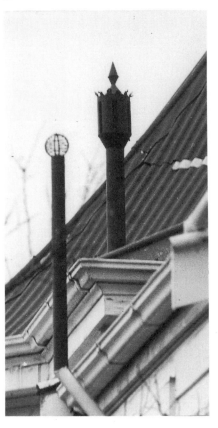 

145. Soil pipe ventilators, Wanganui.

Without proper municipal drainage, the water closet contributed little to hygiene. In 1877 it was still considered by some in England that a system "for disposing of night-soil by means of a network of underground drains . . . is always more or less of an evil, and one which should be avoided".[36] They preferred the cesspool, the earth closet, and the night-soil collection, with surface water in the streets to carry away the chamber-slops. The drainpipes made by New Zealand brickyards in the early 1860s were not for house drainage — they were needed to drain the land.

In drainage systems, ventilation was needed to carry away noxious gases, and until the problems of sewer ventilation were properly understood, many illnesses and epidemics were caused by toxic gases entering houses through straight (un-trapped) wastepipes. As drainage was introduced in the 1890s and 1900s, houses sprouted vent pipes above the roof, ending in elaborate peaked "helmets" with ventilation openings, or with serrations cut into the end of the pipe and turned out like the leaves of a pineapple.

Once water had been piped to the kitchen, it was a small step to arrange for a system of heating the water as well. The mysteries of hot water were well understood in the age of steam, and the domestic solution in the 1880s was a simple modification of the kitchen range. This was simply extended to include a copper water tank beside the firebox, filled by a bucket from above, with a big brass lever tap fitted at the front to dispense instant hot water. The next improvement was the high pressure water service from a town main supply. A larger separate copper cylinder with corrugated sides was connected to the water supply, and boiler pipes circulated water to and from the firebox of the range. The cylinder was enclosed in an airing cupboard beside the range, and from here hot water was piped to the bathrooms and the kitchen sink.

The coal range (or wood stove) succeeded the colonial oven as early as the 1880s, although colonial ovens were still being made in 1882. Some ranges were brought by colonists from England, and in 1856 "Russell's Celebrated Cooking Stoves"

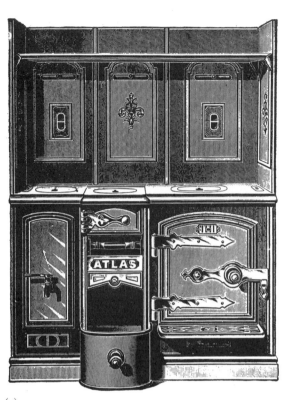

146. Coal ranges:
(a) Atlas coal range with
built in water heater;
(b) Nicholls Bros. "Orb"
coal range.
(c) Troup's Improved
bottom grate

(a)

(b)

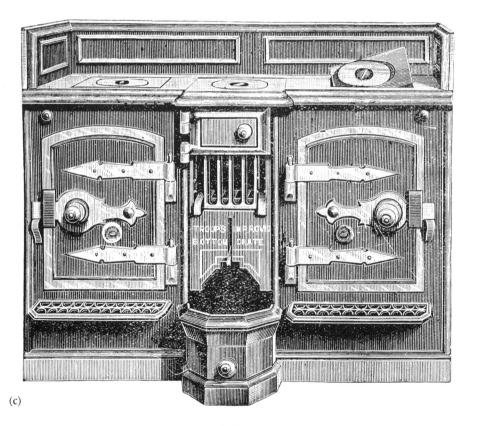

(c)

made in Sydney were on sale in Auckland.[37] In Dunedin, Shacklock's first coal range, the "Orion", was produced in 1873, and others followed. The coal range fitted into a brick chimney with an opening about 1.5 metres high, and the recess could be lined above the hob with glazed decorative tiles, or matching cast iron panels, or the bricks were just painted. The hearth was tiled, or made of smooth concrete with a red wax applied daily, and it was surrounded by a plain iron or brass fender. The small firebox of a coal range could be enlarged by a projecting woodbox to take pieces of wood up to 500 mm long. Above the range, the wire rack with a polished brass edge was used to warm food and dry utensils or even footwear.

Usually the kitchen chimney was built back-to-back with the chimney in the parlour, dining room, or a bedroom. When towns were still small and fuel was plentiful, large wood-burning "cottage

147. The coal range in a Southland farmhouse kitchen, Mandeville.

148. A 1905 kitchen with coal range (note the redundant gas light fitting and the new electric flex and shade). *ATL, Stefano Webb Collection.*

(a)

grates" were the rule. By the 1880s, however, firewood was so far from the larger towns that coal had to be bought for the family fires. Coal fires were most efficient in very small grates, so that the typical parlour or bedroom fireplace of the 1880s and 1890s had a cast iron plate with an arched recessed firebox over a tiny grate, and a flap at the back which was closed when the fireplace was not in use. Many had inset decorative tile surrounds, and the deeply moulded and textured castings were easily built into a brick recess with some rubble and mortar thrown in behind, and the wooden chimneypiece in front. By 1900 larger villas had in addition to the kitchen range, fireplaces in the parlour, dining room, and in at least one bedroom. It was these that were used to heat the house.

Coke gas was first made in Dunedin in 1863, followed by Christchurch in 1864, Auckland in 1868, and Wellington in 1871. At first it was used for lighting, and gas lights transformed Victorian homes after dark. But it also came to the kitchen to compete with the coal range. Swedish "Primus" gas cookers were available by 1890 with three burners, on two of which sat a removable oven. A proper gas cooker with a fixed oven was patented in 1884,[38] and thereafter in many town houses, the old range was rooted out of its brick shell and replaced by the new enamelled wonder. For those

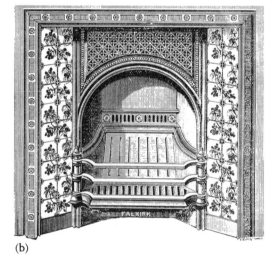

(b)

who preferred to keep their old coal range, there were small bench-top burners with a rubber hose connection, ideal for boiling the kettle without having to stoke up the fire.

Many householders, however, were suspicious of gas, fearing explosions and poisonous vapours, and it was true that when gas-heated air cooled on the iron roof, the acidic condensates caused the roof to corrode more rapidly. Gas lighting in houses and streets became common in towns of the late nineteenth century, with the yellow glow from the "gasoliers" (or gaseliers, or gasaliers) accompanied by a steady hiss. The fittings hung from an elaborate ventilating ceiling rose of fretted timber, cast

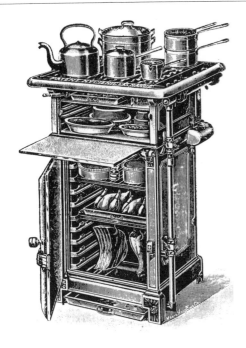

Boiling Burners.

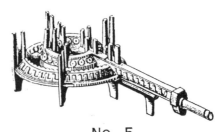

NO. 2.
Width: 6½" Length: 10½"

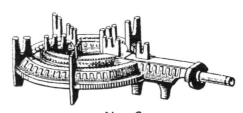

NO. 5.
Width: 6½" Length: 10½"

NO. 6.
Width: 8½" Length: 13½"

(a)

(b)

plaster, or (after 1900) pressed-out metal. Alternatively, they were mounted on wall brackets. Extravagant shapes were invented using the curves of the brass or copper gas tube, and the burner was screened by a thin frosted glass "chimney". Later, the patent gas incandescent mantle greatly increased the amount of light from gas, but it was not until the 1880s that electricity was available as an alternative source of light.

Electricity changed the appearance of houses and streets. Telephone wires, strung along poles in the street since the early 1880s, were joined by thicker power cables, and in existing houses iron conduit pipe was run up walls and across ceilings between switches and light fittings. In new houses, of course, the conduit was hidden in the framed walls, and only the shining brass or porcelain switch on its varnished wooden plaque, and the clear glass globe hanging under its white conical china shade could be seen. On some of the fittings, the flex ran through a pulley on a china counter-weight filled with lead shot, and over a ceiling pulley — allowing the height of the lamp to be adjusted by touch.

In a Victorian middle-class country which had always had a "servant problem", piped water, gas, and silent electricity were an incalculable blessing to the houseproud woman.

Artistic Gas Fittings

Patent Reversible Fittings for Upright or Inverted Burners in Oxydised Copper Finish ✍
Special Wide Spread Inverted Fittings for dining Rooms

151. Gas fittings:
(a) bench top burners, from Brinsley and Company catalogue, 1921;
(b) pendant gas light fitting.

i. Colour and finishes

In the 1860s and 1870s colours on New Zealand houses were usually quiet and restrained. The range of coloured paints was limited, and the fashion was for soft hues taken from the landscape. "Pluck from the ground the roots of the grass, and the colour of the earth thereon will be the colour of the house,"[39] said Andrew Jackson Downing in 1880. After the 1880s, however, scientific explanations of the relationships between colours encouraged an adventurous use of paint, and American writers, including Calvert Vaux and Henry Hudson Holly, supported a new fashion for harmony based on strong contrasts. One of the most influential theorists was Christopher Dresser whose twenty-seven axioms and rules of colour were quoted in *Shoppel's Modern Homes*.[40]

Wooden houses needed paint for weather pro-tection, and the profusion of ornamental detail on later houses was an opportunity for invention and individuality. Holly suggested that exterior trims "should be a darker shade of the same [colour as the walls], or a deeper colour, to give them prominence and assist in bringing out the design, though they should be rather in harmony than in violent contrasts."[41] One of his exterior colour schemes had walls of neutral buff, the walls of a recessed porch in deep ultramarine green, trimmings of Indian red relieved by lines of black, and a coved ceiling of brilliant blue.[42]

Calvert Vaux argued for variety to avoid monotony — "It is entirely insufficient to use only one or two shades of colour for each house. Every rural building requires four tints to make it a pleasant object in the way of colour."[43]

Early photographs of New Zealand houses sug-

152. Painting the villa: (a) early photograph showing the complexity of the original paint scheme; *ATL Stefano Webb Collection.*

(b) contrasting colours on alternate sheets of iron on the verandah roof. *Matakohe Museum.*

gest that experimental philosophies of house painting were often put into practice here, but the particular colours used can now only be deduced from the evidence of paint scrapings. Christopher Cochran's book *Restoring a New Zealand House* gives a range of colours for houses built between 1860 and the mid 1880s: soft fawns, greens, red-browns, and yellows for walls, with off-white for ornament. From the mid 1880s to 1914, he suggests additional darker and richer colours for weatherboards, with trims picked out in maroon, chocolate, or green.[44] Galvanised iron roofs were almost always painted red, a dark shade if the local Nelson haematite oxide was used, but a much brighter shade if the paint was based on imported English oxide. A popular colour scheme for roofs — especially the verandah roof — was to paint alternate sheets with contrasting red and white paints. All paints used lead as a drying agent, both inside and out, and it was usual for the painter to arrive with a keg of white lead and drums of linseed oil and to make up his paints on the job.[45]

Inside the house each room was decorated with its own colour scheme, so that odd combinations of colour often came together on opposite sides of a door between two rooms. Christopher Dresser offered typical colour schemes incorporating decorative designs on ceiling, cornice and dado. For example:

A good room would be produced by [a] pattern . . . on the ceiling in dark blue and cream colour, by the cornice being coloured with a prevalence of dark blue, the walls being cream-colour down to the dado; the border separating the dado from the wall being black ornament on a dull orange colour and by the dado being chocolate with a black rosette upon it, the skirting boards being bright black . . . If the room is high a bordering may run around the upper portion of the wall, about three to four inches below the cornice . . . in dull orange and chocolate . . . Walls are papered in middle-class houses. I must not object to this universal custom; but I do say try to avoid showing the joinings . . . Avoid all papers in which huge bunches of flowers and animals or the human figure are depicted. The best for all purposes are those of a *simple* geometric pattern . . . "powdered" or placed at regular intervals over a plain ground.[46]

In the kitchen, pantry and scullery, plaster walls were painted, and wooden walls were painted or

153. (a) A parlour or sitting room of c.1905. *ATL, Head Collection.* (b) A Dunedin sitting room. *AIM.*

varnished. In the 1890s wallpaper friezes above the picture rail were common, and skirtings and architraves were picked out in two colours, sometimes divided by a fine gold line. All wallpapers were pasted to hessian "scrim" tacked to the rough lining boards with thin white tape to prevent sagging, and this prevented the paper being torn by movement in the boards. A popular effect on plain walls was obtained by painting through a home-made stencil, to get a repeating pattern along the top of the wall.

Doors, if not painted, were stained and varnished, or "grained" — a technique which mimicked the natural appearance of a "high quality" wood such as oak or walnut. In some large houses door panels were painted in monochrome with rural scenes or floral arrangements. Kauri floors were stained black where a rug would not cover the boards, and in the kitchen and bathroom and sometimes the hall, linoleum covered the whole floor. Wooden fire surrounds were usually painted — a favourite colour was black, with grooves and other details picked out in gold. An alternative finish was "marbling", where paint was carefully applied and combed or streaked to resemble stone.

Wallpaper and woodwork, however, were only a background for an immense array of portable property which settled heavily on shelves, mantlepieces, tables, chairs, stands, picture rails, cabinets, plate racks, and the floor. In some rooms the only visible surface left was the ceiling — even the windows were obscured with plants and painted glass "vitremanic" screens. The most common ceiling in ordinary houses was board and batten — 300 mm boards with moulded cover battens from the catalogues. In grander houses the ceilings in the best rooms were plastered over timber lathes fixed to the ceiling joists, and sometimes workmen were brought from Italy to do the ornamental plasterwork. Ceilings were sometimes papered, but after 1900 the most popular decorative ceilings were the Wunderlich Company's pressed "art metal" panels. Ernest Wunderlich first imported zinc ceilings into Australia in 1885, and then began to manufacture his own sheets from mild steel. His company also imported the Marseilles terracotta roof tile, and both products were sold in New Zealand by the agents, Briscoe and Company.

Briscoe's catalogue *Beautiful Homes and Public Buildings in New Zealand* proclaimed the "artistic emphasis" and "generous spaciousness" of a well-planned ceiling. Under their ceilings there was:

> no annoyance of broken bric-a-brac or other damaged valuables, nor have the household staff continually to be sweeping up pieces of fallen plaster and whitewash. Thus happiness reigns where discontent once held sway.[47]

As well as on the ceiling, more than 300 patterns of pressed metal sheets were used for the cornice, the wall, and the dado, and even light fittings of pressed copper were available. Outside, pressed metal sheets were fixed to the gable end walls as a decorative lining, either direct to the framing, or in more adventurous designs such as a semicircular arch with a concave soffit. Stamped metal gave a highly decorative finish at comparatively low cost and it could be easily installed by local tradesmen. One of the more bizzare products of the company was "Wunderlich's Imitation Rockface Galvanised Steel Sheeting . . . specially suited to districts that are subject to earth tremors".[48]

The art metal dado competed with timber boarding and thick embossed papier mâché sheets which gave an effect similar to the Wunderlich sheets at a lower cost, while patterned linoleum, which was really a floor covering, was used in bathrooms to make a washable dado. Christopher Dresse singled out this feature for particular praise.

> I like the formation of a dado, for it affords an opportunity of giving apparent stability to the wall by making its lower portion dark; and furniture is invariably much improved by being seen against a dark background. The occupants of a room always look better when viewed in conjunction with a dark background, and ladies' dresses certainly do.[49]

Very little furniture was built into the house — at most a cupboard beside the range, no higher than the dado, or later, a tall airing cupboard. Much greater use was made of movable fittings — wardrobes, dressers, sideboards, and chests of drawers. The "housewife's mania for built-in cupboards"[50] was the product of a later period — the Victorian family, like magpies, preferred to gather their possessions about them.

154. Plan of a typical single
bay cottage.

PLANNING AND FORM

The kinds of weatherboard houses which were
built in this country in the 1850s changed little
during the 1860s, and it was only in the 1870s that
ordinary houses began to get appreciably bigger. In
England the term "villa" had been borrowed from
Italian country houses along with the language of
classical architecture. At first "villa" referred to "a
country house for the residence of an opulent person".[51] By the time New Zealand was settled, however, it was commonly used to describe a comfortable surburban house, and it was this usage that
was brought to New Zealand. In the 1860s land
agents' advertisements offered "villa sites" for
sale[52] —and villas were set apart from cottages by
their size and cost. "Villa" is used here to refer to
later Victorian houses of more than four or five
rooms, typically built in the suburbs, and after the
1870s often elaborately decorated. "Cottage", on
the other hand, refers to any simple smaller house
of the same period.

The planning of nineteenth century villas was
not very complicated, but it is difficult to discuss
it separately from their building form, which was
complicated. As houses grew larger and popula-
tions in the towns increased, privacy became more
highly valued and protected, and the idea of a public
"front" and a private "back" space influenced the
arrangement of rooms, entrances, and finishes.

In the four-room cottages of the 1860s and
1870s, the two front rooms were the living room
(parlour) and the best bedroom, with the kitchen
and another bedroom at the rear. The privy was
tucked away in a far corner of the section, and later
there was an outhouse for the laundry near the back
door. In small houses the front door opened into
the parlour which served as a thoroughfare to the
other rooms. In these smaller houses the roof was
typically a pyramid or long hip, or a wide gable, or
perhaps a narrow hipped rectangle with a back
lean-to — forms which persisted from the colonial
days, but differed from their predecessors in detail
and style. The strict rules of symmetry applied both
in elevation and in plan, just as they did in very
large and expensive houses. By contrast, houses
which might be described as "working home-

steads" often showed an asymmetrical exterior which concealed a chaotic plan.

The slightly larger or "better class" four-room cottages had the added refinement of a passage between the front rooms joining the front door to the kitchen at the rear. Unless the house was correspondingly wider, the passage cut down the size of the parlour. In a small house, the parlour could be made bigger either by reducing the size of the back bedroom or by extending the parlour beyond the front wall. There were two important consequences of this second choice. First, the symmetry of the front was lost, especially if the roof of the projecting bay ended in a gable; and second, the simple gable or hipped roof no longer coped with the now irregular plan. The lost symmetry could, of course, be restored by projecting bays on both sides of the front door, as in the H or U plan colonial houses.

At the same time, as ordinary houses began to get bigger, the hall ran deeper into the plan, with rooms ranged more or less equally on either side. To cover this enlarged plan and its extended bay with a simple short-span roof, parallel gables along the plan turned and met at the front, with hipped corners, and with a rainwater gutter between them. This highly flexible device allowed houses to be longer without any added roof problems, and more importantly, where rooms projected at the front, the ridge on one or both sides could simply continue forwards. This was the basic form of the *centre gutter villa*, and the bay villa houses.

By the 1880s the single bay villa or cottage had become a recurring type, particularly in Auckland. Bays were often added to older square-plan houses, often so discreetly that the junction can hardly be noticed. Plans had scarcely changed, except to get longer by one or two rooms. The kitchen remained at the end of the hall under a lean-to roof, with a "back kitchen" or "scullery" where the washing-up was done, and a pantry (beside or behind the cooking kitchen). The plans published in timber merchants' catalogues followed this pattern, but in large houses with servants, the kitchen was sometimes in a separate building joined to the house at the rear, via a butler's pantry and the dining room.

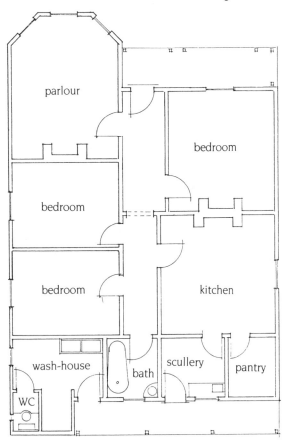

155. Plan of a typical single bay villa.

156. The evolution of the
villa — square villas:
(a) centre gutter, Gisborne;
(b) pyramid, Dunedin;
(c) hipped gable, Rotorua.

157. The evolution of the
villa — single bay villas:
(a) flush bay, Devonport;
(b) factory bay window,
Gisborne;

(c) faceted bay, Devonport;
(d) full gabled bay,
Devonport.

159

158. The evolution of the
villa — double bay villas:
(a) hipped faceted bays,
Gisborne;
(b) gabled faceted bays,
Hawera;

(c) square bay windows,
Wellington;
(d) gabled square bays,
Devonport.

159. Bays added to older
houses — the obvious and
the subtle:
(a) gable cottage, Waihi;
(b) "catslide" cottage, Banks
Peninsula;

(c) square cottage,
Devonport;
(d) centre gutter villa,
Devonport.

160. The evolution of the
villa — corner bay villas:
(a) gable and return hip,
centre gutter roof
—Gisborne;
(b) gable and return gable,
pyramid roof — Wanganui;
(c) gable and return gable,
centre gutter roof
—Gisborne.

161. The evolution of the
villa — corner angle bay
villas:
(a) turretted corner, centre
gutter roof — Gore;
(b) corner window, hipped
gabled roof — Devonport;
(c) door at corner, faceted
pyramid roof —Wanganui.

162. Centre gutter villas
—basic forms.

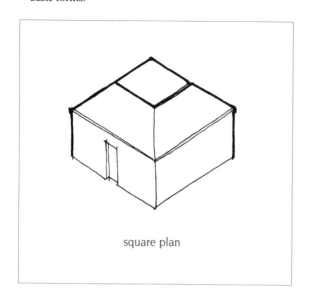

square plan

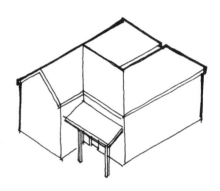

single bay flush

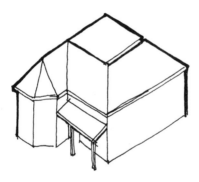

single bay faceted

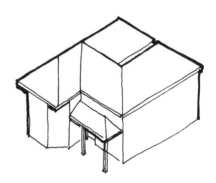

single bay hip over

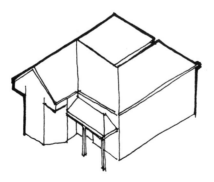

single bay gable over

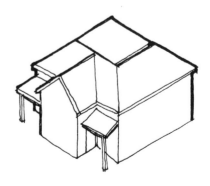

centre bay

By the 1890s the dining room had been adopted in middle-class homes as one of the "best" rooms. Its logical place was about the middle of the house, and here it was dignified by a larger than usual window of two or three sashes in a row, or by a projecting bay. The bay solution required the roof to follow suit, and so the *corner bay villa* was created — a type of house found logically on many street corner sections. A very early example of this type is "Trecarne", built in 1877 near Cambridge. This form showed a new kind of symmetry, based not on the centre line of the hall and front door, but on the diagonal axis through the hipped corner. This axiality was emphasised in later villas by an angled bay window at the corner with a gabled roof above — the *corner angle bay villa* — or by a turret; or finally, by placing the front door at the corner.

Symmetry, however, was not always observed. Wellington's two-storey hillside houses often had an off-centre axis centred on main rooms with the hall and porch to one side, or they simply dispensed with an axis altogether. Typically, these houses were built like a double bay house cut down the centre, with one half stacked above the other, and with "half a hall" down one side on each floor. Sometimes the entrance wandered down the side of the house, but otherwise the typical villa features were there — bay windows, verandahs or porches, turrets and all.

In the 1890s the bathroom was finally allowed into the house. Because it was small, it sat at the very end of the hall, occupying little more than the width of the hall itself. The lavatory moved to the back verandah, or into the laundry in its outhouse, or under the lean-to at the back. All these migrations took place under the accommodating centre-gutter roof in its various common forms, until the 1900s when the hip roof reappeared. This form had certain practical advantages — centre gutters

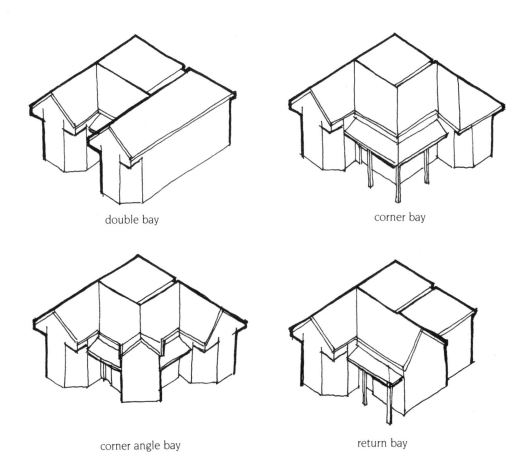

double bay

corner bay

corner angle bay

return bay

169

163. Pyramid villas
—basic forms.

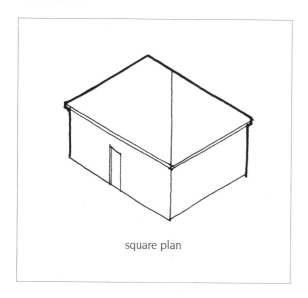

square plan

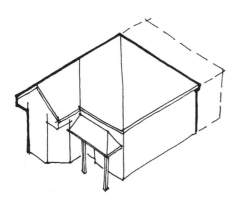

single bay

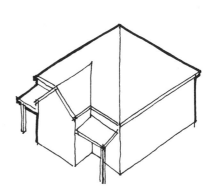

centre bay

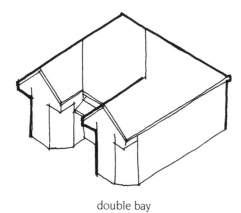

double bay

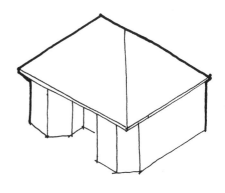

roof over double bay

had proved to be incontinent once the galvanised iron gutter decayed, especially when drifted snow melted and outlets were choked with leaves. Also, the taller hipped roof had a more imposing mass than the uniform ridge height of the earlier type. It proved to be just as flexible as the centre-gutter roof and sprouted bays in every direction. The *hipped villa* was joined around 1900 by the hipped gable roof (a hip roof with a small gable at one or both ends of the ridge), which also went through the full repertoire of bays and turrets.

The characteristic projecting bay of the bay villa house had developed gradually from a plain flush gable in the 1860s to a gable with a factory-produced bay window on the end under a hip or gable roof in the 1880s. At some stage in the 1890s this manufactured window became part of the wall itself and extended across the full width of the bay, so that the projecting room ended with diagonal corners and a narrow end wall, with a double-hung window in each corner. At first the bay roof was hipped to each angle of the faceted bay, but later the more common solution was a rectangular plan hip, gable, or half-hip ("snubnose") roof over the diagonal corners, "supported" by decorative non-structural eaves brackets. Part of the formal variety of corner bay houses came from the mixing of hip and gable on either bay, and of the bay end walls underneath — faceted with diagonal corners, square with re-entrant corners, or flush without modification. Other bay variations included multiple windows in the end walls (double, triple, or "Chicago"), or the Otago-Southland device of separate hipped or gabled roofs over the bay windows.

Finally, in the 1900s planning broke away from the simple but authoritative regime of the central hall. The repeated use of the bay form had created

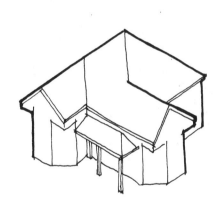

return bay

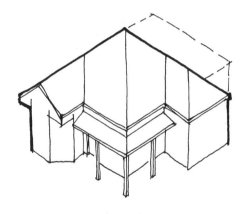

corner bay

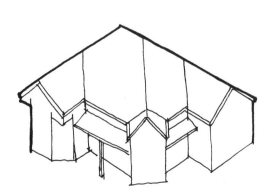

corner angle bay

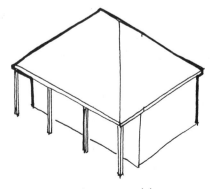

roof over verandah

164. Hipped gable villas
—basic forms.

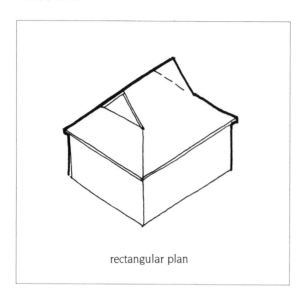

rectangular plan

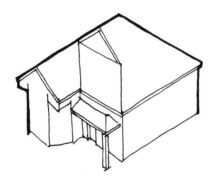

single bay

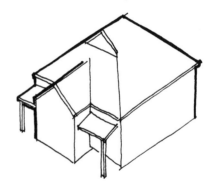

centre bay

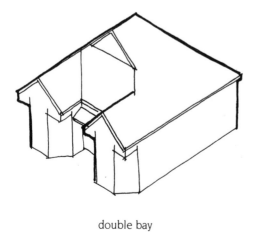

double bay

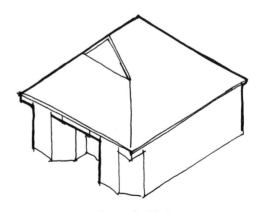

roof over double bay

internal vacuums in the plan which were filled by rooms in new and unconventional relationships. The hall became a servant of the rooms instead of a dictator, and powerful American notions of open planning and new kinds of joinery appeared in houses, which in other respects preserved the image of the late Victorian villa.

A summary of the range of formal possibilities for villa houses, based on their roof forms and variations in the treatment of the bay, is as follows:

1. FORM OF MAIN ROOF:
1.1 centre gutter
1.2 hip
1.3 hipped gable

2. COMBINATION OF BAYS:
2.1 no bays
2.2 single bay
2.3 double bay
2.4 corner bay
2.5 corner angle bay

3. END WALL OF BAY:
3.1 flush
3.2 faceted bay
3.3 square bay

4. ROOF OF BAYS:
4.1 hip
4.2 gable
4.3 snubnose

Further formal variation came from a range of optional extras:

verandahs were common to the villa, but some South Island houses had only a recessed entrance porch;

lean-tos were usually built in to the original design, but could be omitted and/or built on later;

two-storey villas repeated details of the standard type on both levels.

With all this choice, there are more than 6,000 possible variations to the villa house.

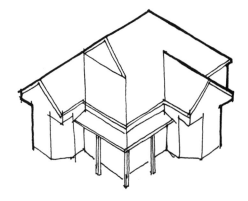

corner bay

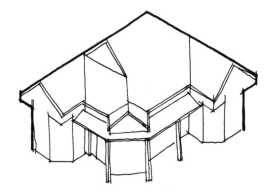

corner angle bay

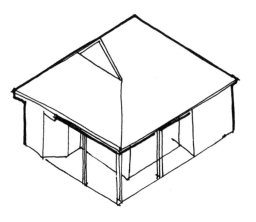

roof over return bay

165. "Up-and-down" houses, Wellington.

(a)

(b)

(c)

(d)

166. Wellington houses
—details:
(a) side entrance;
(b) corner entrance porch;

(c) bay windows;
(d) verandahs and false
parapet.

(a)

167. Classical influences:
(a) timber "quoins",
Dunedin;
(b) moulded window hood,
Wellington;
(c) arched pediment,
Wanganui;
(d) "acroteria", Gisborne
(since removed).

(b)

(c)

(d)

STYLE

The "Battle of the Styles" (Gothic v. Classical) in nineteenth century English architecture ended in an uneasy truce about 1845, when it was generally agreed that Gothic architecture was suitable for churches and for the rustic cottages of the wealthy or their tenants, and Classical styles most suited public and institutional buildings. The middle class were unmoved by these distinctions, however, and they borrowed freely for their houses from both the Gothic and the Italianate repertoires.

The researches and writings of A.W.N. Pugin spread the Gothic gospel to foreign parts including New Zealand, where by 1860 there were already a number of good houses in the "Carpenter Gothic" style. The distinguishing feature of Gothic architecture was the gable, ornamented in the carved mediaeval style that Pugin had made popular, and the preferred direction was up — tall narrow windows (lancets), steep pitched roofs, and openings finished in a pointed arch.

Italianate was the language of Classical architecture, and in this style the typical roof was hipped and low-pitched. Horizontal lines were emphasised, and openings were often finished in a round or flat arch or with a moulded "pediment" — and they were defined by moulded trims. The Classical orders — Doric, Ionic, and Corinthian — governed decorative detail, and columns or pilasters were important structural devices. Axiality and symmetry were important principles in the design and planning of Classical buildings.

From 1860 to the early 1900s New Zealand villa houses took on both aesthetic philosophies, and gave them a unique quality by reproducing in wood the full decorative arsenal of Gothic and Italianate motifs, together with any others that took the fancy of the designers, the builders, and the owners. The timber merchants promoted the fashion in their catalogues by copying in wood every detail of European masonry construction. Mouldings, architraves, brackets, keystones, dentils, and rusticated weatherboards which mimicked the stone buildings of Greece and Rome were applied promiscuously with arched or pointed windows to New Zealand villas of the 1870s onwards.

In the beginning styles in New Zealand reflected an austerity of thought and means, as well as the sheer technical difficulty of hand-working the ornament. Once machine moulding began in the 1860s however, the trade had a licence to make what it pleased, and society showed its approval by adorning its houses with these machine-made symbols of progress and prosperity. The cottages of the working class remained small and modestly ornamented, but the affluent middle class built ever larger villas with façades bedecked with cast iron, fretwork, and turnery, especially on the verandah and the bay.

Fretwork still retained something of the quality of the Gothic tracery from which it derived, and even the early cast iron work kept the lightness of hand-wrought iron. Some of the classical references provoked the disapproval of the *literati* though, particularly the practice of ornamenting corners with false quoins of wood with moulded edges to imitate stone construction. Henry Hudson Holly wrote in 1863:

> remember the maxim "truthfulness in building" . . . Do not carve stone details out of wood, nor, with false pride, attempt to make it resemble something else . . . falsehood and imitation give indisputable evidence of vulgarity of taste.[53]

The Italianate style, as befitted a masonry style of construction, was in Victorian hands heavy and massive. The roof crept out from the wall supported on fat *modillions* (brackets), and lines of thick mouldings represented the classical frieze. Timber quoins at the corners, pediments over the windows, architraves with keystones, and hefty turned balusters, weighed down the facade — especially in some Wellington houses. On some still elegant houses, a pleasant conceit was to add *acroteria* (or "terminals") cut out of sheet iron or zinc and fixed to the gutters at corners and in the centre of the facade.

In the New Zealand villa Italianate brackets, friezes, and architraves, with Gothic gables, bargeboards, and ornament were adopted as elements of the villa style itself, just as other stylistic events were absorbed as soon as they reached New Zealand. In America new decorative styles were being constantly spawned in the heady atmosphere of late Victorian eclecticism, but only faint echoes were heard here — except for the "Queen Anne" or "Free Classical" style.

Queen Anne, or "the Red Queen" as Robin Boyd has called it, competed with High Victorian Gothick in exuberance and the freedom with which forms were borrowed and arranged. The style was inspired by the work of the architects J.J. Stevenson and Norman Shaw around 1870, when they reintroduced red brick into the cold stone neighbourhoods of London. Ornament was reduced, but building masses became more complex, and classical details were paraphrased, if not parodied, with complete freedom. The turret, often found on the New Zealand corner bay villa, came from Queen Anne, and was enthusiastically accepted here in the 1880s after the style had become *passé* abroad. Other signs of the Queen's presence here were fancy shingles in the gable-end wall (often simulated in weatherboard), divided margins in the top sash of double-hung windows (or more commonly, separate divided fanlights above), decorative crests

on the roof, slender chimneys with bulbous tops and terracotta inserts, turned verandah posts, and coloured cast glass. The arrival of Marseilles tiles from Australia coincided happily with that of Queen Anne, and the bright orange terracotta roofs with their moulded ridges and terminals fitted exactly the mood of the Queen Anne villa.

A contemporary and highly popular American development was the so-called "Eastlake" style attributed to Charles Eastlake, an English architect, whose book *Hints on Household Taste* first published in 1868 had had an enormous influence on domestic furniture.

His robust furniture designs were transposed into a domestic building style in America, not unlike Queen Anne, but distinguished by more ornate carved and turned ornament and scrollwork. Eastlake decoration can be seen in the interlocking spindlework and knobs of verandahs and gables on many New Zealand villas of the 1900s, and in false verandahs over bay windows or under a

168. (Opposite) A large
house in Queen Anne style
— Fitzroy House,
Christchurch. *ATL*.

169. "Queen Anne"
influences:
(a) divided window
margins and tiled roof,
Wellington;
(b) turrets, Dunedin;
(c) the arch and divided
fanlights, Gisborne.

projecting main roof. Another typical feature was the fan-shaped bracket at the top of turned verandah posts, and in the eaves brackets of the bay roof.

Another American style of the same period was the "Eastern Stick" style, characterised in weatherboard houses by flat boards laid over the outside to suggest framing and bracing. In New Zealand these "stickwork" motifs were applied sparingly to the villas, with struts and diagonal scroll-cut brackets supporting the eaves of the bay roof, and sun screen hoods over windows, and patterns of curved stickwork on gable end walls. In larger houses massive turned structural posts supported heavy curved or scalloped brackets to prop up

(a)

170. "Eastlake" influences:
(a) spindle work, Devonport;
(b) spindle fan and frieze, Gisborne;
(c) spindles and scrollwork, Devonport.

171. (Opposite) "Eastern Stick Style" influences:
(a) stick work on gable ends, Wanganui;
(b) stick "framing", Wellington;
(c) Judge Seth-Smith's house, Auckland. AIM.

(b)

(c)

verandahs and first-floor porches. Some houses, such as Judge Seth-Smith's in Remuera, showed a clear familiarity with the style.

These late American styles shared many features, and at the end of the Victorian era in New Zealand they combined with the more complex house forms (especially the corner-angle bay villa) and the Marseilles tile roof to produce the short-lived "Edwardian" villa style. In these houses echoes of the earliest New Zealand homesteads were evoked in verandahs sheltered under a main roof which swept down much closer to the ground than in any Victorian villa. This was one of the liberating effects of a piped water supply in towns

(a)

(b)
(c)

now that the eaves no longer had to be high enough to fill rainwater tanks:

> a 600 gallon tank . . . cannot collect water from eaves that are less than 10 feet above [floor] level, a height which necessitates rooms being considerably more than 7 feet 6 inches between floor and ceiling, and which prevents the long sweep of a roof, almost to the ground, which is a picturesque feature in so many houses . . . the copying architect, with little or no initiative, is hampered when he wishes to force on a practical client the latest bit of picturesque architecture culled from some modern English or American publication[54]

The "carpenter-architects" were no longer called on to design houses from a simple formula and a catalogue of mouldings. Clients now came to them with imported plan books from America or Australia, or ideas borrowed from the work of English-trained architects. In New Zealand local architects and draughtsmen were soon producing their own plan books:

> the New Zealand designer utilises our own climatic advantages . . . in a way no outside architect could equal. Effective use of materials most economical in this country is another strong point of commendation about the "made in New Zealand" design.[55]

One of the earliest and most prolific plan-book designers was the architect G.W. Phillips, who published plan books and specifications for houses of different sizes between around 1909 and 1913.* The style of his houses is best described as transitional and eclectic — most of his designs were in the Edwardian villa style, but the later designs were clearly influenced by the American bungalow. The houses in *Laidlaw Leeds' Plans of Houses* were more conservative in style, and based on traditional centre gutter and hipped villa forms, with solid-bracketed verandahs, bracketed eaves, and Italianate chimneys. *New Zealand Homes, 60 Practical Designs*, published around 1915 by Jas. Christie, offered straightforward late villas, indisputable bungalows, and a large number of houses of mixed descent.

With these transitional houses the villa style in New Zealand came to an end, unable at last to accommodate overseas ideas which conflicted with so many of its basic qualities. Its form was now hopelessly fragmented; the eaves bristled with exposed rafter ends, and of the surviving ornamentation, brackets and friezes were reduced to solid boards with a few holes and shaped edges, ending finally as plain tapered boards stuck to posts and roof beams. Everything was now so coarse and heavy that it was more the thickening of age than adornment.

The Victorian villa in New Zealand had served its people well, and expressed perfectly the exuberance and energy of an age of invention and achievement. The villa was the reward of the self-made man, and whatever its shortcomings it has proved itself remarkably flexible in use and design, in housing four or five generations of New Zealand families.

*His publications included *Designs for New Zealand Homes and Residences; New Zealand Homes and Bungalows* in three volumes for houses of three and four rooms, five rooms and six rooms; and *Details and Specifications for New Zealand Homes, Bungalows, Residences, etc.*

PART III

THE BUNGALOW
AND BEYOND

1910~1940

Introduction

After 1910 the starch and lace of Victorian villas in New Zealand gave way to a more casual, homespun style imported from America — the Californian Bungalow. In suburbs such as Sandringham, St Kilda and Miramar, acres of flat land were criss-crossed by streets lined with bungalows, their wide windows shaded by low sweeping gable roofs. As the roof lines came down, hemlines went up; established patterns of life and behaviour were shattered by the Great War, and as the war ended a new generation looked for a better way of life.

For a decade they found it in greater mobility and leisure, and more comforts in the home. Towns which had expanded rapidly in the first decade of the century with the advent of the electric tram surged ahead once more in the 1920s as the economy revived. More and more of the population became town dwellers and private motor car ownership, which had reached 3,000 in 1911, soared to 103,000 by 1927. This new flexible personal transport changed all the rules governing the location, size, and growth of towns.

Large laconic American cars made new settlements possible in previously remote parts of the country. Science entered the home through wires, pipes, and invisibly, through the "ether" — and New Zealanders danced to the gramophone, listened to the news on the wireless, and turned on hot water in the kitchen and bathroom.

The Depression in the 1930s, however, undermined national confidence and the self esteem of thousands who could not get jobs or who found their jobs degrading. House building plummeted, and the few houses that were built at that time were sober and severely simple.

New hope came with the election of a Labour government in 1935, and the State began to build houses — solid and sensible. Private house builders turned to the novel exotic forms of the *Spanish Mission* and *Moderne* houses — film-set facades covering old plans. Like the villa before it the bungalow reflected this recurring cycle of binge and austerity in New Zealand economic affairs. At its height it was exuberant and informal, spacious and well-built, while in the depths of the Depression those that were built were dour and withdrawn.

The first bungalows in New Zealand were the work of architects, but the style was so quickly taken up by local builders that by 1914 the villa had had its day. The builders' inspiration came from plan books — American, English, Australian and then New Zealand — which flowed steadily onto the shelves of the nation's bookstalls.

Simple design and a more relaxed lifestyle gave the bungalow its appeal to a generation force-fed on the formality and ornamentation of late Victorian houses. Simplicity of appearance suggested cleanliness and efficiency and more obscurely, a "scientific" approach to domestic affairs. "The bungalow is simply a scientifically designed habitation for men", claimed *Bungalow Magazine* in 1914. Moreover, the bungalow was inexpensive, and an "artistic" style of house — "Many people hold the idea that to build an artistic house necessitates spending a large sum of money. Often the reverse is the case."[1] It was through an imaginative and clever use of simple materials and objects that the bungalow aesthetic was achieved.

This then was a house for the people — a house in which aesthetic and pragmatic needs were satisfied at a cost the masses could afford. The bungalow style was not just a way of building, it was also a new way of life.

The Californian bungalow

172 A bracketed cottage; from A.J. Downing's *The Architecture of Country Houses*, 1880.

"The question has often been asked. . . . What do you term a Californian Bungalow?'

"A typical Californian Bungalow must necessarily have wide overhanging eaves, and be designed in the Mission Style of Architecture —namely, everything plain and heavy. Special features are also commodious porches and wide low windows. In designing a Bungalow care should be taken to avoid waste space — typically a labour saving house for the housewife."

— KIBBLEWHITE, c 1924.

AMERICAN ORIGINS

The direct inspiration for these houses came from the west coast of North America. The rise of the bungalow style of building there is interesting in itself, and its origins are claimed variously as Japanese, Indian and in some of its forms Spanish American. Each of these traditions contributed to the bungalow, but the style that emerged was distinctively Californian.

The word "bungalow" was borrowed from the English who in turn acquired it from the India of the Raj. An Indian *bangla* was a traveller's rest house — a sort of rudimentary motel with a verandah, central hall, and rooms of the simplest kind. The use of the term in England, however, had come to mean "neither the sunproof squat house of India, nor the rough log hut of colder regions" but an "artistic little dwelling, cheaply but soundly built with proper regard to sanitation and popped down in some pretty little spot with just sufficient accommodation for our particular needs."[2]

In America it is recognised that the American bungalow owes more to Japanese models than it does to the buildings of India, for all the apparent similarities. In fact, it was only around 1910 that a resemblance was noted between the East Indian bungalow and the new low-slung American houses. Essentially the bungalow was "an unassuming dwelling containing no more than an absolutely necessary number of rooms",[3] and that it stood for "a simple unaffected sort of life . . . a gayer and less formal kind of setting".[4]

Historically, it is possible to sense the beginnings of the Californian bungalow in some of the designs of Andrew Jackson Downing, especially his "bracketed" and "Swiss" cottages. The shallow chalet-style roof was an essential element of the bungalow style, even to the brackets tucked under the overhanging gable roof. Downing's planning too had some of the openness and continuity of the twentieth century bungalows.

Contemporary sources for the earliest bungalows can also be found in the *Shingle* style and *Stick* style houses of the eastern states of America, each of which developed independently of European models. Stick style buildings expressed their internal framework in "stickwork" applied to the exterior walls, with a vertical emphasis; and in the 1890s on the west coast of America, architects such as Bernard Maybeck and the Greene brothers reworked the stick style into horizontal lines, still with the structure made visible on the outside. Shingle style contributed not only its characteristic wall covering to the bungalow, but also a tradition of interior spaces which flowed together and mingled with the outside in deeply recessed porches.

It has been suggested that the bungalow style in the USA was an architects' style, as in the extraordinary work of Maybeck and the Greenes. Their houses show a clear Japanese influence in low-pitched over-sailing roofs, the direct expression of timber construction, and an emphatic connection with the ground where rubble construction rose up in walls and chimneys, binding each house to its site. But these buildings were also part of a wider aesthetic (even philosophical) movement peculiar to the time and place. California was a meeting place of many cultures and architectural traditions, and the Californian bungalow borrowed and adapted freely from those traditions that best suited local conditions.

As the bungalow style became popular in America, a literature of appreciation promoted its ideals of economy, simplicity, and scientific and artistic design. Plan books produced exclusively by architects in the nineteenth century now appeared mass-produced by mail order companies such as the Radford Architectural Company, Sears Roebuck and Company, E.G. Stilwell and Company, and many others. Their catalogues of plans sold in thousands, and their drawing offices worked full time to produce the drawings ordered by their readers. Periodicals dedicated to the "bungalow ideal" argued the merits of the style as "architectural logic exemplified in home building,"[5] and just as nineteenth century influences moved freely around the edges of the Pacific Basin, so in the early twentieth century American plan books soon reached Australasia.

THE CALIFORNIAN BUNGALOW IN NEW ZEALAND: STYLE

In New Zealand the term "bungalow" was widely and casually used as a fashionable buzzword in the local building industry — particularly in land agents' advertisements — so that for some time it meant little more than "not villa". In practice, many houses dubbed "bungalow" in the 1910s were just late villas with bungalow trimmings.

These "Transitional" houses were still planned as villas, and outside they were still clad in weatherboard, or occasionally brick, but the roofs were flatter and the boxed eaves had given way to exposed rafter-ends without fascia boards. The verandah remained in its traditional position, but under an extension of the main roof supported by plain posts with solid tapering wooden "wings" instead of the elaborate turned and fretted decoration of a decade earlier. Bay windows persisted, but often as no more than a "box" window propped on brackets, and the old double-hung sashes were replaced by new-fangled casement-and-fanlight windows (a peculiarly New Zealand foible).

The Transitional houses — villa in substance, bungalow in manner — have been largely rejected as an illegitimate by-product of change in popular taste. At their worst they were timorous, awkward and ill-proportioned, but the best of these houses deserve recognition for the skill with which two

173. A typical Transitional house Devonport.

aesthetic philosophies were reconciled in satisfying and convincing buildings.

The battle of the two styles was brief, and after 1918 no speculative builder with any commercial sense would have bothered to advertise a new house in the villa style. As late as 1915 some local plan books such as *Laidlaw Leeds' Plans of Houses* showed designs in a stripped-down Transitional style aimed clearly at a rural conservative market; and in Jas. Christie's *New Zealand Homes 60 Practical Designs* of 1915 there was not one identifiable Californian bungalow illustrated. On the other hand, G.W. Phillips had produced four books of plans by 1913, and there were unmistakable Californian style houses in his later designs.

The builders depended at first on the imported plan books and periodicals, and reproduced designs from the plans and elevations published in America. Architects warned that "the slavish copying of plans from cheap publications is . . . a dangerous practice,"[6] but those who could not afford the architect's service had to rely either on the plan books or the builder's own sketch on dog-eared cartridge paper. In 1924, R.W. Kibblewhite claimed in his *Popular Modern Homes* to have adapted the Californian bungalow to the New Zealand conditions, yet in 1931 there was still a search for a local character — "we have the Californian Bungalow, the Spanish Mission, the Italian and English types . . . (why not) a New Zealand type of bungalow?"[7]

In the plan books great emphasis was placed on the cheapness of standard plans. "The cost of plans, specifications and quantities is only a fraction of what the architect would charge for plans alone" claimed Laidlaw Leeds' catalogue. "Buy standardised plans and save money" urged Harry Ratcliffe, a Wairoa architect: and Jas. Christie reminded his customers: "I furnish stock plans for all styles of houses, which if drawn to order would cost you four times as much as I charge".[8]

Whatever their origins or their merits, the plan books offered New Zealand housebuyers unprecedented freedom to choose a plan tailored to their needs and pockets, and in a style which they fancied — an architecture of consensus.[9]

When the Bungalow style left California for

New Zealand it took with it the low pitched gable roof with wide eaves, wide deep porches, heavy beams and thick tapered piers, massive chimneys, and shingles for the walls. In the hands of New Zealand builders bungalows soon acquired bow and bay windows, casement-and-fanlight windows, corrugated iron on the roof, and weatherboards on the outer walls.

The roof gave the house its form. Until about 1925 the gable roof had covered most bungalows, usually as a dominant single span parallel to the street or at right angles to it. Secondary roofs covered porches on all sides — offset on the gable end wall, appearing out of the main roof at the sides, or simply as an extension of the main roof. As plans became more complex, overall forms were fragmented, and gables wandered off in all directions until the main roof was lost in a confusion of bargeboards and ridges. But gradually through the 1920s the hip roof returned, exerting a steadying influence, and by 1930 it had almost replaced the gable, or reached a compromise in the *snubnose gable* roof.

Although the Bungalow style used plain and simple finishes, there could be a surprising amount of decoration, usually as flourishes on construction

174. Two "bungled" villas: (a) Gisborne — a bungalow porch, chimney, and box window on an 1890s villa. (b) Mt Eden — an 1890s villa with bungalow roof and porch.

details. Typical were the scalloped ends of the bargeboards and the row of projecting blocks (false ceiling joists) at the base of the gable wall — a carry over from the villas. The gable wall itself was often shingled, as were the bay and bow windows, and like them it was usually finished in a bell-cast — a curved flare outwards at the base. On the gable was this was sometimes carried further to form a sunhood over the windows below. Almost every gable sported a ventilator — a louvred opening shaped as a square, a diamond, or a circle, and in many houses the weatherboards in the apex were simply replaced by trelliswork. In other houses a window was used instead (even where there was no first floor), or a "clerestory" window was built into the main roof under a flat or gable "dormer" roof.

175. (a) An American plan company advertisement from *Bungalow Magazine*, 1914.
(b) A Northcote (Auckland) house of c. 1920.

176. (Top) A "confusion of bargeboards and ridges".

177. (Above) Scalloped bargeboard ends.

Porches were enclosed by a variety of balustrades; solid and built of weatherboards, brick, stucco or shingles; or open with wide flat baluster boards pierced by an incised floral motif. At the corners of the porches the roof was supported by massive piers or pylons which tapered upwards from a wide base. In California (and sometimes in New Zealand), these were built of stone or brick, but more often the local version mocked the original with hollow weatherboarded boxes. The pylons carried the roof on short stubby posts (as many as three each), but eventually they ended up as posts themselves with perhaps a slight taper in the top half. The porch span was often as much as six metres, and especially in stucco houses could be formed as a shallow arch. Arches were not strictly part of the bungalow style (although important in later Spanish Mission houses), yet arched porches were common in New Zealand bungalows and some late houses used an arch motif as a decoration on the flat gable wall.

178. A typical gable ventilator.

179. (Below) A roof clerestory window.

180. Bungalows with porches — the pylon and the arch:
(a) Dunedin;
(b) Rotorua;
(c) Wanganui;
(d) Wanganui.

(a)

(b)

(c)

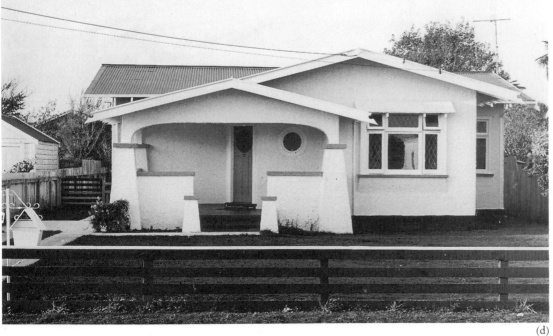

(d)

180. (Cont.) Bungalows with porches — the pylon and the arch.
(e) Devonport;
(f) Grey Lynn.

Fireplaces moved to outer walls (often in company with the fireside inglenook), and the chimney rose up from heavy haunched shoulders to end with a wide flat capping plate. In larger houses the chimney could be massive and sculptural, but more often it was a simple square roughcast shaft.

Apart from the pitch and shape of roofs, it was in the design and position of windows and doors that bungalows differed most from villas. In the Transitional period and in some provincial areas such as Gisborne, double-hung windows persisted, but in odd combinations such as unequal sized sashes with the top divided into squares. The fanlight of the late villas, introduced to improve ventilation, was retained in company with the casement — the fanlight was hinged at the top, the casement at the side. This combination was unique to New Zealand bungalows, and for larger rooms casement-and-fanlight were simply multiplied to give more light and ventilation so that it was common to find seven or eight windows in a single opening.

The bay window of the villa also continued in the bungalows, at first as a modest window seat, but quickly evolving into curved bow windows which billowed voluptuously out of the wall, and which owed more to the Arts and Crafts houses of English architects than to the bungalow style. Bow and bay windows were often combined at the corner of a room to make a glazed "drum", recalling

181. (Left) Inglenook and chimney, Devonport.

182. (Below) Bow windows:
(a) five-light, Wellington;
(b) six-light, Devonport.

183. Corner bow window,
Point Chevalier.

(a)

(b)

the turrets of Queen Anne style. A popular conceit of the mid twenties was a miniature bow window of glittering bevelled glass leadlights, fitted in the wall beside a chimney, or perhaps the entry hall.

In the early bungalows, as in the later villas, the fanlight was an opportunity to display coloured cast glass leadlights. Designs based on the Art Nouveau style of formalised floral motifs linked by sinuous vines were repeated in the front door and often in internal doors. In late bungalows the coloured glass was replaced by clear or frosted bevelled glass in leaded Art Deco patterns of chevrons, stripes, circles and zigzags. In the hall, or on one wall of the living room, fixed windows featured leadlight seascapes or rural scenes.

184. Mini bow windows:
(a) Devonport;
(b) Devonport.

185. (Right) The bungalow and its matching fence, Epsom.

196

a. Siting and gardens

New bungalows sat in orderly rows along new streets around the urban fringes of established towns, but there was a new rhythm to the layout of the houses. On each property the house kept a generous distance away from one side boundary, and sooner or later this space was occupied by a new kind of outhouse — the motor garage. Motor cars were expensive to buy and maintain and decent shelter was essential to protect the investment. Garages were seldom very grand and usually followed the house by a year or two, or three. It was this simplicity that appealed to the Christchurch poet Mary Ursula Bethell when she wrote:

My garage is a structure of excessive plainness,
It springs from a dry bank in the back garden,
It is made of corrugated iron,
And painted all over with brick-red.

But beside it I have planted a green Bay-tree.
— a sweet Bay, an Olive, and a Turkey Fig,
— a Fig, an Olive, and a Bay.[10]

The garage could readily be planted out, but a more arduous task for those who built on rough subdivision land was to make a garden out of the property.

First the land had to be fenced. Rudimentary three-wire fences were strung up and planted out with macrocarpa or yew hedges which have since grown into immense shaven green walls. Some fences were built to match the house in brick perhaps, or stucco, or were selected with gates from the crinkly wire and wrought iron frames in the Cyclone catalogue. Those who took *The Craftsman* spirit to heart tried their hand at rustic fences and garden furniture using the ubiquitous manuka, and in many suburbs there was an abundance of loose fieldstones to be gathered which made excellent dry walls "to be shelter from winds, shade from the burning sun".[11]

The emphasis in bungalow gardens was on informality and a genial chaos of plants close to the house and growing over porches and pergolas. Native trees and shrubs were often planted where a generation before they had been rooted out and replaced with those of Mother England. Exotic plants now came from subtropical and alpine regions — rhododendrons, hibiscus and bougainvillaea — and rockeries were popular.

The front gate lay discreetly to one side and a gravel or concrete path wound up to an entrance porch at the side of the house. Lawns were broken

186. Cyclone fencing and
gates:
(a) fence (with sparrow
iron below), Christchurch;
(b) double gates, Grey
Lynn.

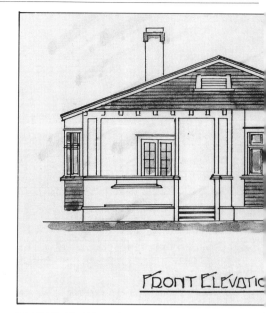

FRONT ELEVATIO

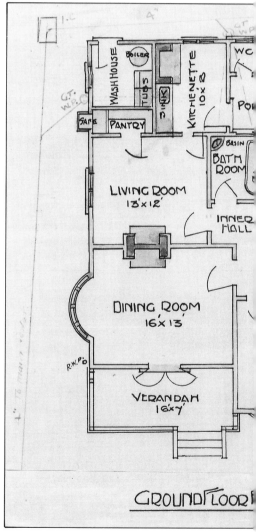

GROUND FLOOR

up by shrubs which partly concealed the house
from the street and gave modest privacy to
porches.

b. Planning

Changes in the stylistic wrapping of the bungalow
were echoed as dramatically inside. Rooms took on
new names, new shapes, and found new positions
about the house, now much less dependent on a
formal face to the street. Visitors could expect to be
introduced at the side of the house, leaving the
front for private outdoor living.

Early bungalow plans were more relaxed and
less confining than in villas, with projecting wings,
bay windows and porches on all sides. But the most
fundamental planning stage in the shift from villa
to bungalow was the size and position of the hall or
passage.

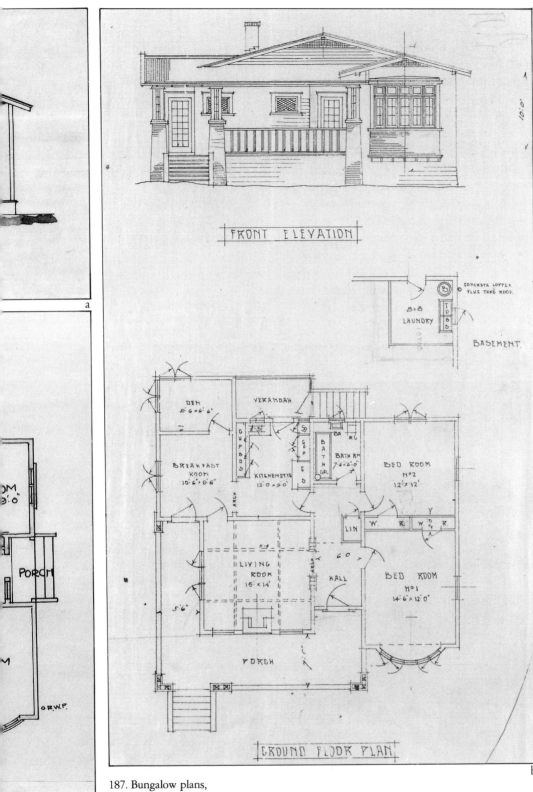

FRONT ELEVATION

BASEMENT.

GROUND FLOOR PLAN

187. Bungalow plans,
Devonport:
(a) 1920 (Left);
(b) 1924 (Right).

In the last villas the passage had shrunk to a vestibule at the front door with a narrow offshoot deeper into the house. In the bungalows this vestibule became the "hall", often a room in itself, and the passage which ran off to one side no longer determined the positions of other rooms. Coat cupboards and linen presses were built into every niche and corner, and in some two-storeyed houses, the stair wound up around a spacious entry hall, rather in the manner of an English country house.

The true open planning of the American prototype was rarely adopted in New Zealand bungalows — the climate was not cold enough to justify central heating, nor was it so warm that the entire house could be heated from the living room fireplace. Anyway, New Zealanders still valued their privacy. As a compromise, sliding doors separated living room and breakfast room, the kitchen

opened directly off the breakfast room and "a certain amount of inter-communication [was] acceptable provided the bedrooms and bathrooms [were] skilfully arranged".[12]

The very names of the rooms suggested a different lifestyle — "living room" for parlour, "breakfast room" for dining room, "kitchenette" for kitchen (now combined with scullery), "laundry" for washhouse. Verandahs became "porches" and there might be two, three, or even more of these. Apart from the entrance porch there was often a sun porch off the living room, a back porch off the kitchen (perhaps with tradesmen's delivery cupboards), and a great novelty imported from America along with the fad for healthy scientific living — the sleeping porch. This was really an outdoor room, sometimes at first floor level, where beds were kept in the summer months. For privacy,

188. Sliding doors between rooms — optional open plan. *ATL, McAllister Coll.*

189. The first floor sleeping porch (note also the inglenook and chimney), Hawera.

canvas blinds could be lowered; for comfort, mosquito net curtains could be drawn; for warmth, concertina windows such as the Easifold type could be fitted.

Rooms were now smaller but more carefully planned, and in many houses what was described as "the housewife's mania for cupboards" led to better use of the available space. So bedrooms had built-in wardrobes (admittedly small), the kitchenette might have a small table with fixed seats built into an alcove for "snacks", and efforts were made to plan for a logical sequence of tasks in the preparation of food — a popular topic in the women's pages of magazines: "a dinky little kitchenette and a breakfast room adjoining must be in the plan. And the kitchenette must have plenty of cupboards and proper sliding bins".[13]

Between the kitchenette and the breakfast room a handy "pass through" or servery with panelled or leadlight doors was neatly framed and built into the wall, often as part of a bank of china cupboards. More cupboards for firewood were built in beside the fireplaces, which once more moved to the outside wall as they had in the earliest European houses in New Zealand. This helped to reduce the overall bulk of the house, although more heat was lost to the outside.

Perhaps the most successful feature of classic bungalows was the "ingle" or "inglenook" — a deep alcove in the living rooms where seats were built in around a fireplace with small windows and bookshelves on either side of the chimney. Here the cosy informality of the bungalow ideal, centred on the familial hearth, made the living room genuinely livable.

The importance of the bathroom in everyday life can be seen from its location at the heart of the typical bungalow plan. Once an inconvenient and often uncomfortable chore, bathing now became a luxury to be enjoyed daily: "the bathroom should not only be devoted to cleanliness, but regarded as a haven of rest and recuperation from the activities of the day".[14] No longer a cramped spartan room under the back lean-to, or at the end of a long hall,

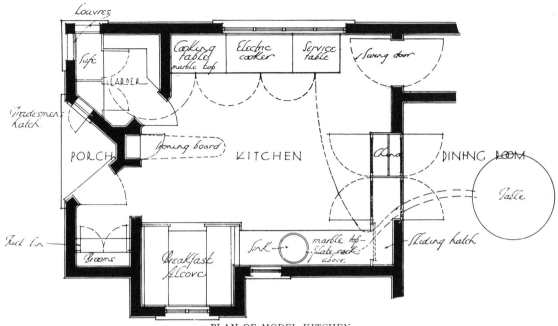

PLAN OF MODEL KITCHEN
The dotted line indicates the progressive sequence of operations in preparing food for the
table, and returning dishes, etc., to the sink.

190. A kitchen showing the work sequence and breakfast alcove — from *NZABR*, August 1926.

191. (Right) The inglenook —inside. *ATL, Steffano Webb Coll.*

the bathroom and its accomplice the lavatory now occupied a central position, close to bedrooms for convenience and to the kitchen for economic plumbing. For some, "all this preoccupation with the bath and its attendant luxuries indicate[d] the complete weakening of our moral fibre".[15] Nevertheless, the bathroom had acquired a social status and a hedonistic appeal it has not since lost. Together with the hall, the bathroom was the major advance in the planning of the New Zealand bungalow.

c. Construction

By about 1910 supplies of the New Zealand kauri, of which most villas were built, had become desperately scarce because of the huge exports to Australia. Timber merchants began to mill greater quantities of other native species such as rimu, but to offset the shortage they also imported timber from overseas.

In America bungalows were built from indigenous oregon, cedar and redwood, and these timbers

had become part of the style. As bungalows became more popular in New Zealand, exotic timbers arrived in large shipments and even villas of the early 1910s were built of oregon and cedar, as well as other species imported for joinery, including hoop pine, baltic pine, Australian blackwood, American oak, maple and cottonwood. Cedar was brought in not only in solid baulks, but in vast quantities as sawn shingles, an essential element of the Bungalow style in California. By 1927, however, it was claimed that there were adequate local timbers for ordinary small house construction, except that baltic pine, redwood or oregon were still recommended for doors and windows. In 1928 Kibblewhite could recommend for one of his standard plans heart rimu panelling with rewa rewa covering battens, heavy puriri beamed ceilings with kauri panels between, and Canadian redwood shingles stained dark green for the roof.

Although bungalows looked very different from villas, their construction was much the same and this continuity of technique helped ease the New

Zealand house out of its old shell and into the new. Some changes were needed for fixing new sheet linings, but the light wooden frame continued to be the most common form of house construction throughout this period.

Changes in foundations began as early as 1910 when glazed ceramic piles were produced to replace the usual totara or puriri house blocks, but even after cheap concrete piles became available around 1920 wooden blocks remained in use well into the decade. Solid concrete foundation walls were another development to give the support required for stucco finishes and to prevent cracking. In the house frame itself, horizontal pieces called "nogs" (or "dwangs" in the south) were widely used to support the edges of new sheet linings. The average wall height dropped about 0.6 metre to around 2.75 metres, and the pitch of the roof correspondingly fell from the usual 30 degrees or more to between 15 and 20 degrees.

Rafter spacings increased from 0.9 metre to as much as 1.2 metres in cheaper houses, with dummy rafter ends between showing in the exposed eaves, and it was not unusual to find 75 x 50 mm purlins sagging across the increased span.

There were other construction materials for walls. Brick was the most common alternative, particularly in the south, and several companies developed new large earthenware building blocks such as "Mastertile" or Glenbrook's "constructional tiles". The brick companies widely advertised the fireproof qualities of brick construction, and also developed reinforcing bricks to resist earthquakes. Concrete was also used in several forms including concrete blocks, solid walls poured *in situ* and numerous patented systems such as the "Veandhor" from Wanganui.

However, weatherboards were still the most common wall covering and the details and fixing were the same as on villas. But around 1920 the

192. A battened Fibrolite-
covered bungalow,
Gisborne.

heavy "boxed" corner began to give way to the more subtle "mitred" corner, where walls met on a fine serrated edge and each joint in the boards was covered by a folded metal *soaker* (an American invention of 1914). Weatherboards were generally carried to the ground, but on level sections especially it was usual to fix plain 150 mm wide vertical boards below floor level, with a 25 mm gap between and the boards sloping outwards to the ground.

Fully shingled bungalows were rare, but it was even more unusual to find a house in New Zealand without some feature covered in shingles. "Shingles suggest rusticity" said *Bungalow Magazine,* and rustic bay and bow windows and gable walls were particularly popular here.

The most significant technical advance in building materials during the bungalow period, however, was the development of sheet lining materials inside and out. Sheet linings offered cheap, maintenance-free, self-finished wall coverings at a time when costs were rising and timber was scarce.

Asbestos cement sheets were imported from England under the "Poilite" brand name, and later from Australia as "Fibrolite". The sheets, which were 5 mm thick and from 45 cm to 1.2 metres wide, could be cut easily in their "green" (uncured) state, and were quickly fixed with nails. They did not need painting and were claimed to be fireproof. The manufacturer even recommended Fibrolite for interiors — "the intrinsic charm of the walls and ceilings lined with 'FIBROLITE' Asbestos Cement Sheets . . . is always in fastidious good taste [and] is restful and pleasing to the eye".[16] Joints in exterior sheets were usually covered by timber battens, but another solution widely adopted in New Zealand was to use the sheet as a base for a cement plaster finish known as stucco.

Stucco was a common finish for cheap masonry buildings, but in America it was adapted to wooden framed houses by covering the frame with a *lath* of perforated metal ribs, or oregon battens in diagonal layers. In New Zealand stucco was applied directly to sheet materials such as asbestos cement, two local products — Konka board and Gibraltar sheathing — and a variety of imitations.

Konka was first used in Wanganui in 1912 as a patented concrete sheet 91 x 76 cm in size by 15 mm thick. The uncured sheets were fixed to the frame in rows with joints staggered and filled with mortar. Joints and corners were covered with strips of hessian dipped in cement and water to help the plaster coat stick. The stucco was mixed with "Pudlo" waterproofer, "the only substance which can be relied upon to give an entirely satisfactory result . . . [and which] will never fail to make any concrete work absolutely waterproof".[17]

Another building board first made as a base for stucco was Gibraltar sheathing — large sheets of gypsum plaster with a paper covering were coated with bitumen and fixed to the frame, with steel mesh over corners and joints.

Some houses were finished entirely in stucco, others contrasted plaster surfaces with brickwork, and many other houses of mainly brick construc-tion used small areas of stucco for effect. Chimneys too were stuccoed directly on to precast concrete sections. Stucco was the basic wall finish on Span-ish Mission and Moderne style houses in the 1930s.

In the dry Californian climate, low-pitched bun-galow roofs were clad in wooden shingles or tiles, but in New Zealand shingles were uncommon on roofs and if tiles were used (as in Australia) a steeper pitch was advisable to keep the rain out. Corrugated iron allowed the New Zealand roof to be as shallow as the original. There were other roofing materials including asbestos cement slates and corrugated asbestos cement. Welsh slates and Marseilles tiles remained popular, particularly for English style houses.

Asbestos cement slates were laid diagonally, giv-ing the roof a distinctive diamond pattern. Ridges and hips were finished with Marseilles ridge tiles and their brick orange colour contrasted so strongly with the grey of new "slates" that a red-brown slate was developed to diminish the contrast.

193. Brick and Konka
board construction, ready
for stucco finish, Wanganui.
ATL, Deuton Collection.

194. Asbestos cement
"slates" with Marseilles tile
ridge capping, Wellington.

Corrugated asbestos cement came to New Zealand in 1925 as "Big Six", with wider and deeper corrugations than in iron sheets. "Big Six" was intended as an industrial finish and had limited use in houses of the time.

Bungalow roofs transformed the textures of the New Zealand suburban landscape. Wide overhanging eaves cast deep shadows marking the rise and fall of shallow rooflines along the street, in contrast with the steep repetitive roofs of the villas and their menacing finials.

d. Services

By the end of the Great War electricity was accepted as a safe and efficient alternative fuel to gas in domestic appliances. It quickly proved more versatile than gas as more and more household appliances were electrified. "The modern wife . . . won't have 'mucky old ranges' " claimed a contemporary magazine:

A gas stove will be tolerated, but an electric stove will be better and cleaner . . .
Electric cookery has become a possibility for all. No longer need the tired housewife clean fire stoves, scrub saucepans and throw away unpalatable food. The appearance of the electric range leaves nothing to be desired. As a general rule ranges are finished in shiny black enamel, with a high oven to save stooping and with hot plates at the side.[18]

There was, however, still some nervousness about this invisible form of energy. Some believed that electricity was discharged from electric sockets even when nothing was plugged in, and were suspicious of this "non-supervised method of cooking". Until about 1926 switches consisted of two buttons — "on" and "off" — later replaced by "tumbler" or "toggle" switches and radium switches which glowed in the dark.

In 1914 Turnbull and Jones advertised appliances made by the Hotpoint Electrical Heating Com-

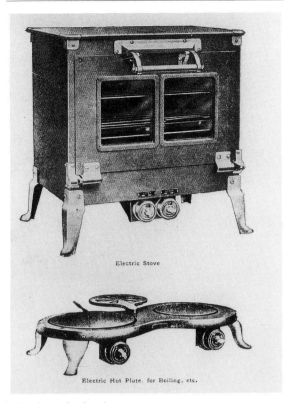

Electric Stove

Electric Hot Plate. for Boiling, etc.

195. An early electric
oven and electric hot plates.

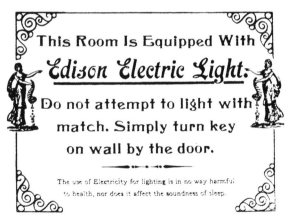

This Room Is Equipped With
Edison Electric Light.
Do not attempt to light with
match. Simply turn key
on wall by the door.

The use of Electricity for lighting is in no way harmful
to health, nor does it affect the soundness of sleep.

196. "Edison Electric
Light". *ATL, Evening Post
Coll.*

pany of Ontario, rejoicing in such names as El
Grillo, El Stovo and El Tosto ("transforms part of
the starch into dextrin; makes it more nutritious,
more digestable, more delectable"). By the mid
twenties just about every domestic appliance had
been electrified, including water heating, and by
1937, according to *Building Progress* magazine, it
was "generally considered folly to build a house at
the present time without installing a hot water
service".[19]

Gas remained popular, however, and cheap
—especially for water heating — and gas califonts
appeared above the bath or kitchen sink in polished brass jackets. Effective gas cookers were
developed from rather primitive beginnings and
the new cookers often replaced the villa's old coal
range, which was rooted out of its tiled alcove to
make way for the new technology. Although both
gas and electric ranges were self-contained units
designed to go anywhere in the kitchen, the practice of providing a tiled recess persisted in many
bungalows, where the cooker sat glowing on its
plinth like some polished, hissing Buddha.

Every house had its safe, a framed box with
fly-screened openings propped on the outside of a
south-facing wall. This was an effective way of
keeping food fresh and many are still in use today.
With the bungalow came the ice chest, a wooden
box lined with metal and built into a recess near the
back door. In the late 1920s electricity made refrig-
eration available to many house owners, and
"home refrigerating sets" could be bought to fit an
existing ice chest. These used a brine tank kept at a
temperature between 16^0 and 24^0 F in an enamelled steel box with a wooden outer case. Some of
these gave off disagreeable amounts of carbon diox-
ide and ammonia, but in 1928 true refrigerators
were on sale in New Zealand, which needed only
electricity and running water and were presentable
enough to go in the kitchen itself:

> The Electrolux refrigerator . . . 5'10" in height
> by 27" in width and 23" in depth . . . is very
> handsomely finished in white enamel while the
> door hinges and fastenings are nickel plated.[20]

In the laundry, if electric or gas hot water were
not available, the old built-in copper was replaced

207

by a new pre-cast concrete model with a round lightweight concrete flue. Washing machines were added to the list of electric amenities, some with an electrically driven wringer. One washing machine without a wringer had "an internal perforated metal basket which, in operation, whirls within the closed washer and in ten minutes washes and rinses the clothes, blues them, and leaves them wringer-dry".[21]

Early machines were supplied in elegant wooden cabinets on castors, but later models fitted into more utilitarian round drums of brass or galvanised steel.

The introduction of so many mechanical appliances during the bungalow period released women from a great deal of drudgery, though not necessarily from the onus of keeping a tidy and clean house. "The bungalow is planned first for the convenience of its intended occupants, housework is reduced to its simplest terms and all matters of modern life are considered."[22]

197. Gas caliphont and gas stove, 1923. *ATL.*

Bungalow interiors were transformed by a flood of manufactured sheet materials which poured onto the market. Some were made from compressed wood fibre (Beaverboard, Upsonboard, Celotex, Donnaconna), others of gypsum plaster (Gibraltar board, Triumph and Maxwell boards). Even asbestos cement was offered — "the perfect combination of Art, Utility, and Economy".[24]

Where a timber finish was wanted English Venesta plywood, or cheaper Amiwud with "the same appearance as the finest grained timbers" was available.

Wallpaper on scrim over rough lining was regarded as unhealthy, and "harbours for Vermin, Dust, Disease", whereas Maxwell Board for instance was claimed to be "Clean, Strong, Sanitary, Fireproof and Everlasting, Mouse and Vermin Proof . . . not affected by weather conditions: Fog, Damp Atmosphere, Sun or Shock . . . it is as permanent as the pyramids".[25]

Joints in sheet linings were covered by timber battens, so that walls and ceilings were crisscrossed by a lattice of dark-stained wooden strips or beams. In the hall, living room and breakfast room, walls were panelled to door height and above this a narrow "plate shelf" ran around the room with ornamental treasures on display. The wall above was painted, or more commonly covered by an extravagant wallpaper frieze on which Art Nouveau motifs flourished. Alternatively, timber battens divided the upper wall into panels trimmed with a narrow paper frieze.

The panelling took everything in its stride and doors, windows, cupboards and fireplaces all fitted in without fuss. Like the plate shelf, the mantelpiece was supported on brackets over a brick or glazed tile fire surround. Ceilings too were panelled, and the typical bungalow featured heavy beams and joists (some hollow) supporting plasterboard or compressed fibreboards in the living rooms. Some of these sheets had textured and patterned surfaces, but it was the beams which gave the bungalow ceiling its character.

In bedrooms ceilings were battened or just wallpapered, and walls were papered from floor to ceiling with a picture rail instead of a plate shelf to divide the frieze along the top. In early bungalows, kitchens and bathrooms were match-lined with

198. Laun-Dry-Ette electric washing machine. *ATL, Gordon Burt Coll.*

e. Finishes and furniture

In the bungalow it was important to have harmony between the house and its fittings, and the keynote was simplicity — in theory if not in practice. Plain natural finishes were preferred and colours and textures were carefully considered in each room according to its use and position in the house.

For the first time, timber as a construction and finishing material was valued for its natural grain and colour, instead of being made to resemble moulded plaster or carved stone. Ironically, New Zealand native timbers were less desirable than exotic species such as oak, oregon and redwood which were part of the style in America. So wooden floors and walls were stained dark to conceal their natural colour — "a good way with rimu is to stain it with bi-chromate of potash solution, then oil and varnish. This gives a deep rich tone, bringing up the grain".[23]

tongued and grooved boards, painted typically with five coats of best white lead paint. Later, special sheet linings such as Sanitas board were developed for these rooms.

Architraves around doors and windows were now much plainer than the deeply moulded trims in the villas. Most common was a plain board, either with a shallow bevel over half its face, or simply tapered upwards while the architrave over the head of the opening tapered each way from the middle.

Panelled walls in the bungalows were generally stained dark, but most other surfaces were light-coloured and this contrast was an important feature of interior colour schemes. Ceilings were painted and walls either painted or covered in wallpapers known as "Art papers". Matt paints were usual for walls and ceilings except in service rooms where lethal doses of lead paint where applied to resist water.

Colour schemes were worked out on a mixture of artistic and pragmatic principles, with generous advice published in magazines and plan books. Kibblewhite, for instance, wrote of one of his designs:

> This little place is a real Bungalow Home . . .
> The interior finishings are carried out in strictly "Mission Style" architecture. Heavy beam ceilings with heavy panelling in the Living Room, Breakfast Room and Hall. Art papers, with finishing timbers in Bed Rooms white enamelled. Kitchen and Bath Room also in white enamel. Other woodwork finished in deep rich brown.[26]

The *New Zealand Architectural and Building Review*, recognising that the kitchen is often the warmest room in the house, recommended dove-grey woodwork with butter colour panels decorated with medallion designs in bright blue:

> Generally the warm colours are cheering and hospitable, while most cool colours are peaceful and soothing. Grey wood-work as well as being

For the outside, contrast was still the rule. Light-coloured weatherboards or stucco were set against dark green or brown facings, green stained shingled walls were framed in white, and in brick houses, white painted stucco could be set against red brickwork with wide black joints.

Bungalow hardware (door handles, window catches, etc.) also came from North America during the twenties, usually with an electroplated finish to resemble antique bronze. But after 1932, as a result of the Ottawa Trade Conference, New Zealand gave preference to British products, from high quality cast bronze fittings to cheap brittle Bakelite fittings for Moderne houses.

In the bathroom and on sink benches, shiny ceramic tiles promised perfect cleanliness. For the kitchen, *terrazzo* (a traditional Italian material) was introduced in 1927 by a British company using Italian labour and marble, in spite of a plea to "train New Zealand lads, aye! and lassies into these 'arts and crafts'".[28] Terrazzo was a type of concrete containing high quality stones, ground and polished to a high gloss for floors and benches.

On wooden floors large bordered carpets or scattered rugs covered the bare boards in living rooms and bedrooms, and English and "Scotch" linoleums in six feet wide rolls were sold for kitchens and bathrooms in a vast range of patterns imitating tiles, parquet and a league of national carpets.

Furniture was robust and simple, and wooden arms and legs were assembled with a minimum of elaboration. Many pieces were modelled on so-called Mission style furniture from California, and oak was favoured for its strength and distinctive grain. Typical of such furniture was the Morris chair with an adjustable reclining back, and upholstered in denim, hessian or patterned moquette. Armchairs were soft and comfortable and also covered with striped or floral moquettes, and cane chairs and tables could be carried out onto porches for casual outdoor seating. "A small tea table for the porch is indispensable," advised the *NZABR,* "as are also easy chairs, a goodly supply of cushions, and if possible, a good hammock."[29]

Where the characteristic Victorian posture had been straight-backed and proper, bungalow furniture encouraged its users to lie back and sprawl.

199. The bathroom —porcelain, ceramic tiles, chrome tubs and mirror glass — "perfect cleanliness". *ATL, Gordon Burt Coll.*

200. The panelled hall with leadlight doors and plate shelf. *ATL, Steffano Webb Coll.*

practical is soothing, and the touches of bright blue in the decorative motifs are very happy.[27]

For living rooms the choice might be a black and white "magpie" effect, or an oriental colour scheme of black and scarlet for the most intrepid. Multi-coloured rooms were considered to be most distinguished, but difficult to achieve.

English houses 1910-1935

BRITISH ORIGINS

The earliest Californian bungalows built in New Zealand were designed by local architects, but most architects in the 1910s and 1920s looked to Britain for inspiration, and many sneered at the "monstrosities, so-called American Bungalows". Their clients were successful and anxious to display their new wealth in houses reminiscent of the "old country".

Although they admitted that "much [might] be learned in the way of labour-saving, sanitation and other details from the American house", they were equally certain that "the English house [gave] the beauty of line, repose and simplicity that should forever be associated with an Englishman's idea of Home".[30]

British architects had been working for wealthy middle-class clients since the 1860s in what had become known as the Arts and Crafts style. This was a movement which grew out of the Gothic Revival and its prophets — Voysey, Webb, William Morris and others — were deeply interested in traditional handcrafted construction and the moral worth of honest toil. They took for their models the cottages and farmhouses of rural England, and built large expensive country houses reminiscent of the simple houses of the poor. They created a domestic architecture which managed to look as if it had always been there, and which appealed to a deep-seated English sense of unity between house and garden.

In late nineteenth century England, however, these privileges could not be reserved for the rich alone, and the vernacular revival spread to large-scale housing through the new *Garden City* movement and its chief advocates Barry Parker and Raymond Unwin. Entire towns were built at Letchworth, Bournville and elsewhere, with modest houses surrounded by generous gardens, wide streets and parks. The houses were much smaller than the original Arts and Crafts buildings, but they were not just scaled-down copies. Their architects designed sensible houses with convenient and practical rooms "large enough to be healthy, comfortable and habitable".[31]

Both the Arts and Crafts and Garden City movements were influential in America, where British architects such as Parker, Baillie-Scott and Ashbee wrote regularly for magazines like *The Craftsman* and the *Ladies Home Journal*. All this contributed to the developing bungalow style, which shared the concern for plain handworked materials and simple domestic comfort.

The same notions fell on fertile ground in suburban New Zealand, where the quarter acre was now firmly established as the unit of new development in towns. Some architects —notably J.W. Chapman-Taylor — built in the pure Arts and Crafts manner, but most New Zealand architects quickly adopted the Garden City aesthetic which gave to their clients a happy sense of continuity with the past. These influences merged in a local idiom which was increasingly affected by elements of the American bungalow style — exposed rafters, bell-cast weatherboards, and so on. But the real lesson of the English house was that each country must develop its own vernacular tradition, and it was left to New Zealand builders to produce a version of the *English Cottage* style for those of more modest means who still cherished an Anglo-Saxon lineage.

ENGLISH COTTAGE STYLE

With the obliging help of the plan book designers, builders mimicked the work of the local architects with considerable accuracy. What they called *English Cottage* style was generally a two-storeyed (or often 1½-storeyed) house with the steep pitch of the main roof sweeping low to the ground over a porch, and broken by dormers and lesser roofs.

201. A house in the Arts and Crafts style.(J.W. Chapman-Taylor architect), Takapuna.

202. A 1920 plan-book house in the English Cottage style, from R.W. Kibblewhite's *Popular Modern Homes*, Devonport.

Often the change of floor level was marked by a change of wall covering. For the upper wall this might be exposed black-painted stickwork over a white sheet material to give a vaguely Tudor effect. At the same time the upper floor might be "jettied" (i.e. slightly cantilevered) beyond the lower level in the manner of old Elizabethan houses. A modest bell-casting served the same purpose especially where the walls were weatherboarded.

Small fully divided casement windows, reminiscent of the early colonial houses, were preferred without the bungalow's fanlights. For a Tudor effect, it was only necessary to substitute diamond pane leadlights and perhaps a small projecting

203. English Cottage style,
Wellington:
(a) jettied first floor and
oriel windows.
(b) half-timbering and oriel
window; Tudor.

"oriel" window to emphasise a stair. Arches were popular at the front door and in the front entrance porch, especially with brick or stucco construction. The roof was tiled with Marseilles terracotta tiles, or very occasionally English *rosemary* tiles, or shingled with diagonal asbestos cement slates or, as always, there was corrugated iron.

A related style was the *Swiss Cottage* with its characteristic steep roof rising from the ground floor walls to enclose two or even three storeys. Here again the first floor was jettied, usually only in the gable end wall, and this was emphasised by large shaped brackets. On some of these houses, upper walls were embellished with a lattice of stickwork incorporating scroll-edged raised panels, but in other respects they differed little from the English Cottage style.

In their planning, English Cottage style houses were very like bungalows on two levels. Much the same sort of lives were lived in them, except that wealthier owners might have a live-in maid. Accordingly, kitchen, breakfast room and living room crowded round the hall on the ground floor, with the possible addition of a study or den. Like the bungalows and the original English houses, the living room had its bay window and sometimes an inglenook, and sliding doors joined it to the breakfast room.

The scale of the hall was in proportion to the owner's means, never quite certain whether it was a proper room or simply an overgrown coat cupboard with a stair. The staircase could be rather grand, with several turns and landings before finally reaching the first floor bedrooms sheltering attic-like under the steep roof. In the best houses the stairhall rose through the full height of the house with a gallery at the first floor landing. Bathroom and lavatory shared the first floor with perhaps an additional w.c. under the stair or near the back door. Beyond the kitchen were laundry and coal store, and on the back porch special cupboards for daily delivery of groceries, meat and bread.

Finishes for these houses varied according to the effect the owner wanted. In some cottage style houses, the exterior "English" appearance was duplicated indoors with period furniture and plaster mouldings on walls and ceilings. For most, however, bungalow decor was an acceptable compromise, with perhaps less panelling, lighter colours and more wallpaper.

In the garden English Cottages naturally favoured the familiar deciduous trees of Britain, with flowering shrubs hiding the base of the house, and paths which passed between herbaceous perennial borders. Lawns were carefully planned to present the house from the best angle and shrubs were moved to one side — "Why not let us have a large sward instead of a shrubbery interspersed with grass?"[32]

THE NEW ZEALAND BUNGALOW-COTTAGE

As the American and European styles fused together in the late twenties, the vigorous gestures of the Californian bungalow were subdued. Massive porches vanished or atrophied to a shadow at the entrance, or were simply drawn into the body of the house as a recess. Overall forms were simplified and became less fragmented, and the single dominant roof returned, now with the hip roof increasingly preferred to the gable.

Rafters were once more boxed in at the eaves, and a continuous fascia ruled a dictatorial line around the tops of walls. Bay windows were reduced to a nominal projecting box or a shallow faceted bulge with a flat roof. Brick and roughcast were common, especially in the south, with brick to sill height or to the horizontal *transom* of the fanlight, and plaster above.

New Zealand houses entered the Depression of the 1930s with only vestiges of their Californian and English origins preserved. They had acquired a conservative character that was as nearly indigenous as anything previously produced in this country, and which persisted in New Zealand domestic building for at least three decades.

204. New Zealand
bungalow-cottage style:
(a) recessed porch and
faceted bay window,
Wellington;
(b) minimal porch, and box
window, Devonport.

Exotic interludes 1930~1940

SPANISH MISSION STYLE

In America the bungalow emerged as a distinct building style around the turn of the century, but Southern California had long been settled by descendants of native Indian people and their Spanish conquerors of several centuries earlier. In this hot, dry, treeless region a way of building had evolved which combined indigenous mud brick construction and traditional Spanish motifs to create an architecture well suited to an arid climate. The ingredients of these buildings were thick plastered adobe with half-round Spanish tiles along the top of parapet walls, large courtyards surrounded by deep arcaded verandahs, narrow deep-set windows, wrought iron gates and security screens, and roofs that were flat or hipped simply behind the parapet.

In 1922 an English professor of architecture, Leslie Wilkinson, introduced this style to Australia where it became instantly popular as the *Spanish Mission* or sometimes *Mediterranean* style. The style had already been brilliantly interpreted in New Zealand in the Auckland Grammar School of 1913-16, and in 1925 W.H. Gummer used it in his house at 46 Mountain Road. Quickly gaining popularity Spanish Mission style featured clearly in the 1931 *Home and Garden Services* plan book. These houses brought a little excitement and novelty to a conservative and depressed market, and even if they did not appeal to all tastes, "the beauty of straight lines heightened by a few arches ... [was] becoming more and more appreciated in New Zealand".[33]

In New Zealand adobe was replaced by plastered concrete or Konka board, Spanish tiles by half

drain pipes, and the courtyard by a walled garden. The flat roof hidden behind a parapet had "a great deal to commend it in-so-much that it produce[d], to us, novelty of design". It could be "relieved with porches having tiled roofs and better still, the main roof [could] be of iron, built in the lean-to style with its attendant economy, but hidden behind the surrounding parapet".[34]

This frank admission of deceit was a remarkable contrast to the honesty and directness of the bungalow philosophy. Spanish houses appealed to a minority taste and were often built on leftover sites in earlier bungalow subdivisions or as one of a variety of competing novelties in new developments.

205. Spanish Mission Style
— arches, half-round tiles, ventilation pipes, window grilles, parapets, stucco:
(a) (Left) Devonport;
(b) (Above) Papakura;
(c) (Right) Mt Eden;
(d) (Below) Whakatane.

ENGLISH COTTAGE REVIVAL

A second English Cottage style can be identified as a contemporary of the Spanish Mission style in New Zealand. In many ways these houses were similar to the Spanish house; the distinguising features were the roofs, gabled and preferably asymmetrical, sweeping down low over an entrance porch. A shingled panel on the gable end wall indicated 'Olde English' while painted stick-work signalled a 'Tudor' variant of the style.

Whereas Spanish houses were generally single storeyed, English Cottages were often 1½ storeyed. A small bay window at ground level was permissible and casement windows were usual, often in groups of three with an arch over the middle sash. The glass was once again divided: "Let us glaze each sash with four panes instead of one" suggested *Home and Garden Services*, "Bother the cleaning — it is the effect we want."[35]

(b)

(a)

206. English Cottage
revival:
(a) Devonport;
(b) Epsom;
(c) Ellerslie.

(c)

INTERNATIONAL STYLE
AND MODERNE

The *International* style as the name suggests was another import. It was an architects' style and did not reach the mass-housing market in New Zealand. It was an architecture of great intellectual purity, expressed in prismatic forms, hard edges and minimal surface modelling. Roofs were flat, walls were flat, and windows were large, continuous and flush with the wall surface.

In New Zealand a number of young architects, among them Robin Simpson, H. Hall, H.L. Massey and Ernst Plischke, practised the International style with wit and skill and a determination to reconcile the crisp unbroken forms with weatherboarded frame construction.

Ordinary house buyers and builders were intrigued, sensing that these houses were in some way appropriate to an age of jazz and chromium plate, and the process of "cultural diffusion" ensured that superficial features of the style filtered through into ordinary house design. Of course, it was not necessary to adopt the open planning of the originals, it was simply a matter of a new kind of elevation to an old plan, and the local version added a few delights of its own.

These populist houses in the Moderne style were necessarily flat roofed with the roof concealed behind a parapet as on the Spanish houses. Later examples, learning perhaps from experience with leaks dispensed with the parapet so that the roof lay like a large inclined slab extending beyond the walls. Corrugated iron could be safely laid to a pitch as low as 5 degrees behind parapet walls, but where the roof became a terrace, water was kept out by various forms of paper and fibre, heavily coated with bitumen and heat-sealed over a wooden floor. Two-and even three-storyed houses were common and often the roof of a lower level formed a terrace or porch for the upper. The parapet ran unbroken

207. Slab roof Moderne without parapet, Herne Bay.

208. Moderne style stucco:
(a) Dunedin;
(b) Rotorua;

208. Moderne style stucco:
(c) Papatoetoe;
(d) Papatoetoe;

(e) Ellerslie;
(f) Dargaville.

209. Weatherboard
Moderne, Northcote.

210. Moderne — the
"Waterfall" effect, Ellerslie.

across the front and down each side as far as the
back wall. In practice, it usually stepped down once
or twice on its way to the rear and occasionally
flicked up light-heartedly in the centre of the front.
The walls themselves were usually stuccoed with a
lightly textured surface, but inevitably there were
attempts to reproduce the style in weatherboard.
To relieve the utter flatness of stucco walls it was
common to add a few coloured horizontal plaster
bands above the windows — three was a popular
number — and these might be continuous on all
elevations, or broken into short strips over each
window, or again just at corners. The bands contributed to a sense of the horizontal which was

understood to be proper to the Moderne style, but
they were also in part a rebellion against the puri-
tanical plainness of the international prototypes.
Other defiant gestures included decorative plaster
motifs at corners, on chimneys and above windows
and the entrance — rising suns, planets, circles,
squares, lozenges, wedges and even sailing ships.

To reinforce the horizontal emphasis, corners
frequently disappeared as one wall swung round in
a giant curve to meet the adjacent wall, taking with
it a long strip window. In some larger houses these
curved walls were repeated two or three times as
the house stepped back from the street. This
resulted in flowing elevations which earned such

houses the nickname of "Waterfall" style.

Windows were made up in multiples of casements (with no fanlights), and each sash was divided horizontally into three or four panes, as was the front door. For lesser rooms double casements at the side were sufficient, but for added distinction at the front a circular or semi-circular window might be included by the front door or in the door itself. Above the entrance a small cantilevered flat roof sheltered the narrow, shallow porch from which semi-circular concrete steps radiated in tiers.

So powerful were these jazzy elevations that many older houses — villas in particular — were de-roofed and forced into a stucco straitjacket in an attempt to "Moderne-ise" them. The results have usually been unfortunate; the hybrid houses have suffered from disturbing problems of scale and from the worst features of both original and revised styles.

In Moderne houses there were no dramatic advances in planning. The best made use of the freedom allowed under a nearly flat roof and were carefully planned with layouts similar to their bungalow

211. Moderne interiors.
AIM — Sparrow Photo.

contemporaries. Less well-designed examples reverted to the narrow central passage with plain four-square rooms set out on either side. Many were built during the Depression and cheapness was readily confused with economy.

Finishes, however, were in stark contrast with the dark panelled richness of the bungalows. Many of the decorative foibles of Moderne houses were inspired by another aesthetic fashion from overseas known as Art Deco. As the name suggests this was a decorative style, concerned with surfaces; it was most highly developed in commercial buildings such as skyscrapers and new cinema buildings, where reality was suspended on and off the screen in elaborate dramatic facades and interiors. Art Deco was a style of lines and layers with geometric designs being particularly common.

Ordinary cinema-goers, therefore, returned home to their own private film sets of smooth plastered walls and ceilings with deeply moulded cornices (where wall meets ceiling). Everywhere the zigzag outline of the Art Deco skyscraper was repeated as a decorative motif — in fabrics, on wallpaper and linoleums, in stepped plaster mouldings and on light fittings and furniture. Even the

tiled fire surround was stepped. New materials appeared moulded in a machinelike angularity and surfaces in the house were harsh — tiles, glass, steel, Bakelite, plaster, terazzo and chrome plate. Interior colours were equally austere, with black and white combining with chrome plate on hardware and light-fittings. Creams and ochres offered a warmer if somewhat drab decor, with highlights provided by brown bakelite door handles and the mottled ceramic tiles of the fire surround.

Outside, the houses were often stark white, after the International model, with decorative motifs picked out in cream, green or black. The geometric discipline of the house was firmly imposed on the garden, with concrete paths running straight from door to gate flanked by narrow borders of annuals, or just grass. Obedient yew trees stood on either side of the door, and standard roses formed a guard of honour along the path or occupied neat geometric beds in the centre of the lawn.

Moderne was an ephemeral and quirky style and although it was inspired by a respectable architectural philosophy, local owners and builders added their own flourishes to produce individual, endearing houses with all the qualities of folk art.

State houses 1905~1945

In 1905 the Workers' Dwellings Act was passed. This allowed the State to set aside land, and for the first time to build houses for lease to workers at modest rentals. Thirty-four designs were selected from 150 submitted by local architects, but the workers were reluctant to rent these houses in some areas because of cost and poor public transport. A second Act passed in 1910 increased the loan limits and encouraged tenants to buy the houses over a period of twenty-five years. A maximum cost was set at £600 pounds and the booklet of plans that was published showed houses in the Transitional style. The Housing Act of 1919 increased the cost limits further, and the Department of Labour produced more designs in a loose English bungalow style, although applicants could present their own designs for consideration. These early State houses were, however, still beyond the

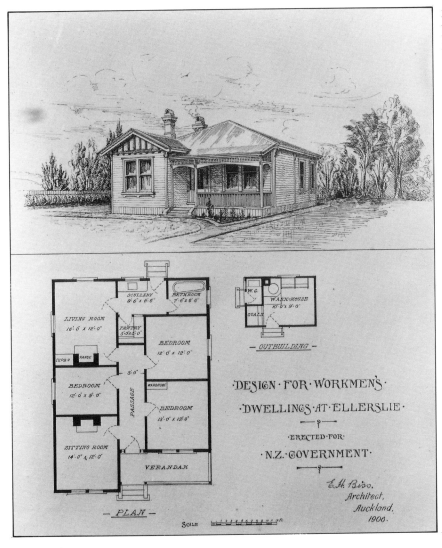

212. Plan and perspective view of a Workers' Dwellings Act (1905) house by the architect E.H. Biss.

227

213. Workers' Dwellings Act (1905) houses at Ellerslie.

reach of many, and relatively few were built (about 650 between 1905 and 1919, and a further 600 up till 1934).

The newly elected Labour Government of 1935 decided to make State rental housing available once more and established the Department of Housing Construction with its own architectural staff. The policy was to build well-designed houses of good materials and to let them to worker tenants at very low rentals. The department's architects produced a range of well-planned houses which developed from the late bungalows of mixed American and English origins, taking a compact form and stripping away the last remnants of porches, bay win-

dows, pergolas and verandahs. Roofs were mostly hipped and tiled with only a nominal overhang at the eaves. Windows were casements with high sills (no fanlights), and walls were brick veneer for permanence and low maintenance, or weatherboard for economy.

The State architects toyed with the International style with more precision than the builders' Moderne, but the brick-and-tile hipped roof aesthetic predominated and became a solid base for government and private housing for at least two decades. These houses were born of a desire to build well but not extravagantly and by 1940, 9395 State houses had been built in regimented subdivisions from a range of more than 300 plans. So although no two houses in a street needed to be identical, the economics of standardised details produced a controlled aesthetic which left no room for self-expression or eccentricity.

These safe but unspectacular houses were a God-send to many New Zealanders in the aftermath of a depression, but as always in this country there were restless souls who sought their own salvation. In the late thirties young architects such as Paul Pascoe and Vernon Brown built houses which grew out of the New Zealand landscape and acknowledged a New Zealand style of life. They adapted the ideals of the Modern Movement in fresh unassuming houses which owed little to the fashions of England and America. They set standards of planning which became commonplace only many years later. For the first time local architects designed local buildings of a high standard of ordinariness which could be set comfortably in any New Zealand town or city suburb, yet which held the beginnings of a more exuberant and experimental way of making houses. It was in these low-slung, well-planned houses that New Zealand architects first began to find themselves "at home" in their own country.

> I do not dream of Sussex Downs
> or quaint old England's quaint old towns:
> I think of what will yet be seen
> in Johnsonville and Geraldine.[36]

Glossary
of building terminology

NOTE: Words listed here are explained as generally understood in present-day New Zealand. The precise meanings of some terms derived from classical architecture are not necessarily those commonly used today.

adobe	or "mud brick" — large moulded blocks of *cob* mixture, dried in the air, and laid like bricks with a clay mortar, to form thick walls
angle stop corner	a solid timber piece fitted at the outside corners of weatherboarded walls and against which the weatherboards finish — cf. *boxed* corner
architrave	a wooden (usually) board fixed as a frame around an opening in a wall, and covering the joint between the wall and the lining in the opening
balloon frame	an American system of frame construction in which *studs* run full height in walls, and intermediate floors are supported from the cast iron sides of studs or from secondary *plates* on the face of the studs — cf. *platform* frame.
balustrade	a panel beneath the handrail of a stair or verandah, made up of an arrangement of boards or shaped pieces of wood (balusters), or cast iron; most often as a decorative element
barge board	a board covering the exposed edge of a gable roof — very often decorated
bearer	the lowest member in the house frame, sitting directly on the foundations
bed moulding	a moulded timber bead fixed around the edge of a timber panel in a door or on a wall, and set *within* the opening made for the panel — cf. *bolection* moulding
bolection moulding	a moulded timber bead fixed around the edge of a timber panel in a door or on a wall, and set partly within the panel opening but overlapping the edge of the opening
boxed corner	boards fixed over weatherboards at outside corners of a house to exclude water — cf. *angle stop corner*
came	a flexible lead strip for joining pieces of glass (i.e. for "lead lighting")
casement	a hinged window — usually hinged at the side but sometimes at the top or the bottom — cf. *sash*
cast iron	iron building components formed by pouring molten iron into prepared moulds — cf. *wrought iron*
"catslide" roof	see "saltbox"
"Chicago" window	a composite window made up of centre panel and two narrow side panels — usually double hung sashes — named for a typical office window in Chicago in the 1890s
clerestory window	a window located above the main roof line, or high on one wall
cob	a mixture of clay, water, chopped straw or grass (in New Zealand tussock or wiwi), and often animal manure, all

231

thoroughly mixed and trodden in layers to form walls

cornice an ornamental moulding around the edge of a ceiling to cover the junction between wall and ceiling

dado a special treatment of the lower part of an internal wall; for decorative effect, or to resist damage by furniture, etc.

deal the nineteenth century name for a plain board, usually up to about 40 mm thickness

dormer a small window letting light into an upper floor through the roof, with its own small roof, in a variety of forms

double-hung (sashes) counter-balanced windows where each *sash* is balanced by a weight connected to it by a cord which runs over a pulley set in the window surround

eaves the projection of the roof beyond the walls; hence:
"flush eaves" — no projection
"boxed eaves" — projecting roof lined on the underside or soffit

fanlight a small opening window over a larger casement or sash window (originally a semi-circular window above the entrance in Georgian houses with fan-shaped radiating glass panels)

fascia a board under the edge of the roof at the *eaves*, to support spouting and to divert water away from the wall

finial a tall narrow shaped projection at the apex of a gable roof in nineteenth century houses

flashing folded metal strips fixed around junctions in roof coverings to prevent entry of water; also around openings in walls for the same purpose

gable the triangular shaped wall at the end of a ridged roof, i.e. of a "gab roof"

hip (roof) the junction between two roof planes, usually a line from ridge to eaves

jamb part of a wall either side of a door or window opening

joist horizontal framing member supporting a floor or ceiling

key (in plastering) the roughening of a surface to be plastered, to enable the plaster to grip the surface

lath a thin strip of wood, usually fixed to framing as a base for plastering

light a pane of glass within a divided window; the window is described by the number of *lights* it contains — for example, a 6-light *sash*

matchlining (matched lining) thin *tongued and grooved* boarding with edges angled to form a V at joints; widely used to cover interior walls and ceilings, especially in kitchens and bathrooms

modillion a wide, shaped and carved bracket supporting the boxed *eaves* of the roof

mortise a rectangular hole cut into a piece of wood to receive the corresponding shaped end *(tenon)* of another piece which is to be joined to it

newel a carved or turned post at the top and bottom of a stair, to which the handrail is attached

nog (or dwang) a short piece of framing timber fixed tightly between *studs*, to which lining materials are fixed

pan iron flat iron roofing sheets with edges turned up against adjacent sheets and covered over to exclude water

pediment a triangular or arched false "gable" above a door or window

pilaster a simulated rectangular column, or half column built into a wall

232

pisé — a mixture of earth, small gravel, and very little water, rammed into prepared forms with a special tool (a *pisoir*). An ancient construction revived in France in the eighteenth century — rarely used in N.Z.

plate (in wall framing) — horizontal framing members at the bottom and top of the wall

platform frame — the usual system of frame construction in New Zealand *studs* run only one storey height in walls and finish under a top *plate* — cf. *balloon* frame

pugmill — a mechanical device used to break clay down in preparation for brickmaking

purlin — a roof framing member fixed over the rafters, and to which the roof covering is fixed

quoin — a large masonry block, usually stone, placed at the corners of buildings and copied in timber on many New Zealand houses where it was sometimes referred to as "long and short" work

rising damp — moisture from the ground drawn up into masonry walls through capillary action

saddle poles — straight tree branches lashed together at one end and placed over the ridge of a roof to prevent thatch or bark coverings from blowing away

"saltbox" roof — (or "catslide") — a *gable* roof with lean-to additional rooms, where the roof runs direct from gable ridge to lean-to eaves

scantlings — nineteenth century term for framing timbers — i.e. thicker than about 50 mm

sash — window usually sliding vertically (*double-hung*) — cf. *casement*

scriber — a thin batten with one edge cut to the shape of the wall covering material and fixed to the edge of an *architrave* or *boxed corner* to exclude water

shake — a thin board slightly tapered in thickness and fixed in layers and rows as a roof covering — shakes were split by hand from solid timber — cf. *shingle*

shingle — a machine sawn *shake*

skillion (roof) — a single-pitch roof or "lean-to" attached to a building to enclose extra rooms; also knowns as a *skilling*

skirting — a timber board fixed around the edge of a room to cover the junction between wall and floor

soaker — a folded metal sheet nailed over joints in weatherboards, especially at the mitred corners of a wall

stucco — a coat of plaster applied over a wall surface as both decorative and weathering finish

stud — a vertical wall framing member

tenon — the end of a piece of wood reduced to fit a corresponding hole in another piece (*mortise*)

tongue and groove — shaped edges on interlocking boards — one edge with a groove cut out, one edge with a corresponding projecting tongue

transom — a horizontal division between parts of a window

truss — a carved bracket used to support mantelpieces, arches, etc. inside the house

valley gutter — a metal drain formed under the roof covering where two roof planes meet on an "internal" angle

wattle and daub — walls made of wickerwork or woven *wattles* (thin branches) and plastered by hand with mud or clay thrown on both sides

wrought iron — iron strap shaped and joined (i.e. *wrought*) by hand in the forge — cf. *cast iron*

Notes and references

Introduction

1. W. Hurst Seager, "Architectural Art in New Zealand", *Journal of Royal Institute of British Architects,* vol. VII, No.19, September 1900, pp.480-491.
2. Frederick de Jersey Clere, "Domestic Architecture in New Zealand", *Studio Year Book of Decorative Art 1916* pp.121-136.
3. W.H. Seager, op. cit., 1900. p.480.
4. James Fitzgerald, *The Nature of Art: A Lecture,* 1868, p.12.
5. F. de J. Clere, op. cit., 1916, p.122.
6. Ibid, p.122.
7. Anon., "The Trend of House Design", *Building Progress,* December 1938, p.15.
8. R.K. Binney, "In New Zealand — The English Tradition", *The Architectural Review,* vol. LVI, No.336, May 1927, p.172.
9. A.P. Pascoe, "Houses", *Making New Zealand* (ed. McLintock), vol. 2, No. 20, 1940, pp.6-31.
10. Ibid, p.24.
11. G. Rawlinson, introduction to *The Godwits Fly* by Robin Hyde, 1980, p.ix.
12. Order in Council, 1970.
13. R.B. Cooke et al, *Housing in New Zealand: Report of the Commission of Inquiry,* 1971, p.90.
14. C. Fearnley, "Colonial Houses", *New Zealand's Heritage,* 21, 1972, pp.572-578; and J. Stacpoole, "Architecture in the 1870s", *New Zealand's Heritage,* 45, 1972, pp.1239-1244.
15. J. Stacpoole, *Colonial Architecture in New Zealand,* 1976.
16. C. Cochran, *Restoring a New Zealand House,* 1980.
17. George Eliot, *Adam Bede,* Signet, 1961, p.455.

1. The first houses 1800-1860

1. N. Prickett, "An Archaeologist's Guide to the Maori Dwelling", *New Zealand Journal of Archaeology,* vol. 4, 1982, p.111-147.
2. W.B. Monkhouse, *The Voyage of the Endeavour 1768-1771* (ed. J.C. Beaglehole), 1968, p.584.
3. Robert McNab, *Historical Records of New Zealand,* 1908, p.114.
4. N. Prickett, op. cit., 1982, p.140.
5. Marion du Fresne, *Early Eyewitness Accounts of Maori Life 2* (trans. I. Ollivier), 1982, p.133.
6. J. Banks, *The Endeavour Journal of Joseph Banks 1768-1771* (ed. J.C. Beaglehole), 1962, p.418.
7. Captain James Cook, *The Voyage of the Endeavour 1768-1771* (ed. J.C. Beaglehole), 1968, p.60
8. Captain Raven in Robert McNab, op. cit., 1908, p.114.
9. S. Northcote-Bade, *Colonial Furniture in New Zealand,* 1971, p.14 note 3.
10. E.J. Wakefield, *Adventure in New Zealand from 1839 to 1844,* vol. I, 1845, pp.44 and 330-1.
11. J.C. Bidwell, *Rambles in New Zealand,* 1841, p.3.
12. E.J. Wakefield, op. cit., vol. I, 1845, p.186.
13. Edward Markham, *New Zealand or Recollections of It* (ed. E.H. McCormick), 1963, p.41.
14. Ibid, p.40.
15. See J. Stacpoole, *A Guide to the Waimate Mission House,* 1971, for an account of the Mission station.
16. Lady Martin, *Our Maoris,* 1884, p.41.
17. W. Yate, *An Account of New Zealand,* 1835, p.196-7.
18. S. Marsden, in E.J. McNab, op. cit., 1908, p.121.
19. Ibid, p.73.
20. R.A. Cruise, *Journal of a Ten Months' Residence in New Zealand,* 1824, p.261.
21. Augustus Earle, *Narrative of a Residence in New Zealand* (ed. E.H. McCormick), 1966, p.65.
22. Sir J. Vogel in the *Official Handbook of New Zealand 1875* gives figures of 13,128 for 1843 and 26,707 for 1851.
23. E.J. Wakefield, op. cit., vol. I, 1845, pp.196-7.
24. Ibid, p.466.
25. E.J. Wakefield, *The Hand Book for New Zealand,* 1848, p.446.
26. Stevan Eldred-Grigg, *A New History of Canterbury,* 1982, pp.29-30.
27. E.J. Wakefield, op. cit., 1848.
28. G.B. Earp, *New Zealand: Its Emigration and Gold Fields,* 1852.
29. C. Hursthouse, *New Zealand, the "Britain of the South",* 1861.
30. E.J. Wakefield, op. cit., 1848, p.446.
31. S. Northcote-Bade, op. cit., 1971, p.32.
32. R.M. Ross, "Waitangi Treaty House", *Historic Buildings of New Zealand: North Island,* 1979, p.49.
33. Letters from New Plymouth.
34. T. Simpson, *Kauri to Radiata,* 1940, pp.72-3.
35. E.J. Wakefield, op. cit., vol. I, 1845, p.200.
36. *Daily Southern Cross,* 27 July 1849, p.3.
37. See Alex Bowman, quoting Mr Westenra's recollections, in his thesis "The Study of the Historical Development of Domestic Architecture in Canterbury, New Zealand", 1941, p.54.
38. C. Hursthouse, op. cit., 1861, p.269.
39. Sir J. Vogel, op. cit., 1875, p.240.
40. E.B. Fitton, *New Zealand, Its Present Condition,* 1856, p.283.
41. E.J. Wakefield, op. cit., vol. I, 1845, pp.380-1.
42. E. Dieffenbach, *Travels in New Zealand,* vol. II, 1843, p.7
43. C. Hursthouse, op. cit., 1861, p.202.
44. S. Northcote-Bade, op. cit., 1971, p.34.
45. C.F. Innocent, *The Development of English Building Construction* 1916, pp.125 and 135.
46. A.D. Best, *The Journal of Ensign Best 1837-1843* (ed. N.M. Taylor), 1966, p.226.
47. S. Northcote-Bade, op. cit., 1971, p.19.
48. From a settler in Otago to his parents in *Letters from Otago 1848-1849,* 1978, pp.33-34.
49. Ibid, p.43.

50. T.L. Buick, *The French at Akaroa*, 1928, p.150.

51. J.C. Andersen, *Old Christchurch in Picture and Story*, 1949, p.65.

52. A.P. Pascoe, "The Study of the Early Buildings in the Canterbury Settlement of New Zealand", 1935, p.49.

53. Howard & Heber Lakeman in *Letters from Otago 1848-1849*, 1978, p.25.

54. R.W. Brunskill, *Illustrated Handbook of Vernacular Architecture*, 1978, pp.50-51.

55. E.B. Fitton, op. cit., 1856, pp.244 and 247.

56. E.C. Studholme, *Te Waimate, Early Station Life in New Zealand*, 1940, p.1.

57. O.A. Gillespie, *South Canterbury: A Record of Settlement*, 1958, p.259-60.

58. C. Godley, *Letters from Early New Zealand 1850-1853* (ed. J.R. Godley), 1951, p.159.

59. C.F. Innocent, op. cit., 1916, p.136.

60. E. Richmond (ed.), "Letters of the Richmond Atkinsons", t/s, 1942, p.140.

61. R. Reid, *The Shell Book of Cottages*, 1977, p.185.

62. G.B. Earp, op. cit., 1853, p.220.

63. Herries Beattie, *Early Runholding in Otago*, 1947, p.77.

64. E.B. Fitton, op. cit., 1856, p.246.

65. C.W. Hursthouse, op. cit., 1861, p.202.

66. A.P. Pascoe, op. cit., 1935, p.49.

67. M.B. Lewis, *Victorian Primitive*, 1977, p.43-50.

68. A.D. Mead, *Richard Taylor Missionary Tramper*, 1966, p.122-3.

69. See G.F. Wilson, "A Pictorial Survey of Housing in New Zealand", *Design Review*, vol. 2, Nos 3-6, 1949, p.50.

70. B. Harper, *Petticoat Pioneers: South Island Women of the Colonial Era*, Book 3, 1980, p.172.

71. W.T. Pratt ("An Old Colonist"), *Colonial Experiences*, 1877, p.71.

72. For an account of Pompallier House see R.M. Ross, *A Guide to Pompallier House*, 1970.

73. Ibid, pp.13-14.

74. E.J. Wakefield, op. cit., vol. I, 1845, pp.295 and 422.

75. J.M. Stacpoole, op. cit., 1971, p.38.

76. See H.D. Mullon, *Letters from New Plymouth 1843*, 1968, p.77.

77. See Charles Brown, bricklayer, in *Letters from Settlers and Labouring Emigrants in the New Zealand Company's Settlements of Wellington, Nelson and New Plymouth*, 1843, p.44.

78. E.J. Wakefield, op. cit., vol. II, 1845, p.161.

79. From a settler in Otago to his parents, *Letters from Otago 1848-1849*, 1978, p.33.

80. C. Heaphy, *Narrative of a Residence in Various Parts of New Zealand*, 1842, pp.86-7.

81. A.H. Reed, *The Story of Early Dunedin*, 1956, p.52.

82. H. Knight, *Otago Peninsula*, 1979, p.58.

83. R.S. Burn, *The Colonist's and Emigrant's Handbook of the Mechanical Arts*, 1854, pp.92-94.

84. A. Drummond, *Married and Gone to New Zealand*, 1960, p.78.

85. E.J. Wakefield, op. cit., vol. II, 1845, p.307.

86. *Auckland Times*, 1 March 1843.

87. E.B. Fitton, op. cit., 1856, pp.244-5.

88. C. Godley, op. cit., 1951, p.41.

89. For an account of stone houses in England see R.J. Brown, *The English Country Cottage*, 1979, pp.159-193.

90. M. MacGregor, *Etiquette and Elbowgrease*, 1976, p.5.

91. *The Canterbury Colony: Its Site and Prospects*, Hocken Reprint Series No. 2, 1976, p.59.

92. C. Hursthouse, op. cit., 1861, p.201.

93. A. Marjoribanks, *Travels in New Zealand*, 1845, p.81.

94. W. Yate, op. cit., 1835, pp.36-51.

95. Ibid, p.51.

96. J. Adam, *Twenty-five Years of Emigrant Life in New Zealand*, 1876, p.37.

97. See *Letters from Otago 1848-1849*, 1978, p.34.

98. C. Godley, op. cit., 1951, p.21.

99. R.S. Burn, op. cit., 1854, pp.43-6.

100. C. Hursthouse, op. cit., 1861, pp.202-3.

101. T.W. Leys (ed.), *Brett's Colonists' Guide and Cyclopaedia*, 1883, pp.16-17.

102. S. Butler, *A First Year in Canterbury Settlement and Other Early Essays* (eds. H.F. Jones and A.T. Bartholomew), 1923, pp.176-7.

103. *Letters from Otago 1848-1849*, 1978, p.34.

104. P. Freeman, *The Homestead: A Riverina Anthology*, 1982, pp.16-17.

105. E.J. Wakefield, op. cit., vol. I, 1845, p.412.

106. G.G. Thornton, *New Zealand's Industrial Heritage*, 1982, p.18.

107. E.J. Wakefield, op. cit., vol. II, 1845, pp.160, 439, 281.

108. D. Scott, *Inheritors of a Dream*, 1962, p.35-36.

109. A. Bowman, op. cit., 1941, p.51.

110. C. Godley, op. cit., 1951, p.170.

111. Ibid, p.74.

112. Sir J. Vogel, op. cit., 1875, p.55.

113. P. Nicholson, *The New Practical Builder and Workman's Companion*, 1823, p.206.

114. J. Gwilt, *An Encyclopaedia of Architecture*, rev. Papworth, 1881, p.1339.

115. Sir J. Vogel, op. cit., 1875, pp.214 and 240.

116. C. Hursthouse, op. cit., 1861, p.202.

117. "An Old Emigrant", "Emigration to New Zealand or the Emigrant's Handbook", (MS.), 1863, p.11.

118. Sir J. Vogel, op. cit., 1875, p.119.

119. G.B. Earp, op. cit., 1853, p.222.

120. C. Godley, op. cit., 1951, p.32.

121. J. Fitzgerald, op. cit., 1868, pp.11-12.

122. C. Godley, op. cit., 1951, p.85.

123. G.B. Earp, op. cit., 1853, pp.222-3.

124. E.C. Studholme, op. cit., 1940, p.194.

125. Acland in A.P. Pascoe, op. cit., 1935, p.45.

126. E.J. Wakefield, op. cit., 1848, p.446.

127. G.B. Earp, op. cit., 1853, p.218.

128. E. Dieffenbach, op. cit., vol. I, 1843, pp.37-8.

129. R.S. Burn, op. cit., 1854, p.42.

130. W.T. Pratt op. cit., 1877, p.15.

131. E.B. Fitton, op. cit., 1856, p.80.

132. C. Hursthouse, op. cit., 1861, p.269.

133. C. Godley, op. cit., 1951, p.44.

134. P. Nicholson, op. cit., 1823.

135. R.S. Burn, op. cit., 1854, pp.73-7.

136. Advertisement in the *New Zealand Directory for 1866-67*, p.24.

137. Sir J. Vogel, op. cit., 1875, p.240.

138. E.J. Wakefield, op. cit., 1848, p.446.
139. Lady Martin, op. cit., 1884, p.12.
140. Sir J.L. Campbell, *Poenamo: Sketches of the Early Days in New Zealand,* 1881, pp.154-6.
141. A.P. Pascoe, op. cit., 1935, p.53.
142. Sir J. Vogel, op. cit., 1875, p.240.
143. For an authoritative account of colonial furniture see S. Northcote-Bade, *Colonial Furniture in New Zealand,* 1971.
144. C. Hursthouse, op. cit., 1861, p.448.
145. *Letters from Otago 1848-1849,* 1978, p.38.
146. J.C. Andersen, op. cit., 1949, p.66.
147. R.S. Burn, op. cit., 1854, pp.98-100.
148. T.W. Leys, op. cit., 1883, p.561.
149. R. Sales distinguishes "built-in" and "built-on" lean-to roofs in his B.Arch sub-thesis "Early N.Z. Settler Cottages 1850-70".
150. E.B. Fitton, op. cit., 1856, p.246.
151. R.S. Burn, op. cit., 1854, p.2.
152. C. Godley, op. cit., 1951, pp.289-90.
153. C. Hursthouse, op. cit., 1861, p.271.
154. J.M. Freeland, *Architecture in Australia: A History,* 1968, p.75
155. C. Godley, op. cit., 1951, p.226.
156. S. Northcote-Bade, op. cit., 1971, p.24.
157. A. Rapoport, *House, Form and Culture,* 1969, pp.1-8.

II. Victorian villas and cottages 1860-1910

1. J.A. Froude, *Oceania or England and Her Colonies,* 1886, p.247.
2. E.J. Wakefield, op. cit., vol. II, 1845, p.160.
3. Advertisement in *Auckland Almanac and Directory,* 1856.
4. Advertisement in *Chapman's New Zealand Almanac,* 1861.
5. Advertisements in the *New Zealand Almanac Advertiser,* 1864.
6. J. Bathgate, *New Zealand Its Resources and Prospects,* 1883, p.77.
7. A. Clayden, *A Popular Handbook to New Zealand,* 1886, pp.165 and 167.
8. T. Kirk, the Conservator of State Forests, quoted by R.C.J. Stone in *Makers of Fortune,* 1973, p.97.
9. Ibid, p.111.
10. Penman, unpublished recollections of the building trade in the early twentieth century, collected by J.T. Diamond, pp.4-6.
11. *Daily Southern Cross,* 10 January 1865, p.1.
12. Anon., *The Province of Otago,* 1868, p.51.
13. Advertisement in *The Southern Provinces Almanac, Directory and Year-Book for 1862.*
14. G.G. Thornton, op. cit., 1982, p.120.
15. G. Herbert, *Pioneers of Prefabrication,* 1978, p.37.
16. Advertisement in *Wise's Directory of New Zealand,* 1875-6, p.178.
17. Advertisement in *Chapman's Auckland Directory,* 1873-4, p.446.
18. E.J. Wakefield, op. cit., 1845, vol. I, p.446.
19. J.M. Freeland, op. cit., 1968, p.108.
20. Advertisement in *The New Zealand Almanac — 1866,* p.66.
21. C. Tomlinson, *Illustrations of Useful Arts and Manufactures,* 1858, p.66.
22. A. Polak, *Glass, Its Makers and Its Public,* 1975, p.167.
23. F. de J. Clere, op. cit., 1916, p.122.
24. Advertisement in *Chapman's New Zealand Almanac — 1862,* p.63.
25. Advertisement in *Wellington Almanac,* 1879, p.63.
26. H. Budden, *A Colonial Nurseryman's Catalogue,* reprinted 1979.
27. See R.O. Clark's *Illustrated Price List* for "Patent Earthenware House Block with Bricks", 1904, p.47.
28. F. de J. Clere, "Reminiscences of Architectural Practice", *NZIA Journal,* April 1935, pp.20-21.
29. R. Moxley (ed.), *The Province of Otago,* 1868, p.51.
30. See *Mitchell's Building Construction,* 1959, p.225.
31. *Beautiful Homes and Public Buildings in New Zealand,* Briscoe and Company Ltd, c.1905, p.15.
32. Advertisement in *Cleave's Auckland Directory, 1890,* p.xxxix.
33. Penman M.S., op. cit., c.1960, p.2.
34. Advertisement in *The Wellington Almanac,* 1879, p.65.
35. Advertisement in *The Auckland Director,* 1882, p.28.
36. E. Dobson, *Pioneer Engineering,* 1877, pp.126-127.
37. Advertisement in *The Auckland Almanac and Directory,* 1856.
38. R. Boyd, *Australia's Home,* 1968, p.37.
39. A.J. Downing, *Cottage Residences,* 1880, p.201.
40. G. Shoppell, *Shoppell's Modern Homes,* 1890, p.10.
41. H.H. Holly, *Modern Dwellings in Town and Country,* 1878, p.26.
42. Ibid, p.27.
43. C. Vaux, *Villas and Cottages,* 1864, p.68.
44. C. Cochran, op. cit., 1980, p.62. Two Australian books give additional detailed colour schemes for houses of the period and would be relevant to New Zealand: I. Evans, C. Lucas and I. Stapleton, *Colour Schemes for Old Australian Houses,* 1984; H. Tanner, P. Cox, P. Bridges and J. Broadbent, *Restoring Old Australian Houses and Buildings,* 1975, appendices I and II.
45. Penman M.S., op., c.1960, p.6.
46. C. Dresser, *The Technical Educator,* vol. II, c.1900, p.120.
47. Briscoe and Company Ltd., c.1905, p.13.
48. Ibid, p.53.
49. C. Dresser, op. cit., c.1900, p.120.
50. Anon., "Homes and Architecture: Book Plan Copying Dangerous", *New Zealand Architectural and Building Review,* 30 Sept. 1927, p.9.
51. J. Gwilt, op. cit., 1881, p.1339.
52. *Weekly News,* 30 July 1864, p.20.
53. H.H. Holly, *Holly's Country Seats,* 1863, p.29.
54. F. de J. Clere, op. cit., 1916, p.123.
55. Anon., "Dominion Homes", supplements to *Progress,* 1915, p.1.

III. The bungalow and beyond 1910-1940

1. Keyes, Mann & Co., *Modern Homes of New Zealand*, 1917, p.2.
2. R.A. "Bungalow" Briggs, *Bungalows and Country Residences*, 1901, p.v.
3. C. Lancaster, *The Japanese Influence in America*, 1963, p.104.
4. R.R. Phillips, *The Book of Bungalows*, 1920, p.40.
5. M.D. Hite, "Defending the Bungalow", *Bungalow Magazine*, January 1914, p.43.
6. Anon., "Homes and Architecture: Book Plan Copying Dangerous", *NZABR*, 30 Sept. 1927, p.9.
7. J.L. Hanna, *Modern New Zealand Homes*, 1931, p.22.
8. Jas. Christie, *New Zealand Homes, 60 Practical Designs*, 1915, p.12.
9. E.W. Rogerson uses this expression in his unpublished M.A. thesis "Cosy Homes Multiply", 1976, p.138.
10. M.U. Bethell, "Detail", *An Anthology of Twentieth Century New Zealand Poetry*, (ed. V. O'Sullivan), 1976, p.11.
11. M.U. Bethell, "Erica", op. cit., p.12.
12. Anon., "Homes and Architecture: Book Plan Copying Dangerous", *NZABR*, 30 Sept. 1927, p.9.
13. Ibid, July 1926, p.6.
14. J.L. Hanna, op. cit., p.30.
15. J.L. Hanna, op. cit., p.30.
16. James Hardie & Co. Catalogue, *The Home You Want: The Fibrolite Bungalow*, c.1920s, p.8.
17. Advertisement in *The N.Z. Building Record*, July 1924, p.24.
18. Anon., "The Modern Home: What the Modern Wife Wants", *The N.Z. Building Record*, 15 July 1926, p.6.
19. Anon., "Hot Water Services", *Building Progress*, vol. II, No. 4, April 1937, p.6.
20. Anon., "Refrigerators", *NZABR*, 29 February 1928, p.13.
21. Anon., "Electricity in the Home", *NZABR*, July 1926, p.30.
22. M.D. Hite, "Defending the Bungalow", *Bungalow Magazine*, January 1914, p.40.
23. B. Hooper, "The Model House — And how to obtain it!", *N.Z. Architectural & Building Review*, 10 June 1926, p.18.
24. James Hardie & Co. Catalogue, op. cit., c.1920s, p.9.
25. Advertisement in supplement to *N.Z. Building Record*, 15 July 1925.
26. R.W. Kibblewhite, *Practical Book on Bungalows*, c.1928, p.23.
27. Anon., "One Woman to Another", *New Zealand Architectural & Building Review*, August 1926, pp.30-32.
28. Anon., "Mosaic-Terrazzo", *N.Z. Architectural & Building Review*, 30 July 1927, p.15.
29. Anon., "One Woman to Another", op. cit., August 1926, pp.30-32.
30. Anon., "Homes and Architecture", op. cit., 30 September 1927.
31. B. Parker & E.R. Unwin, *The Art of Building a House*, 1901, p.3.
32. J.L. Hanna, op. cit., p.48.
33. Ibid, p.18.
34. Ibid, p.22.
35. Ibid, p.42.
36. Denis Glover, "House Thoughts", *Thirteen Poems*, 1939.

Bibliography

Early accounts and early settlers

Adam, J. *Twenty-five Years of Emigrant Life in New Zealand*, Edinburgh, 1876.

Bagnall, A.C. & G.C. Peterson, *William Colenso, His Life and Journeys*, A.H. & A.W. Reed, Wellington, 1948.

Banks, J. *The Endeavour Journal of Joseph Banks 1768-1771*, ed. J.C. Beaglehole, Angus and Robertson, Sydney, 1962.

Beaglehole, J.C. *The Voyage of the Endeavour 1768-1771*, Cambridge University Press, Cambridge, 1968.

Best, Abel Dottin. *The Journal of Ensign Best 1837-1843*, ed. Nancy M. Taylor, Government Printer, Wellington, 1966.

Bidwell, John Carne. *Rambles in New Zealand*, W. S. Orr & Co., London, 1841.

Butler, Samuel. *A First Year in Canterbury Settlement and Other Early Essays*, eds. H.F. Jones & A.T. Bartholomew, Jonathan Cape, London, 1923.

Campbell, Jessie. "Letter from Wanganui", 4 December 1842, (typescript in Alexander Turnbull Library).

Campbell, John Logan. *Poenamo: Sketches of the Early Days in New Zealand*, Williams and Norgate, London, 1881.

The Canterbury Colony, Reprint Series No. 2, Hocken Library, Dunedin, 1976.

Carter, C.R. *Life and Recollections of a New Zealand Colonist*, R. Madley, London, 1866.

Cruise, R.A. *Journal of a Ten Months' Residence in New Zealand*, Longman, Hurst, Rees, Orme, Brown and Green, London, 1824.

Darwin, Charles. *The Voyage of the Beagle*, J.M. Dent and Sons Ltd, New York, 1980.

Dieffenbach, Ernest. *Travels in New Zealand* (2 vols), John Murray, London, 1843.

Earle, Augustus. *Narrative of a Residence in New Zealand*, ed. McCormick, The Clarendon Press, Oxford, 1966.

Fitzgerald, James. *The Nature of Art: A Lecture*, The Independent Office, Wellington, 1868.

Fitzroy, Robert. *Remarks on New Zealand*, W. and H. White, London, 1846.

Fuller, Francis. *Five Years' Residence in New Zealand*, Williams and Norgate, London, 1859.

Gisborne, William. *The Colony of New Zealand*, E.A. Petherick & Co., London, 1888.

Godley, Charlotte. *Letters from Early New Zealand 1850-1853*, ed. John R. Godley, Whitcombe & Tombs, Christchurch, 1951.

Heaphy, Charles. *Narrative of a Residence in Various Parts of New Zealand*, Smith, Elder and Co., London, 1842.

Innes, C.L. ("Pilgrim"). *Canterbury Sketches*, Lyttelton Times Office, Christchurch, 1879.

Letters from Otago 1848-1849, No. 4 in *Victorian New Zealand*, Reprint Series, Hocken Library, Dunedin, 1978.

Letters from Settlers and Labouring Emigrants in the New Zealand Company's Settlements of Wellington, Nelson, and New Plymouth, Smith, Elder & Co., London, 1843.

McNab, Robert. *Historical Records of New Zealand* (2 vols), Government Printer, Wellington, 1908.

Marjoribanks, Alexander. *Travels in New Zealand*, Smith, Elder and Co., London, 1845.

Markham, Edward. *New Zealand or Recollections of It*, ed. McCormick, Government Printer, Wellington, 1963.

Martin, Lady. *Our Maoris*, Society for Promoting Christian Knowledge, London, 1884.

Mead, A.D. *Richard Taylor Missionary Tramper*, A.H. & A.W. Reed, Wellington, 1966.

Ollivier, Isabel (trans.). *Early Eyewitness Accounts of Maori Life 2*, National Library of New Zealand, Wellington, 1982.

Petre, The Hon. Henry William. *An Account of The Settlements of The New Zealand Company*, Smith, Elder and Co., London, 1842.

Polack, J.S. *New Zealand: Being A Narrative Of Travels & Adventures* (2 vols), Richard Bentley, London, 1838.

Pratt, W.T. ("An Old Colonist") *Colonial Experiences*, Chapman and Hall, London, 1877.

Simmons, Alfred. *Old England and New Zealand*, Edward Stanford, London, 1879.

Taylor, Rev. Richard. *Te Ika a Maui; or New Zealand and its Inhabitants*, Wertheim and MacIntosh, London, 1855.

Wade, W.R. *Journey In The Northern Island of New Zealand*, George Rolwegan, London, 1842.

Wakefield, E.J. *Adventure in New Zealand from 1839 to 1844* (2 vols), John Murray, London, 1845.

Yate, William. *An Account of New Zealand* (1835), A.H. & A.W. Reed, Wellington, 1970.

Almanacs, yearbooks, handbooks & newspapers

Algar, F. *A Handbook To Auckland*, Australian and New Zealand Gazette, London, 1867.

"An Englishman and A Colonist". *Emigration to New Zealand*, Jarrold and Sons, London, 1876.

"An Old Emigrant". "Emigration to New Zealand; or The Emigrant's Handbook", (MS.), 1863.

Bathgate, John. *New Zealand Its Resources And Prospects*, W. & R. Chambers, London, 1883.

Burn, Robert Scott. *The Colonist's and Emigrant's Handbook of the Mechanical Arts*, Blackwood and Sons, Edinburgh and London, 1854.

The Canterbury Colony — Its Site and Prospects, No. 2 in *Victorian New Zealand*, Reprint Series, Hocken Library, Dunedin, 1976.

Clayden, Arthur. *A Popular Handbook to New Zealand*, Wyman & Sons, London, 1886.

Earp, George Butler. *New Zealand: Its Emigration and Gold Fields*, Geo. Routledge & Co., London, 1852.

———*The Emigrant's Guide to New Zealand*,

Geo. Routledge & Co., London, 1849.

The Emigrant's Guide to New Zealand, Stewart and Murray, London, 1848.

Fitton, E.B. *New Zealand: Its Present Condition*, Edward Stanford, London, 1856.

Hursthouse, Charles. *New Zealand, the "Britain of the South"*, Edward Stanford, London, 1861.

Isitt, F. Whitmore. *New Zealand: As It Was In 1870/As It Is In 1880*, Haughton and Co., London, 1880.

Leys, Thomson W. (ed.). *Brett's Colonists' Guide and Cyclopaedia*, Henry Brett, Auckland, 1883, 1887.

May, Joseph. *May's Guide to Farming in New Zealand*, G.T. Chapman, Auckland, 1869.

The New Zealand Year-Book 1886-87, London, 1886.

Pratt, W.T. ("An Old Colonist"). *Colonial Experiences*, Chapman and Hall, London, 1877.

The Province of Otago, The Provincial Government, Dunedin, 1868.

Puseley, D. ("An Englishman"). *The Rise, Progress & Present Condition of New Zealand*, W. Hall, London, 1858.

Silver, S.W. & Co. *Emigration Guide*, The Company, London, 1850.

Stevens, G. & D.H. Bartholomew (comps.). *New Zealand Directory for 1866-67*, Stevens & Bartholomew, Melbourne, 1866.

Vogel, Sir Julius. *The Official Handbook of New Zealand*, Wyman and Sons, London, 1875.

Wakefield, E.J. *The Hand-Book for New Zealand*, John W. Parker, London, 1848.

Willis, Gann & Co. *The New Zealand Handbook*, Willis, Gann and Co., London, 1864.

Yarborough, Alf. Cooke. *A New Field for Emigration*, Bean, Weble, & Co., London, 1885.

New Zealand & local histories

Allan, R.M. *Nelson — A History of Early Settlement*, A.H. & A.W. Reed, Wellington, 1965.

Andersen, Johannes C. *Old Christchurch in Picture and Story*, Simpson and Williams, Christchurch, 1949.

Beattie, Herries. *Early Runholding in Otago*, Dunedin, 1947.

Buick, T. Lindsay. *The French at Akaroa*, Board of Maori Ethnological Research, Wellington, 1928.

Drummond, Alison & L.R. *At Home in New Zealand*, Blackwood & Janet Paul Ltd., Auckland, 1967.

Drummond, Alison. *Married and Gone to New Zealand*, Paul's Book Arcade, Auckland, 1960.

Eldred-Grigg, Stevan. *A New History of Canterbury*, John McIndoe, Dunedin, 1982.

Gillespie, Oliver A. *South Canterbury, A Record of Settlement*, South Canterbury Centennial History Committee, 1958.

Hall-Jones, John. *The South Explored*, A.H. & A.W. Reed, Wellington, 1979.

Harper, Barbara. *Petticoat Pioneers: South Island Women of the Colonial Era*, Book 3, A.H. & A.W. Reed, Wellington, 1980.

Knight, Hardwicke. *Otago Peninsula*, Dunedin, 1979.

MacGregor, Miriam. *Etiquette and Elbowgrease*, A.H. & A.W. Reed, Wellington, 1976.

Natusch, Sheila. *On The Edge Of The Bush*, Craig Printing Co., Invercargill, 1976.

Prickett, Nigel. "An Archaeologist's Guide to the Maori Dwelling", *New Zealand Journal of Archaeology*, vol. 4, 1982.

Scott, Dick. *Inheritors of a Dream*, Ronald Riddell, Auckland, 1962.

Simpson, H.M. *The Women of New Zealand*, Department of Internal Affairs, Wellington, 1940.

Sinclair, Keith. *A History of New Zealand*, Penguin, Harmondsworth, 1969.

Soper, Eileen L. *The Otago Of Our Mothers*, Whitcombe and Tombs, Dunedin, 1948.

Stedman, G.M. "The South Dunedin Flat: A Study of Urbanisation 1849-1965", unpub. M.A. thesis, University of Otago, 1966.

Stone, R.C.J. *Makers of Fortune*, Auckland University Press, Auckland, 1973.

Studholme, E.C. *Te Waimate, Early Station Life in New Zealand*, A.H. & A.W. Reed, Wellington, 1940.

Von Dadelszen, E.J. *Statistical View of Fifty Years' Progress in New Zealand 1856-1905*, Government Printer, Wellington, 1906.

Waite, Fred. *Pioneering in South Otago*, Whitcombe and Tombs, Dunedin, 1948.

Texts on building methods & technology

Bale, M. Powis. *Woodworking Machinery, Its Rise, Progress & Construction*, Crosby, Lockwood & Son, London, 1914.

Blair, W.N. *The Building Materials of Otago*, J. Wilkie and Co., Dunedin, 1879.

————"The Industries of New Zealand", an address, Christchurch, 1887.

Carter, Bonita. "The Kauri Timber Company 1888-1914", unpub. M.A. thesis, University of Melbourne, 1972.

Dobson, Edward. *Pioneer Engineering*, Crosby, Lockwood and Co., London, 1877.

————*A Rudimentary Treatise on the Manufacture of Bricks and Tiles*, rev. A.B. Searle, Crosby, Lockwood and Co., London, 1921.

Hunt, Robert (ed.). *Ure's Dictionary of Arts, Manufactures, and Mines*, Longmans, Green, and Co., London, 1875.

Innocent, C.F. *The Development of English Building Construction*, Cambridge University Press, Cambridge, 1916.

Polak, Ada. *Glass, Its Makers And Its Public*, Wiedenfeld and Nicholson, London, 1975.

Sale, E.V. *Quest for the Kauri*, A.H. & A.W. Reed, Wellington, 1978.

Sutcliffe, G. Lister (ed.). *The Modern Carpenter, Joiner, and Cabinet-Maker*, The Gresham Publishing Co., London, 1903.

The Technical Educator (4 vols), Cassell and Company, London.

Tidman, Harold W. (ed.). *The Brick and Pottery Bulletin*, Amalgamated Brick and Pipe Company Ltd., Auckland, from 1927.

Tidman, Harold W. (ed.). *Bricks and Pipes*, Amalgamated Brick and Pipe Company Ltd, Auckland, from 1927.

Old texts on house design & architecture

Bicknell, Amos Jackson. *Bicknell's Cottage and Villa Architecture*, A.J. Bicknell, New York, 1878.

——*Detail, Cottage & Constructive Architecture*, A.J. Bicknell & Co., New York, 1873.

Briggs, R.A. *Bungalows and Country Residences*, B.T. Batsford, London, 1901.

Brooks, S.H. *Designs for Cottage and Villa Architecture*, Thomas Kelly, London, 1839.

Downing, Andrew Jackson. *Cottage Residences*, D. Appleton & Co., 1880.

——*The Architecture of Country Houses* (1850), Reprint Dover Publications Inc., New York, 1969.

Eastlake, Charles. *Hints on Household Taste* (1868), Reprint Dover Publications Inc., New York, 1969.

Gwilt, Joseph. *An Encyclopaedia of Architecture*, rev. W. Papworth, Longmans, Green, and Co., London, 1881.

Holly, Henry Hudson. *Holly's Country Seats*, D. Appleton and Co., New York, 1863.

——Modern Dwellings in Town and Country, Harper and Brothers, New York, 1878.

Loudon, J.C. *Encyclopaedia of Cottage, Farm and Villa Architecture and Furniture*, Longman, London, 1836 and 1853.

Nicholson, Peter. *The New Practical Builder & Workman's Companion*, Thomas Kelly, London, 1823.

——*Nicholson's New Carpenter's Guide*, Jones and Co., London, 1825.

Pugin, A.W.N. *Pugin's Ornamental Gables*, Henry G. Bohn, London, 1831.

Shoppell, George. *Shoppell's Modern Homes, Beautiful Homes*, Co-operative Building Plan Association, New York, 1890.

Stephens, Henry and Burn, Robert Scott. *The Book of Farm-Buildings*, William Blackwood and Sons, Edinburgh, 1861.

Stickley, Gustav. *The Best of Craftsman Homes*, Peregrine Smith Inc., Santa Barbara, 1979.

Tomlinson, Charles. *Cyclopaedia of Useful Arts and Manufactures*, Virtue, London, 1886.

——*Illustrations of Trades*, Society for Promoting Christian Knowledge, London, 1860.

——*Illustrations of Useful Arts and Manufactures*, Society for Promoting Christian Knowledge, London, 1858.

Vaux, Calvert. *Villas and Cottages* (1864), Reprint Dover Publications Inc., New York, 1970.

New Zealand catalogues

Bartholomew Bros., Timber Merchants, Catalogue of Mouldings, The Company, Feilding, n.d.

Beautiful Homes and Public Buildings in New Zealand, Briscoe and Company Ltd., Auckland, n.d.

Catalogue of Brinsley & Co.'s Champion Portable Cooking Ranges, Brinsley & Co., Dunedin, 1921.

Catalogue of Houses, Joinery & Woodware, Thomson Bridger & Co., (Dunedin Iron and Woodware Company), Dunedin, n.d.

Catalogue of MacFarlane's Castings, Walter MacFarlane & Co., London, c.1865.

Catalogue of Mouldings, Architraves, Skirtings, Joinery and Turnery Work, Prouse Lumber Limited, Wellington, 1909.

Catalogue of Mouldings, Joinery, Turnery, The Kauri Timber Company, Auckland, 1919.

Cottam & Company's Catalogue of Iron Castings, The Company, London, n.d.

Findlay and Co.'s Illustrated Catalogue, Findlay and Co., Dunedin, 1874.

Glenmore Brick & Tile Manufacturing Coy. Ltd. Catalogue of Clay Products, The Company, Christchurch, c.1930.

Goldie & Sons Catalogue of Mouldings, The Company, Auckland, n.d.

The Home You Want: The Fibrolite Bungalow, James Hardie and Company Ltd., Sydney, n.d.

Waddell, McLeod, & Weir: Catalogue of Mouldings, The Company, n.d.

Wanganui Sash & Door Factory & Timber Company Limited Catalogue, The Company, Wanganui, 1897.

Wells Brothers' Catalogue of Bronze Ormolu and Steel Fenders, Fire Irons, etc,. The Company, Birmingham, n.d.

New Zealand planbooks

Burnett, J. *Pocket-Book of Information for Engineers on New Zealand Railways*, Railways Department, Wellington, 1914.

Christie, Jas. *New Zealand Homes, 60 Practical Designs*, Property & Finance Co., Invercargill, 1915.

Dominion Homes, supplement to *Progress*, Harry H. Tombs Ltd, Wellington, 1915.

Hanna, J.L. *Modern New Zealand Homes*, Home and Garden Services, Auckland, 1931.

Keyes, Mann & Co. *Modern Homes of New Zealand by Architects of Standing*, Keyes, Mann & Co., Auckland, 1917.

Kibblewhite, R.W. *Popular Modern Homes*, the author, Auckland, c. 1924.

——*Practical Book on Bungalows*, the author, Auckland, 1928.

Laidlaw Leeds & Company. *Laidlaw Leeds' Plans of Houses*, The Company, Auckland, c. 1915.

New Zealand Workers' Dwelling Act and *Advances to Workers Act*, Department of Labour, Wellington, 1907.

Phillips, G.W. *Designs for New Zealand Homes and Residences*, the author, Christchurch, n.d.

——*Details and Specification for New Zealand Homes, Bungalows, Residences, etc.*, the author, Christchurch, 1913.

———*New Zealand Homes and Bungalows — 4 and 3 Rooms*, the author, Christchurch, n.d.

———*New Zealand Homes and Bungalows — 5 Rooms*, the author, Christchurch, n.d.

———*New Zealand Homes and Bungalows — 6 Rooms*, the author, Christchurch, n.d.

Ratcliffe, Harry. *30 Plans and Elevations of Selected Bungalows*, the author, Wairoa, 1912.

Tombs, Harry H. *Commonsense Homes for New Zealanders*, Harry H. Tombs Limited, Wellington, c.1920.

The Workers' Dwellings Act 1910, Department of Labour, Wellington, c. 1914.

New Zealand literature on old houses, architecture & components

Bates, H.W. "The Evolution of the Dwelling", *New Zealand Valuer*, vol. 14, Dec. 1957.

Binney R.K. "In New Zealand — The English Tradition", *Architectural Review*, vol. LVI, No. 336, May 1927.

Bowman, Alex. "The Study of The Historical Development of Domestic Architecture in Canterbury, New Zealand", RIBA thesis, Christchurch, 1941.

Clere, F. de J. "Domestic Architecture in New Zealand", *Studio Year Book of Decorative Art*, 1916.

———"Reminiscences of Architectural Practice", *NZIA Journal*, April 1935.

Cochran, Christopher (ed.). *Four Cottages*, New Zealand Historic Places Trust — Wellington Regional Committee Newsletter, vol. 2, no. 3, Wellington, 1980.

———*Restoring a New Zealand House*, New Zealand Historic Places Trust, Wellington, 1980.

Cooke, M.B. *The Age of Houses Illustrated*, Lincoln College, 1972.

Cooke, R.B. et al. *Housing in New Zealand: Report of the Commission of Inquiry*, Government Printer, Wellington, 1971.

Diamond, John T. *Once The Wilderness*, The Lodestar Press, Auckland, 1977.

Fearnley, Charles. "Colonial Houses", *New Zealand's Heritage*, No. 21, Hamlyn, Wellington, 1972.

———*Where Have All The Textures Gone?* John McIndoe, Dunedin, 1975.

———"Houses", *NZIA Journal*, vol. 36, No. 3, March 1969.

Fill, Barbara. *Seddon State Houses — the Workers' Dwellings Act 1905*, Wellington Regional Committee of the N.Z. Historic Places Trust, Wellington, 1984.

Fox, Aileen. *Prehistoric Maori Fortifications in the North Island of New Zealand*, Longman Paul, Auckland, 1976.

Galer, Lois. *Houses And Homes*, Allied Press, Dunedin, 1981.

———*More Houses And Homes*, Allied Press, Dunedin, 1981.

Garrett, James. "Architecture", *An Encyclopaedia of New Zealand*, Government Printer, Wellington, 1966.

———"Home-Building — Our Tradition", *Home & Building*, vol. 21, No. 5, Oct. 1958.

Griffiths, G.J. *How Old Is Our House?* Otago Heritage Books, Dunedin, 1979.

Hammond, Janny. *Bush Carpenters — Pioneer Homes in New Zealand*, John McIndoe, Dunedin, 1979.

Hill, Martin. *New Zealand Architecture*, Department of Education, Wellington, 1976.

Hodgson, T.E.R. *Fire & Decay — The Destruction of the Large New Zealand House*, Alister Taylor, Martinborough, 1978.

Lemon, Daphne & Audrey Bascard. *Taieri Buildings*, John McIndoe, Dunedin, 1970.

———*More Taieri Buildings*, John McIndoe, Dunedin, 1972.

Lowe, David. *A Home In The Wilderness*, The Lodestar Press, Auckland, 1980.

McDonald, Janny. *A Selective Bibliography On Nineteenth Century Domestic and Vernacular Buildings of New Zealand*, National Library School, Wellington, 1976.

McKeon, B.K. *The History of Building Design in New Zealand From Maori Times to the Present Day* (bibliography), National Library School, Wellington, 1959.

New Zealand Historic Places Trust. ed. Francis Porter, *Historic Buildings of New Zealand: North Island*, Cassell and Co., Wellington, 1979.

———ed. Francis Porter, *Historic Buildings of New Zealand: South Island*, Methuen, Wellington, 1983.

Northcote-Bade, S. *Colonial Furniture in New Zealand*, A.H. & A.W. Reed, Wellington, 1971.

Pascoe, Arnold Paul. "Houses", *Making New Zealand*, ed. McLintock, vol. 2 No. 20, Department of Internal Affairs, Wellington, 1940.

———"The Study of The Early Buildings in the Canterbury Settlement of New Zealand", unpub thesis, RIBA, 1935.

Plischke, Ernst A. *Design & Living*, Department of Internal Affairs, Wellington, 1947.

Reynolds, David. *Cottages For Settlers*, Auckland Museum Education Service, Auckland. n.d.

Rogerson, Evan William. "Cosy Homes Multiply 1918-31", unpubl M.A. thesis, University of Auckland, 1976.

Rosenberg, Gerhard. "The Californian Bungalow in New Zealand", *NZIA Journal*, March, 1966.

———*The Evolution of House Design in New Zealand*, School of Architecture, University of Auckland, 1965.

———*Dated List of Some New Zealand Houses Up To 1945*, Department of Town Planning, University of Auckland, 1970.

———*Some Landmarks in the History of New Zealand Housing*, NZIA Conference Papers, 1971.

Ross, R.M. *A Guide To Pompallier House*, Government Printer, Wellington, 1970.

———"Waitangi Treaty Houses", *Historic Buildings of New Zealand: North Island*, Cassell & Co., Wellington, 1979.

Sales, R.M.S. "Early N.Z. Settler Cottages 1850-70", unpubl. sub-thesis/building report for B.Arch. degree, School of Architecture, Auckland, 1970.

Seager, W. Hurst. "Architectural Art In New Zealand",

Journal of Royal Institute of British Architects, vol. VII, no. 19, Sept. 1900.

Stacpoole, J.M. *A Guide to the Waimate Mission House*, Government Printer, Wellington, 1971.

———"Architecture in the 1870s", *New Zealand's Heritage*, vol. 2, pt. 45, Hamlyn, Wellington, 1972.

———*Colonial Architecture in New Zealand*, A.H. & A.W. Reed, Wellington, 1976.

———"The New Zealand Heritage of Buildings", *Comment*, Sept. 1980.

Thornton, G.G. *New Zealand's Industrial Heritage*, A.H. & A.W. Reed, Wellington, 1982.

"The Trend of House Design", *Building Progress*, Dec. 1938.

Wilson, G.F. "A Pictorial Survey of Housing in New Zealand", *Design Review*, vol. 2, no 3, Oct-Nov 1949; vol. 2, no 4, Dec-Jan 1949-50; vol. 2, no 5, Feb-March 1950; vol. 2, no 6, May-June 1950.

Overseas literature on old houses

Addy, S.D. *The Evolution of The English House* (1898), rev. Summerson, London, 1933.

Blumenson, John J-G. *Identifying American Architecture*, American Association for State & Local History, Nashville, Tenn., 1977.

Boyd, Robin. *Australia's Home*, Penguin, Australia, 1968.

Brown, R.J. *The English Country Cottage*, Robert Hale, London, 1979.

Brunskill, R.W. *Illustrated Handbook of Vernacular Architecture*, Faber & Faber, London, 1978.

Bungalow Magazine, The Bungalow Publishing Co., Seattle, 1914-15.

Casson, Hugh. *An Introduction to Victorian Architecture*, Art and Technics, London, 1948.

Evans, Ian. *Restoring Old Houses*, MacMillan, Melbourne, 1979.

Freeland, J.M. *Architecture in Australia: A History*, Penguin, Melbourne, 1968.

Freeman, Peter. *The Homestead — A Riverina Anthology*, Oxford University Press, Melbourne, 1982.

Glassie, Henry. *Folk Housing in Middle Virginia*, University of Tennessee Press, Knoxville, 1975.

Gloag, John. *Victorian Comfort*, Adam and Charles Black, London, 1961.

Handlin, David P. *The American Home: Architecture and Society — 1815-1915*, Little Brown and Company, Boston, 1979.

Herbert, Gilbert. *Pioneers of Prefabrication*, John Hopkins University Press, Baltimore, 1978.

King, Anthony D. *The Bungalow, the Production of a Global Culture*, Routledge & Kegan Paul, London, 1984.

Lancaster, Clay. *The Japanese Influence in America*, Abbeville Press, New York, 1963.

Lewis, Miles Bannatyne. *Victorian Primitive*, Greenhouse Publications, Carlton, 1977.

Lloyd, Nathaniel. *The History of The English House*, Architectural Press, London, 1931.

McArdle, Alma & Deirdre McArdle. *Carpenter Gothic — Nineteenth Century Ornamented Houses of New England*, Whitney Library of Design, New York, 1978.

Maas, John. *The Gingerbread Age*, Rinehart & Company, New York, 1957.

———*The Victorian Home in America*, Hawthorn Books, New York, 1972.

Purdom, C.B. *The Garden City, A Study in the Development of a Modern Town*, J.M. Dent and Sons, London, 1913.

Rapoport, Amos. *House, Form and Culture*, Prentice Hall, Englewood Cliffs, N.J., 1969.

Reid, Richard. *The Shell Book of Cottages*, Michael Joseph, London, 1977.

Scully, Vincent J. *The Shingle Style & The Stick Style*, Yale University Press, New Haven & London, revised 1971.

Stamp, Gavin (ed.). *The English House 1860-1914*, The Building Centre Trust, London, 1980.

Tanner, Howard, Philip Cox, P. Bridges and J. Broadbent. *Restoring Old Australian Houses and Buildings*, MacMillan (Aust.), South Melbourne, 1975.

Unstead, R.J. & W.E. Henderson. *Pioneer Home Life In Australia*, A. and C. Black Ltd., London, 1971.

Williams, H.L. & O.K. *A Guide To Old American Houses 1700-1900*, A.S. Barnes, New York, 1962.

Winter, Robert. *The California Bungalow*, Hennessey and Ingalls Inc., Los Angeles, 1980.

Woodforde, John. *The Truth About Cottages*, Routledge & Kegan Paul, London, 1969.

Wright, Gwendolyn. *Moralism And The Model Home 1873-1913*, University of Chicago Press, Chicago, 1980.

Index

Jeremy Salmond is a practising architect living in Auckland. He was brought up in Gore, and first studied in Dunedin where his grandfather had designed several well-known buildings. After completing a degree in architecture in Auckland, he married anthropologist Anne Salmond, and they travelled overseas for a time. They now live in Devonport with their three children. During a more recent stay in England (1980–81) he worked on an environmental design project in the Norfolk Broads, before returning to Auckland to complete his M. Arch. thesis on which this book is based.

Jeremy Salmond has a particular interest in renovating older buildings, and is the winner of a Monier Design commendation for the renovations to his 1904 villa. A dedicated house-spotter (an activity which takes him to the remote byways of New Zealand), he is also a member of the Auckland regional committee of the Historic Places Trust.